Studies in modern capitalism · Etudes sur le capitalisme moderne

Traditional Romanian village communities

Studies in modern capitalism · Etudes sur le capitalisme moderne

This series is devoted to an attempt to comprehend capitalism as a world-system.
It will include monographs, collections of essays and colloquia around specific
themes, written by historians and social scientists united by a common concern
for the study of large-scale long-term social structure and social change.

The series is a joint enterprise of the Maison des Sciences de l'Homme in Paris
and the Fernand Braudel Center for the Study of Economies, Historical Systems,
and Civilizations at the State University of New York at Binghamton.

Other books in the series

Immanuel Wallerstein: *The capitalist world-economy*
Pierre Bourdieu: *Algeria 1960*
Andre Gunder Frank: *Mexican agriculture 1521–1630*
Folker Fröbel, Jürgen Heinrichs, Otto Kreye: *The new international division of labour*

This book is published as part of the joint publishing agreement established in
1977 between the Fondation de la Maison des Sciences de l'Homme and the
Press Syndicate of the University of Cambridge. Titles published under this
arrangement may appear in any European language or, in the case of volumes
of collected essays, in several languages.

New books will appear either as individual titles or in one of the series which
the Maison des Sciences de l'Homme and the Cambridge University Press have
jointly agreed to publish. All books published jointly by the Maison des Sciences
de l'Homme and the Cambridge University Press will be distributed by the Press
throughout the world.

Traditional Romanian village communities

The transition from the communal to
the capitalist mode of production
in the Danube region

HENRI H. STAHL
University of Bucharest

Translated by Daniel Chirot and Holley Coulter Chirot
University of Washington

1980

Cambridge University Press
Cambridge
London   New York   New Rochelle   Melbourne   Sydney

& Editions de la Maison des Sciences de l'Homme
Paris

Published by the Press Syndicate of the University of Cambridge
The Pitt Building, Trumpington Street, Cambridge CB2 1RP
32 East 57th Street, New York, NY 10022, USA
296 Beaconsfield Parade, Middle Park, Melbourne 3206, Australia
and Editions de la Maison des Sciences de l'Homme
54 Boulevard Raspail, 75270 Paris Cedex 06

This work was originally published in French in 1969 by Editions de L'Académie de la
Republique Socialiste de Roumanie and Editions du Centre National de la Recherche
Scientifique under the title *Les Anciennes Communautés villageoises roumaines*
English translation first published 1980

Printed in Great Britain at the University Press, Cambridge

Library of Congress Cataloguing in Publication Data
Stahl, Henri H.
Traditional Romanian village communities.
(Studies in modern capitalism)
Translation of Les Anciennes Communautés
villageoises roumaines.
'A summary of the three volume work...
Contribuţii la studiul satelor devălmaşe Româneşti.'
Includes index.
1. Cities and towns – Romania – History.
2. Feudalism – Romania – History. I. Stahl, Henri H.
Contribuţii la studiul satelor devălmaşe Româneşti.
II. Title. III. Series.
HT145.R8S713   301.35'2'09498   79-52855
ISBN 0 521 22957 X

Contents

v

vi   Contents

Figures

Tables

Preface

Henri H. Stahl's four decades of field work and documentary research are summarized in this volume on the history and sociology of Romanian communal villages.

Communal villages were characterized by an absence of private control over the means of production. Land was available for all members of the community, though, of course, each owned the fruits of his labour. A fair amount of mythology has arisen through writers trying to find such communities in Europe's past, and to tie them to the cryptic remarks made by Marx about pre-capitalist and pre-feudal societies. But few social historians have ever found such clear evidence as Stahl has that they existed and were very old. None has explained so well under what kinds of ecological and historical circumstances they thrived.

On the basis of loose confederations of such village communities there emerged the early Romanian principalities of the thirteenth and fourteenth centuries. The existence of these states raises two theoretical issues: what modes of production characterized them, and how did they come into being? They were certainly not feudal or slave societies. Nor were they primitive, pre-state, egalitarian societies of the type normally associated with communal arrangements. The combination of such communities and states suggests an 'Asiatic' mode of production. Stahl shows that medieval Romanian states were something never adequately described by Marxist theoreticians, but were what he calls 'tributary' states. While he modestly writes that the Romanian cases were 'unique', they were almost certainly not. His discussion therefore opens a whole new direction for comparative research on early states, and on a mode of production not yet incorporated into Marxist theory.

Communal villages depended on two conditions: low population density and a low degree of outside exploitation. These did not persist together much beyond the late fifteenth century. Exploitation and relative overpopulation spread unevenly, were often not correlated with each other, and in some areas, went through cycles of remission and return. But gradually, the traditional village communities disintegrated, and were replaced by a combination of private property and serfdom. Stahl documents the process 'meticulously' (to use Perry Anderson's description of Stahl's book) and shows how first the growing Ottoman tribute, and later, much more decisively, capitalist market penetration and rapid population growth, destroyed the old solidarities.

Analogous village communities have existed in many parts of the world, and their subjugation to market forces forms an essential part of the creation of the modern world. To have an elegant, theoretically oriented description of the mechanisms at work in this particular case, over five centuries, is a remarkable addition to the general literature on social change and the transition from one mode of production to another. Many colonial and semi-colonial ('peripheral', as they are fashionably called today) societies have had this experience. Stahl's volume adds significantly to the discussion in this area as well.

This book is much more than a first rate empirical and theoretical monograph. There is in it a whole methodological treatise on how to combine ethnographic field work and documentary analysis in order to portray a complex, fluid social reality. Henri Stahl spent many years in the late 1920s and 1930s in Romanian villages. In isolated Carpathian valleys he found extraordinarily archaic communities. In other areas, on important trade routes, or in the plains, he found villages that had been subjected to centuries of outside pressure. Walking over fields, developing a feel for the lay of the land, observing shepherds and peasants, Stahl acquired a sense of rural life that few library-bound historians can approach. Yet, his historical knowledge prevented him from making the anthropologist's error of thinking that everything he saw was the result of unchanging tradition. Far from it. There had been continuous, though irregularly distributed, change from the time of the earliest thirteenth-century records.

No one will ever be able to improve on these studies. The chain of linked changes leading from the present to the past has been decisively broken since 1945. The kind of 'archaeology in reverse' that Stahl practised, reading from his ethnographic evidence to interpret ancient documents, can no longer be imitated in Romanian rural areas. We are fortunate that he was permitted to publish his findings, and to detail his reasoning. They shed light on Europe's rural past, which would otherwise be lost.

But even if it would be difficult to reproduce his style of work in most industrialized countries of the world, there are large areas where similar sorts of analysis might still unlock past social and economic secrets, and permit an improved understanding of the present.

Stahl's work has always been controversial in Romania, and it remains lamentably underadvertised by his country's official social science establishment. This is partly because his findings do not fit a rigid Marxist interpretation of Romanian history. Stahl has long been a Marxist, using economic data, a fine sense of social class and class conflict, and a sound grasp of the theory of changing modes of production to guide his work. He was, in fact, Marxist long before it became profitable to be one in his country. But he has never been a dogmatist.

There is another reason for his semi-ostracism from official historical circles in Romania, and that is his methodological iconoclasm and cross-disciplinary emphasis. In this respect, he closely resembles the French *Annales* school that matured while he was doing his field work. In Romania, however, the exigencies of war and the long intellectual isolation imposed after 1945 prevented the *Annales* model from spreading. Stahl remained alone, an admirer from afar, with little opportunity to interact with the French until the late 1960s. It was a great loss. Even though he had independently developed a similar approach to social history as Marc Bloch and his followers, they could have learned a great deal from each other. As it is, the similarities in style between some of the *Annales* writers and Stahl will impress the reader.

Traditional Romanian village communities is a summary of the three-volume work Stahl published from 1958 to 1965, *Contribuţii la studiul satelor devălmaşe Româneşti* (Contributions to the study of Romanian communal villages). It was first published in Paris thanks to the efforts of Henri Mendras and the Centre National de la Recherche Scientifique. I thank Professor Mendras for his help and encouragement.

DANIEL CHIROT

University of Washington, Seattle

To Margareta Stahl

Introduction

The international framework of the problem and its Romanian aspects

More than all others, those who devote themselves to agrarian studies must, under threat of being unable to decipher the scrawl of the past, more often than not, read history in reverse.

Marc Bloch, *Les caractères originaux de l'histoire rurale française*, Oslo, 1931, p. xii

1 ❧ The international framework of the problem

The problem of the 'second serfdom'

European historians have long pointed out the 'contrast presented by the agrarian regime of Eastern Europe beyond the Elbe and the agrarian regime of Western Europe'.[1] For if 'from the decline of seigniorial institutions Western Europe experienced the emergence of peasant property', it was quite different in Eastern Europe where 'the history of peasants, from the end of the middle ages until quite recently, has only been one of long and progressive decline'.[2]

It is true that in France, from the sixteenth century onwards, serfdom was obsolete and that the former 'serfs' of the middle ages, transformed into 'mortmainers', were subject only to a milder 'seigniorial regime' that was itself on the road to extinction. But as soon as one moves eastward, one finds renewed forms of serfdom, the more severe the newer they are.[3] Thus

1. Henri Sée, *Esquisse d'une histoire du régime agraire en Europe aux XVIII et XIXes siècles*, Paris, 1925, p. 265.
2. Marc Bloch, 'Les deux Allemagnes rurales', *Annales d'histoire économique et sociale*, 1930, volume IX, pp. 606–10.
3. Henri Sée, Armand Rebillon and Edmond Preclin, *Le XVIe siècle*, Paris, 1950.

1

in the fifteenth century, the German peasant was only subject to a few dues in produce and work days; however, he was in fact a free man. The German colonists of Brandenburg, of Pomerania, of Silesia, and of Eastern Prussia were even legally recognized as free. But the victory of the nobility in the peasant wars ended this situation. And it was not only the vanquished peasants of Southern Germany who once again became serfs. From the middle of the sixteenth century the free peasants of East Prussia, Brandenburg, Pomerania, Silesia, and soon those of Schleswig-Holstein were in their turn reduced to a state of serfdom.[4]

So as western serfdom was disappearing a 'second serfdom', or a 'new serfdom' (*eine neue Leibeigenschaft*, to use Engels' terms),[5] that was behind the times was developing and becoming stronger in the east. There were two distinct forms of this development: the return to serfdom of the peasants of Central Germany, who had previously hardly felt any improvement in their situation, and the turn to a new serfdom of the peasants of East Germany who had, until then, been free. This renewal of feudal forms cannot be entirely ascribed to the peasant wars, nor to the Thirty Years' war or the Seven Years' war. Most historians and sociologists agree that the cause was rather the penetration of capitalism.[6] At first sight this might seem contradictory, for it implies that the same cause, capitalism, might have had two opposite effects: the elimination of serfdom in the west, and its creation in the east. Nevertheless, these are the facts: the same social phenomenon of the advent of capitalism can take forms and have effects which are very different depending on the local and historical conditions in which it takes place.

For example, in England it was not small peasant property which arose, as in France, but great estates. In England, where industry first appeared and became dominant, the manufacturers needed large quantities of wool, and to produce it the former feudal owners abandoned cereal production and replaced it with sheep grazing. To do this they had to 'enclose' fields, that is, forcefully seize peasant holdings, thus obliging the peasants to break their ties to the land and

4. F. Engels, notes to *Das Kapital*, by K. Marx, volume I, book III, chapter 8, Stuttgart, 1914, p. 186.
5. F. Engels, 'Zur Geschichte der preussischen Bauern', in Marx–Engels–Lenin–Stalin, *Zur deutschen Geschichte*, volume I, *Von der Frühzeit bis zum 18 Jahrhundert*, Berlin, 1953, pp. 568–78, passim. See also the letters to Marx of 15, 16, and 22 December 1882, in *Briefwechsel*, Berlin, 1950, volume IV, pp. 691, 693, 698; Andrei Oţetea, 'Le second asservissement des paysans roumains (1746–1821)' in *Nouvelles études d'histoire*, volume I, Bucharest, 1955; *Idem*, 'Le second servage dans les Principautés danubiennes (1831–1864)' in *Nouvelles études d'histoire*, volume II, Bucharest, 1960.
6. F. Mager, *Geschichte des Bauerntums und der Bodenkultur im Lande Mecklenburg*, Berlin, 1955, which contains an excellent bibliography on the problem. See also F. Mehring, *Deutsche Geschichte, vom Ausgange des Mittelalters*, Berlin, 1910.

making them 'free' to leave their homes. This went hand in hand with the interests of the manufacturers who needed a proletarian work force; hence the political alliance of the aristocracy with the new bourgeoisie.

The course of events was different in Germany. In the seventeenth century this country was backward and torn by constant war. Its peasants were organized in an outdated way, working their land according to the rules of the agrarian communities, the *Feldgemeinschaften*, dominated by feudal lords to whom they owed dues in produce and in work days. This was enough to sustain the noble class, at least within the limits of a subsistence economy. But as soon as the western capitalist countries began to need cereals which they no longer produced in sufficiently large quantities to feed their cities, western merchants called on the underdeveloped parts of Eastern Europe for the food which their countries lacked. The feudal lords of Germany had to turn to another mode of production in order to meet this rising demand for cereal, a merchandise which brought good prices on the newly created world capitalist market. To do this they seized peasant holdings and turned them into large domains, the *Rittergütter*, which could be more rationally exploited. But since it was a question of cereal production, the English phenomenon in which 'sheep ate men' was not repeated in Germany. Instead, the opposite occurred, and the peasant was tied to the land, thus reducing him to the position of *Leibeigene*. Instead of enclosures there were *Bauernlegen*; instead of emptying villages of their peasant population, villages were filled with serfs tied to the land. Instead of a gentry class there appeared a Junker class which combined in its hands the triple powers of masters of the land, representatives of local justice, and the owners of peasants reduced to virtual slavery (*Grundherr*, *Gerichtsherr*, and *Leibherr*). This was in spite of the barely emerging bourgeois class which lacked a work force.

The renewal of serfdom in Germany was not really a simple return to ancient ways, nor was it, east of the Elbe, the simple repetition of antiquated medieval forms. The influence of the world capitalist market which had set the 'new serfdom' into motion imposed new laws on local social developments. In the first place, a greater supply of cereals had to be provided. In order to do this the old technique of *Dreifelderwirtschaft*, which dated from the high middle ages, had to be replaced by the more modern system of *Koppelwirtschaft* which the Junkers borrowed from the Dutch and transformed according to their needs (the *Preussische Schlagwirtschaft*). In the second place the goal of agricultural production ceased to be oriented toward the acquisition of goods required by a subsistence economy and became oriented to the production of goods which had a price on the world market. This made the feudal demands on the peasant class take on the character of 'primitive accumulation of capital', thus laying the base for future evolution toward capitalist relations.[7]

The phenomenon of a 'second serfdom' is not, however, limited to German territory beyond the Elbe. Certainly, it is here that one finds it in its most meaningful form, justifying Lenin's calling it the 'Prussian road to capitalist penetration into agriculture'. But in fact the same thing happened in many other countries. Russia, Poland, Austria, Hungary, Transylvania, Moldavia, and Wallachia all experienced the same phenomenon in one way or another. Perhaps one might say that in these other cases the phenomenon had the same causes, that is, contact with the world capitalist market. Even the countries that lacked the Baltic ports such as Stettin, Hamburg, Danzig, and Riga, through which the Hanse and then the Dutch exported huge quantities of wheat, still had other ways, over a complex system of roads, to export their merchandise of cereals and livestock. All the countries located between the Black Sea and the Baltic experienced generally the same phenomenon of tardy feudalism, especially from the sixteenth century onwards. This troubling sequence of historical events can only be explained by a similarity in historical conditions.

A whole school of historians does not hesitate to say that the same process of capitalist penetration was at work. Grekov, for example, claims that 'despite the many particular characteristics of developments in these countries, the connecting element is the transformation of agriculture provoked by the general transformation of Europe which caught them in a feudal stage. The common problem, then, was how to raise production and transform it into money by using feudal means.'[8] But according to the members of this school of thought, it was not always the world market which played a key role in South-East Europe, but rather local markets. Certainly, it would be unwise to deny the existence or importance of such markets. Werner Sombart considered them vital for a comprehension of the genesis of western capitalism. However, there

7. Johannes Nichtweiss, *Das Bauernlegen in Mecklenburg, eine Untersuchung zur Geschichte der Bauernschaft und der zweiten Leibeigenschaft in Mecklenburg*, Berlin, 1954. See also S. D. Zakin, 'The fundamental problem of the so-called "second serfdom" in Eastern and Central Europe', Romanian translation from the Russian in *Analele româno-sovietice, Istorie* series, 1958, nos. 1–2. J. Nichtweiss, *Zur Frage der zweiten Leibeigenschaft und der sogenannte preussische Weg der Entwicklung des Kapitalismus in der Landwirtschaft Ostdeutschlands* in *Zeitschrift für Gerschichtswissenschaft*, 1953, no. 5.
8. B. D. Grekov, *Peasants in Russia*, Romanian translation from the Russian, Bucharest, 1952.

must have been specific circumstances which caused these local markets in Eastern Europe to produce a second feudalism instead of a capitalist order. Probably these local markets, situated within feudal systems of backward countries, only became important as links in the intercontinental capitalist markets which had already been created. In the end, then, the same force was at work – the penetration of western capitalism, even if it manifested itself indirectly through local markets.

This introduces an interesting social historical problem, for what is being discussed here raises theoretical questions about the development of all backward societies after their entry into the orbit of more advanced social forms. All 'historical periods' are characterized by the co-existence, within a single 'contact area', of societies located at different levels of development. There have always been countries at the forefront of progress, and others more backward. A 'historical period' necessarily takes on the characteristics imposed on it by the more advanced countries. Those which are more backward fall prey to the 'law of the period'. For example, one cannot conceive of a 'slave mode of production' without a 'barbarian' hinterland which provides the source of slaves who can be seized in war. Rome could not have existed without the 'barbarians'. Nor can the history of the 'barbarians' be understood without reference to Rome. In the same way, during the period in which the western societies were feudal, their neighbours in the hinterlands also became feudal without passing through an earlier stage of the slave mode of production; that is, without having passed through the earlier stages of western history. Today we can observe 'under-developed' countries that have barely attained the level of tribal organization passing directly to capitalist forms, or even socialist forms according to the social spheres which influence them, just as they pass directly from the hoe to the tractor and from the ox cart to the airplane without going through intermediary stages. In an analogous way one must admit that the arrival of capitalism, as a form of social organization, must have had direct as well as indirect effects on the whole of the contemporary world according to what stage the various backward countries had reached.

Marx had already fully understood this problem of the penetration of capitalism and its special effects in different countries (as it happens, precisely while analysing the birth of serfdom in Romania) when he formulated a law which is more general than the immediate problem of the second serfdom: 'But as soon as people', he wrote, 'whose production still moves within the lower forms of slave-labour, corvée-labour, etc., are drawn into the whirlpool of an international market dominated by the capitalistic mode of production, the sale of their products for export becoming their principal interest, the civilised horrors of overwork are grafted on the barbaric horrors of slavery, serfdom, etc.'[9] Hence the work of slaves, or of serfs, can serve capitalist ends in all backward countries as soon as these are brought into the linkages of world capitalist commerce. This permits the formulation of a hypothesis which states that if one finds relations of serfdom coming into being or becoming aggravated in the sixteenth century and in a backward society, this might well be explained by the establishment of direct or indirect contacts with the capitalist world. During the sixteenth century all of Europe formed a single social unit where the laws of the market imposed themselves, more or less, however great were the differences separating the various countries. As soon as goods obtained a price on the world market, as soon as the currencies of international commerce were subjected to the capitalist variations of the gold market, there occurred a penetration of market forces into all those regions of the hinterland which could not, of themselves, have reached this stage. This seems to me to be so undeniable that it is hardly worth opening a debate on the subject.

Romanian aspects of the problem and methodological consequences

It is another problem altogether which we would like to deal with: to define the conditions in Romania that allowed the penetration of capitalism to take place in a unique way, one of interest both to local social history and to the general theory of the emergence and influence of capitalism in the world.

Our study of Romanian social history brought to light, as an essential local phenomenon, as a kind of underlying element, the existence of a large number of communal villages. It is true that village communities of this type were characteristic of the 'Ponto-Baltic' zone, and that several classical works prove the importance of the *Mark* for German[10] history and of the *mir* for Rusasian history.[11] The same social basis of

9. Karl Marx, *Capital*, volume I, edited by Frederick, Engels, New York, 1967, p. 236.
10. Georg Ludwig von Maurer, *Einleitung zur Geschichte der Mark-, Dorf- und Stadtverfassung und der öffentlichen Gewalt*, Reinheim, 1966.
11. A. von Haxthausen, *Studien über die inneren Zustände Russlands*, 1847–52, 3 volumes. See also A. Tschuprow, *Die Feldgmeinschaft. Eine morphologische Untersuchung* (Abhandlungen aus dem Staatswissenschaftlichen Seminar zu Strassburg. Herausgegeben von G. F. Knapp, XVIII), Strassburg, 1902: This remains one of the best treatments of the problem.

village communities can be found in the other countries cited: Austria,[12] Hungary[13] and Poland.[14] This social history may be contrasted with that of the west, where in the early middle ages there was a direct transformation from the slave and colonial latifundia to feudal domains. In the west it was from the beginning a question of a landowning class and their warrior enemies who, by conquest, took over the social status of the landowners, and of a serf class which gradually liberated itself. In the east, on the other hand, the peasants, organized into free village communities, fell into serfdom quite late, to the benefit of a class of nobles either only recently risen from local 'chieftainships' or evolved from conquerors of areas which they had colonized in western fashion. The feudal lords of the east began by exploiting not slaves or conquered peoples but free village communities, by purely fiscal means, and only acquired property rights over the land and inhabitants much later.

The existence of these free village communities explains the particular forms that serfdom took in these regions and the special forms of serfdom explain, in turn, the particular ways in which capitalism made itself felt. A study of this social history is particularly apt in the Romanian provinces because nowhere in the Ponto-Baltic zone were the forms of village communities so recent or typical as in Romania, especially in Moldavia and Wallachia (which we will study almost exclusively). In these two Romanian provinces, the village communities were so alive that even in the mid twentieth century they could be found in large numbers and, in addition, many were still 'free', i.e. they had never had a local lord.

The fact that such communities survived until so recent a period is of the greatest importance, as it made a direct social study possible. This was no longer the case in the rest of Eastern Europe in the twentieth century.[15] This exceptional opportunity for learning the laws of these archaic forms of social life is also important for methodological reasons.

12. Otto Bauer, *Der Kampf um Wald und Weide. Studien zur österreichischen Agrargeschichte und Agrarpolitik*, Vienna, 1925.
13. Károly Tagányi, ' Geschichte der Feldgemeinschaft in Ungarn', *Ungarische Revue*, 1895.
14. Mieroslawski, *Histoire de la commune polonaise du Xe au XVIIIe siècle*, Berlin, 1856; Zygmut Wojciechowski, *L'Etat polonais au moyen-âge; Histoire des institutions*, Paris, 1949.
15. The reader is encouraged to consult my previous works. The most important are: *Nerej, un village d'une région archaïque*, Monographie sociologique dirigée par H. H. Stahl (part of the monograph series on Romanian rural life, published by the Bibliothèque de Sociologie, Ethique et Politique under the guidance of D. Gusti), 3 volumes, Bucharest, 1939; 'L'habitat humain et les formes de la vie sociale', *Arhiva pentru știința și reforma socială*, Year XII, nos. 1–2; 'L'organisation collective du village roumain', *Arhiva pentru știința și reforma socială*, Year XIII; *Contribuții la studiul satelor devălmașe românești* (Contributions to the study of Romanian communal villages), 3 volumes, Bucharest, 1958–65.

The old documents are always enigmatic and difficult to interpret when one wants to reconstruct the forms of rural social life. In any case, the old documents concerning the villages are so laconic and imprecise that they cannot be understood without prior knowledge of the social laws of the village communities. Without knowledge of the communities of recent times, interpreting the old acts would be impossible. Moreover, Romanian historical documents are mainly those written by the boyar class and are about serf villages or those becoming enserfed. If one followed the method stating that 'nothing exists outside the texts', then one might believe that the free villages did not even exist. In fact, some of our historians, believers in this method, do not hesitate to draw this conclusion. However, the free communal villages did exist. Given this fact, it is not only a question of explaining it but also of using it in historical research; first of all, because the recent past and the present constitute the base of all historical reconstruction, and secondly because one has the opportunity of using a second means of research, that of field work, in addition to archival work, where the sociological survey can supplement and lend support to the documents.

Marc Bloch was perfectly right when he said that 'More than all others, those who devote themselves to agrarian studies must, under threat of being unable to decipher the scrawl of the past, more often than not, read history in reverse'.[16] That is what we have tried to do, perfecting a research technique which we have called, since 1928, 'social archaeology'. On the basis of surveys made between 1926 and 1946 we established hypotheses which then underwent historical verification and, inversely, on the basis of our interpretation of the old documents, we have tried to improve our understanding of the discoveries made by direct field research. We must acknowledge, however, that it is difficult to do history in reverse. In the first place, it must be remembered that all social evolution does not proceed uniformly, from one country to another or even, within a single country, from one region to another or from one village to another. Thus direct observation shows the simultaneous existence of different levels of development which seem logically to be different steps of the same evolutionary process. Village communities which are the purest survivals of the archaic type can be found side by side with evolved communities in the midst of capitalist disintegration.

Every sociologist making a direct social study must be an historian, for the need to transform the logical order imposed by the morphological

16. Marc Bloch, *Les caractères originaux de l'histoire rurale française*, Oslo, 1931, p. xii.

study into a chronological order is imperative. Thus, if the oldest forms are truly 'archaic' and are survivors, one must be able to find them 'living' and dominant in past centuries. Studying these centuries, it is surprising to learn that even then there existed the same inequality of different levels of development, depending on the regions or the villages. In the mid sixteenth century, for example, forms of social organization can be found which are more evolved than the surviving forms in the twentieth century.

The only method to use, in order to understand this apparently chaotic muddle of social phenomena which are mixed from century to century and from region to region, is to proceed not only backwards or in reverse, but also forwards, in chronological order, zigzagging from time to time, from century to century, as much forwards as backwards.

One will not find in these pages a strictly chronological account according to the classical historical style of recounting events. As we are attempting to study the origins of social forms, we will try to group forms that seem 'contemporary' by their degree of social maturity, by their sociological similarities if not by the century they belong to. It should be possible from the outset to put forward in the ordinary way the conclusions we have arrived at. But this would be imposing a point of view and ready-made conclusions that we ourselves do not consider as gospel. We think it is better to leave the reader to judge the facts for himself, after we have assembled them, as arguments for an interpretation which seems to us the only likely one. We will follow, then, in our account, the same path which our research took, tracing as clearly as possible the course of our thought and reasoning, often considering contemporary events side by side with past ones so as to understand the logical order and the historical order, the chronology of the process of social formation, while giving for each period a concise table of the existing social forms, some belated and outdated, others dominant, and still others only emerging, containing the seed of future development.

'Free' villages and 'serf' villages

In order to get an overview of the village communities of Wallachia and Moldavia, of which some were free and some serf, we have taken as our starting point the statistical data concerning the situation at the moment when the system of corvées was legally abolished in 1864. Boyars and peasants liable to corvées still followed at this time a confused complex of laws and reciprocal obligations, the boyars having to allow the

TABLE 1. *Number and percentage of villages formerly free, serf or mixed*

Free	Serf	Mixed	Total
1,710	5,827	1,462	8,999
19%	64.8%	16.2%	100.0%

TABLE 2. *Proportion of free population in mixed villages*

	Percentage of population free			
	Over 75%	51–75%	25–50%	less than 25%
Number of villages	642	378	271	171
Percentage of villages	43.9%	25.9%	18.5%	11.7%

peasants the use of certain plots of land and the peasants, in exchange, having to give a tithe and some work to the lords. By the Rural Law of 1864 two-thirds of the land of each village was granted to the peasants, exempt thenceforth from the payments of tithe, while the boyar became the absolute owner of the remaining third, free from any obligation to cede any land to the peasants. As for the labour dues, they had to be repurchased by the peasants in cash. There were 511,896 corvée peasants who benefited from this law.[17]

Unfortunately, no general survey of the population was made at the time, so that we have no information on the non-corvée peasants who were not affected by the Rural Law. An attempt was made to fill in the gaps during the survey of 1912 (i.e. forty-eight years later) by listing separately the descendants of old serf (corvée) peasants.[18] Thus it was found that there were 463,534 households of former serfs (65.7%) and 241,665 households of non-serfs (34.3%). This population lived in 5,827 formerly serf villages and 1,710 free villages. In addition there were found 1,462 mixed villages, where serfs and free men lived side by side (table 1). The 1,462 mixed villages had a free population with the proportions as shown in table 2. In total, 1,020 mixed villages had an absolute majority of 'free' peasants (69.8% of such villages). What is the social history of these diverse categories of peasants, some free, some serf? Was it an old free peasant class that fell partially into

17. Leonida Colescu, *La loi rurale de 1864 et la statistique des paysans devenus propriétaires*, Bucharest, 1900.
18. Petre Ponti, *Statistica răzeșilor* (Statistics of the free peasants), Bucharest, 1921.

TABLE 3. *Percentage of free villages in 1722, 1831 and 1912 (Oltenia)*

	Percentage of free villages		
Counties	1722	1831	1912
Gorj	61.7	57.4	45.0
Vilcea	55.5	51.0	46.9
Mehedinți	41.2	39.2	27.2
Dolj	40.7	22.9	9.2
Romanați	22.3	16.1	7.4
Total	48.0	38.6	28.9

serfdom? If one had old statistical data, it would be easy to know. Unfortunately, the fiscal censuses date only from the first half of the nineteenth century and, moreover, they do not correlate either among themselves or with the data of 1912. It is most difficult to draw satisfactory conclusions.

However, we possess a partial census established in 1722 by the Austrians[19] at the time when they controlled 'Little Wallachia', comprising five counties west of the Olt River. This census, called 'Virmontian' after the name of the Italian administrator who made it, established two categories of villages, those which had lords and those which had none. There were found to be 350 free villages, or 48.0%, out of a total of 729 villages. If one compares, at least for this region, the data from 1722 with the later pertinent information, the result is as shown in table 3.

The decrease in free villages is evident. All the more so considering that the first data, furnished by the census of 1722, point to a strong trend toward enserfment of the villages. For, among the 379 villages registered as serf villages, there were 129 which had only recently come 'under the protection' of a boyar or which had simply been 'occupied' by force by some powerful person. Though unfortunately we lack similar information for the whole country, it may be supposed that the same decline of free villages was generally taking place.

It will be important to see if the historical documents confirm this thesis, which seems so likely: that is, that the free communal villages existed from the beginning of the state and that they were subjected over the course of history to a process of enserfment, which nevertheless did not succeed in enserfing all of them, even though the process began long ago.

19. C. Giurescu, *Materiale pentru istoria Olteniei sub austriaci* (Materials on the history of Oltenia under the Austrians), volume II, Bucharest, 1909, pp. 304–30.

2 ⚜ Hypotheses concerning the genesis of the Romanian feudal states

Cartography of the zones of free and serf villages

The statistical data established on the basis of census of 1912, although not totally reliable, do constitute a particularly interesting document from the historical point of view as soon as one interprets them geographically, taking into consideration not only their numerical values but also their spatial distribution. One has only to look at fig. 1 to see that a whole series of problems appear that would have escaped us if we had not taken this approach. Thus one sees that the free villages are concentrated in certain zones of the country where they are predominant. There are even 'zones without lords', where the free peasants make up the absolute total. On the other hand, there are also 'zones of serfdom', where free peasants do not exist or where, at most, they are but rare exceptions. And there are regions where free and serf villages co-exist. These diverse types of villages are sometimes so inter-mixed in the same geographical areas that any hypothesis of two civilizations confronting each other, giving birth to two distinct social histories, or of the decisive influence of geographic conditions, falls flat. The hypothesis of a difference in agricultural techniques could not be seriously considered either, for free and serf villages had the same agricultural level, the same economic occupations and the same work procedures, as we shall see.

We will then have to call upon other purely social circumstances to explain this phenomenon of the co-existence, in the same territories, in the same geographic and cultural conditions, of such contradictory social phenomena as those of the free and serf villages. What is remarkable is that the mass of free villages is found deep in the mountainous regions, the sub-Carpathian depressions and the hills where the earliest political states were born. This is proved by an act of 1247 and by the internal documents of the fourteenth century which

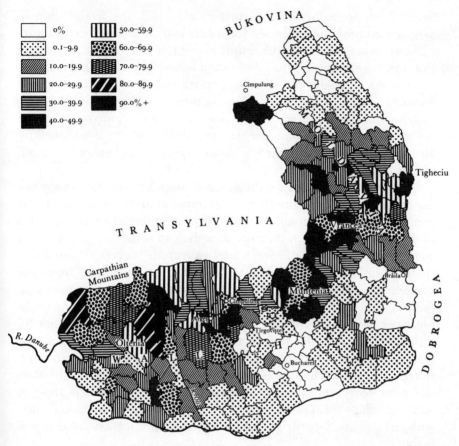

Fig. 1. Percentage of free villages according to the census of 1912.

indicate this as being the region where the state, properly called 'the Romanian country', also called 'Muntenia' (Land of the mountains), was founded. It is from this base that the Carpathian boyars threw themselves against the Tartars to reconquer the Danubian plain, a region of mostly serf villages. At first, this situation seems paradoxical: it is certain that any 'feudal' state implies the existence of a class of lords with access to a mass of villages exploitable by tithes and corvée labour, rich enough to assure the life of the warriors, the masters of the state. How was it possible, then, that the 'free' villages dominate at the moment when the state was born? This problem would be insoluble if one committed the error of believing that there was only one way to exploit an agrarian population: that known in the west, where the feudal lords were landowners, receiving as such the feudal dues in produce and labour. Actually lords can exploit village communities without owning them, by the simple imposition of a tribute, according to a state fiscal system. Thus, the central head of the warrior class could command a repressive state fiscal apparatus and distribute the 'national revenue' – if one can call it such – to the members of the seigniorial class, without owning the land, which continued as the patrimony of the communal villages. A basis for the state could then be established by an ascendancy over the men without actual possession of the land, except in a nominal fashion.

But this brings us to a troubling conclusion, because it goes against the opinion that was formerly very widespread among historians: that the 'feudalism' of Romania resembled western feudalism on the basis of the theory of eminent domain according to which a 'lord' bestows on a whole hierarchy of vassals and subvassals 'benefits' containing 'immunities' that they hold as 'owners', commanding from the beginning a 'demesne', a *terra indominicata*, and in turn bestowing 'holdings' to their serfs who are liable for tithes and corvées. If this could not have been the form that the 'feudal' order took in Romania (if, arbitrarily, we wish this term to signify any social system where a class of lords exploits a peasant class by tithes and corvée labour and not a system of internal, hierarchic organization of a class of lords),[1] then one must verify the existence of initial fiscal exploitation and show in what way these fiscal rights could be transformed into true feudal ones, with serfdom and lordly rights to feudal land rents in goods, money and labour.

Looking at fig. 1, a literal interpretation is tempting. One notes what might be the avenues of serf villages which cross the mass of 'free' mountain villages, as if the feudal lords, at first exploiting the free villages by taxation, had then pushed foward, making their way through the villages along the valleys leading to the Danube, hurrying toward the plain reconquered from the nomads, where they were able to take full ownership of villages seriously depopulated by the series of wars. The lords then repopulated these villages by colonizing them with peasants who were enserfed by the mere fact of settling on conquered lands.

The map of Moldavia shows us another variation of the same social history. Here, it is the north of the country which is the area of reconquest and serfdom (with a few exceptions, such as the villages of

1. This is far from being the viewpoint of all historians.

Cîmpulung which formed a quasi-autonomous 'republic' near the centre of the state), whereas the south, towards the Danube, is a land of mostly free villages, with two other small 'republics', that of the Vrancea and that of Tigheciu.[2] This confirms the fact that the Moldavian state was formed by an act of reconquest from the Tartars executed by a group of Romanian warriors from Maramuresh on the other side of the Carpathians, not by local lords as in Wallachia. One can explain the nature of the serfdom in the villages of northern Moldavia precisely by the effect of this reconquest and repopuation of a profoundly devastated zone. From this base of 'the country above', the Moldavian state gradually encompassed 'the country below', not by arms but by taxation and slow economic infiltration. The villages in the south of Moldavia could thus survive as 'free' villages, particularly since they also had the role of frontier guards.

Let us add that in Transylvania the facts are even clearer, although less interesting. Here the Hungarians conquered all the Romanian villages. Two races were in conflict, the victorious race reducing to serfdom the vanquished one, leaving only a few free villages, for example, in the region of Fagarash, which for a while was under the domination of the Wallachian State, and the military border zones where Maria Theresa and Joseph II later created the special Frontier Regiments.

Thus, we would be right to conclude, in the first place, that if there was a 'Romanian feudalism' it was of a completely different nature from western feudalism and, in addition, that there were even three distinct varieties of this Romanian feudalism: on the one hand, that of Transylvania, created by the *conquest* of Romanian communal villages, by a Hungarian warrior people, and, on the other hand, two other forms created by the *reconquest* of the nomads, Wallachia's being the work of a local class, Moldavia's that of a class of Romanian warriors from Transylvania. If our hypothesis corresponds to reality, we should find the symptoms of these three types of social development, which, later on, in spite of their different origins, will slowly unify, tending toward the same final stage of belated capitalist penetration.

2. Unfortunately this large number of free peasants in the villages of Cîmpulung does not appear on the map, as in 1912 Bukovina was in the Austro-Hungarian Empire and was therefore not included in the Romanian census.

The archaeological document of village boundaries

Let us proceed a little further in the study of Romania by analysing what are called 'rural landscapes'. We have already had occasion to describe several of their aspects. But we still have to consider a problem of a more visibly archaic nature.

Every rural landscape is in itself a document that the historian ought to understand, as an archaeological testament of a special nature, enabling one to reconstruct past stages of man's social history. Without claiming that the territorial divisions of village communes go back to prehistory or to antiquity,[3] one cannot deny that they have a nature so visibly archaic that people have spoken of the 'eternal order of the fields'.[4] What can the ancient history of these communes be? We can perhaps reconstruct the history, by taking into account the village lay-out.

In Romania there are two types of village communities. One is that of a rectangular geometric lay-out. Just as the French *quartiers* or the German *Gewanne* are divided into clusters of juxtaposed strips (*Hufen*), the territorial complexes of Romania are also formed by a series of long strips arranged parallel to each other. But it should be emphasized that instead of small surface areas divided into individual lots, they are immense geographical spaces, measuring in length and in width more than ten kilometres, compartmentalized into public areas, belonging to human collectives.[5] These village communities can be arranged in a single row or in a series of rows, situated one above another. In Romanian this type of communal arrangement has a very picturesque name. The communes are 'communes under the same yoke' (*înjugate*), 'related' (*însurărite*), or like 'twin brothers' (*îngemănate*).

Let us look closer at this kind of partitioning of a whole region into geometric areas. It is not easily visible to the eye.[6] But the village

3. Roger Dion, *Essai sur la formation de paysage rural francais*,Paris, 1934; Gaston Roupnel, *Histoire de la campagne francaise*, Paris, 1932; Georges Lizerand, *Le régime rural de l'ancienne France*, Paris, 1942.
4. Roland Maspétiol, *L'ordre eternel des champs*, Paris, 1946.
5. Helmuth Haufe, 'Der freibäuerliche Kleinadel der Militärgrenzen', *Deutsches Archiv fur Landes und Volksforschung*, Year II, Book II, 1940. Haufe wants at all costs to see Romania as an area of German influence following an ancient *Drang nacht Osten* wherever one finds a division of the land similar to that of the *Hufen*. Following this way of thinking one might declare the whole surface of the world as an area of 'German cultural influence'.
6. Several remarks are in order here. It is hard to reproduce village boundaries on maps from the written description of the measurements found in the various documents. The peasant surveyors measured in 'lengths walking on the land', going over hills and through valleys in their own fashion without following the methods of modern surveying. There were no plumb lines and there was no way of sighting on a line with the horizon. Areas of equal size measured

Fig. 2. Area of the free villages (1912).

perimeters are observable if one follows the old technique of the peasant surveyors. Thus one sees that all these communes define each other. Each one is but a piece in a larger context. It is therefore only necessary to know the points of intersection between neighbouring communes, forming, depending on the case, a *duplex* or a *quadruplex confinii*. Surveyors laid down as markers stone posts specially cut so that two or four faces (called *pravăţ*) indicated the direction to follow. Thus, from

according to such 'lengths' can appear on a map as if they are unequal. It is just as important to note that measurement was not carried out on abstract surfaces but on real ones whose economic value was unequal. Land of inferior quality had to be compensated with grants of more land since a larger amount was needed to be considered equal to a smaller amount of better land. Also, surfaces were not measured as such. Only the three 'lines' were measured in order to determine the location of the 'corners' of the land.

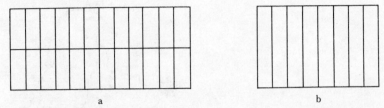

Fig. 3. Types of village boundaries: (a) the 'related' type; (b) the 'twin' type.

the principal 'corner' (*colţ*), called 'cut off' (*cheotoare*), a straight line is taken in the direction indicated by the *pravăţ*, 'width-wise' (*de-a latul*) to meet the stone on the opposite corner, from where one proceeds, at a right angle, following the length of the commune (*de-a lungul*) to meet the third corner, which sends one to the fourth, which points the way back to the first stone, thus 'closing' the contour.

Such geometric perimeters, covering a whole region, cannot be perfect unless the terrain makes it possible. To mark out a hilly terrain, to take account of river courses, of lines where water forms the separation, to avoid swamps and to include hillsides, certain distortions must occur without losing either the principle of the four corners or the total geometric form. At the most, intermediate stones must be added between the four principal corners, of which only two, those of 'the middle' (*mijloc*), serve as geometric points. Once the four corner stones and the two middle ones have been identified, measuring can proceed by a simple enough technique, as it is not necessary to measure the area, only the three 'lines' formed by the distances between the two upper stones, between the two middle stones, and between the two lower stones. There is no need to measure the actual lengths as these are defined by the adjoining territories.

There is no question that the arrangement of the territory of a whole region into communes having the form of large elongated rectangles could be the result of chance or of successive private initiatives. This method of partitioning the land can only be the result of a surveying operation with equal divisions as its goal. As a matter of fact, the boundaries between villages are laid out in such a way that each village benefits from the available economic zones: mountains, hills, fields, forests, watercourses, etc. In some cases, to maintain the equality of the villages, the surveyors had to resort to some rather complicated partitioning, with certain 'closed-in' villages being given passageways across neighbouring communes so that they might have access to the mountains and to sources of water.

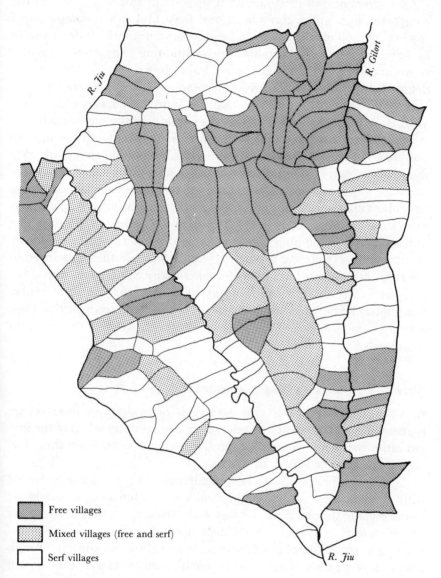

Free villages

Mixed villages (free and serf)

Serf villages

Fig. 4. An actual example of an area with 'twin' territories and 'round' ones; free, mixed, and serf villages co-exist in the region of the Jiu and Gilort valleys in central Oltenia.

Of course, not all of Romania is divided in this way. Next to the complexes of regular communes one may find other complexes of 'round' or 'angular' (*rotunde, colţuroase*) communes which do not seem to have undergone an egalitarian partitioning. For these irregular communes, the method of the 'three lines' does not work. One cannot define their contour without giving a complete description, step by step, 'from sign to sign', noting the 'natural signs', such as watercourses, heights, trees, roads, etc., and the 'man-made signs', such as marking stones, ditches, earth mounds, under which, for later verification, were put coal, cinders, pottery shards and glass. Stones and tree bark with the heraldic sign of the state, the *bos aurus* (*bour*), were also laid where possible.[7] The number of boundary stones needed to lay out these irregular villages was very great; the measurements must be paced out from stone to stone for the whole length of the perimeter. The interior of the angular communes can at most be treated as a certain number of subdivisions of oblong geometric form, which are then submitted to the rule of the 'three lines', which makes many calulcations into strips necessary. But what is very important is that even these irregular communes can be subjected to the same rules of egalitarian partitioning, with the same solution of passageways for the problem of the closed-in communes.

Chronology of the village boundaries

At what period did this vast operation of egalitarian inter-village partitioning take place? One series of arguments dates it before the first formation of the pre-feudal state, probably about the tenth century. The arguments may be stated as follows.

(a) If such operations had been made when the state already existed with a chancellery which could send out written acts, it would be inconceivable that no documentary trace remains. And there is no act which records or even mentions these operations.

(b) The technique of the Romanian surveyors, as we know it through a very large number of old and modern documents as well as by its still common practice among the peasants, is exclusively a technique of

7. We cannot help but recall the surveying techniques of the Romans in the *gromaticii veteres*, who used the same methods. They said that there existed an *agrimensura per extremitatem comprehensi, per strigas et scamnas*, as well as another, the *agroarcifinii qui ulla mensura continentur; finitur secundum antiquam observationem, fluminibus, fospossessore potuerunt obtineri*. See A. Meitzen, *Siedlung und Agrarwesen der Westgermanen und Ostgermanen, der Kelten, Finnen und Slawen*, Berlin, 1895, volume I, the section entitled 'Die römischen Landmessungen und Feldeintheilungen', p. 300.

reconstruction of the old village boundaries: the surveyor limits himself
to finding signs of the old borders and does not even consider in what
way he could establish new ones.

(c) All the old documents, even those of the fourteenth century,
unanimously acknowledge that the village boundaries have existed from
time 'immemorial, if not forever. As, generally, the social memory
retains the great events of collective life for at most four to five
generations, it follows that one must count back at least a hundred years
from the oldest date recorded in the documents to assign a date for the
division of the land into village communes.

(d) One must not lose sight of the fact that, according to the constant
tradition of the old documents, each village commune is organized by
a double (dichotomic) rule: the commune is split in two, lengthwise,
the two halves named 'upper part' and 'lower part'. For a whole group
of old villages in Moldavia, where the reconquest of the territory from
the nomads was more recent than in Wallachia and where the local
social forms kept a more archaic nature than in other provinces, the
documents mention also the existence of two rather enigmatic people
called *knez* and *judec*. In other regions inhabited by Romanians, these
prove to be village chiefs. In those villages with two *judeci*, the coupled
halves of the village territory are designated by the term *judeci*. The
names of the two *judeci* are sometimes used as geographic terms, based
on their eponymous origin, while at the same time they are 'socionyms',
that is, collective names for all those in one half of the village. In spite
of the fact that the mention of double *knez* or *judeci*, that is, of the
coupling of communes, only appears at random in the documents when
it is a question of specifying the shares belonging to each commune or
how to identify a village by the name of the *knez* living there, one can
nevertheless point to a whole group of dichotomic villages, large enough
to be taken into consideration. Examination of a recent edition of a body
of old documents reveals the situation shown in table 4.[8]

The system of dividing into two equal parts is not unknown, for it
corresponds to the whole system of the double clans that the English
sociologists call 'moiety' and Durkheim 'phratrie'. Thus if the old
Romanian communes adopted this dualist system it is because they were

8. All of the statistics and the texts of cited documents come from *Documente privind istoria României*
(Documents relating to the history of Romania) published by the Romanian Academy,
Bucharest, 1951–60. This includes twelve volumes plus a two volume place-name index for
Wallachia from 1247 to 1627 and ten volumes for Moldavia from 1384 to 1620. For later
documents we have used the collection *Documente privind relațiile agrare în veacul al XVII-lea și
XVIII-lea* (Documents relating to agrarian relations in the seventeenth and eighteenth
centuries), Bucharest, 1961 and 1966.

TABLE 4. *Number of dichotomic villages out of total villages mentioned*

Period	Total villages	Dichotomic villages
1390–1449	945	63
1450–1499	971	117
1500–1549	883	231
1550–1599	1455	203

established at a period when the local population was still organized into tribes, and at the time of partitioning the land into village groups the social organization by 'moiety' was kept in mind. This gave birth to a territorial system of the same nature.

This carries us back to the 'time immemorial' of which the documents speak, long before the formation of the state; or, more properly, to the times of tribal organization when the ties of consanguinity formed the basis of all social cohesion. The division into communal lands took place before the establishment of a territorial organization based on 'proximity' rather than blood.

(e) One must also note that many times, in the same territorial complexes, the villages of former serfs and free villages are mixed together. Now, it is very probable that at the time when the territorial division was made, this distinction between free and serf villages did not yet exist. It could not be a case of a seigniorial latifundium with a single holding, covered with serf villages, in the middle of which later on some villages succeeded in freeing themselves from serfdom. It is more logical, rather, to consider that the process was probably inverse, that there was a zone of free villages most of which fell into serfdom, conquered by an emerging feudal class. Only a few villages escaped the take-over. One must thus place this division into village communes in a period when the feudal class was not yet completely formed, thus before the birth of the state. For the state, as opposed to the pre-state tribal formations, presupposes the existence of a class of masters with holdings of a rather sizeable mass of villages, subjected to tributes in tithe and forced labour.

(f) In certain regions of the plain of the lower Danube, steppes and pre-steppes, there are scattered 'mounds' built by the nomads. This has been demonstrated by archaeological findings. They are generally considered to be tombs. Often enough they do contain human bodies, arms and religious objects from ritual barbarian burials. As for their distribution, there are two types of mound formations: some are massed together in a confused group, lacking any discernable order, covering different-sized areas. These are actually gigantic cemeteries. But there are others which are arranged in a rigid geometrical pattern. From a central high mound, there is a whole line of lower mounds. Along this same line, on the map, one invariably finds other series of mounds, farther away and out of sight. These lines reveal a perfect knowledge of the terrain: they fit with the lines where streams separate land or where different geomorphic zones come together, lines which are difficult to make out on the broad steppe. This proves that those who built them were not strangers to the land, and, although 'shepherds', they were entrenched on the land which they occupied relatively permanently. These lines are cut by other lines crossing at right angles, through the points of the 'great mounds', thus forming the basis of a system of triangles of surprising regularity. Is it another example of surveying? This is a tempting hypothesis. In that case, it would have to be a question of inter-tribal land boundaries.

The peasants of today are perfectly aware of these things. They call the lines of mounds *măguri înşirate* (strung mounds) and the meeting points *crucea măgurilor* (cross of the mounds). And, even more importantly, these mounds still serve today, often enough, as reference points for the village communes, with the 'corners' of the communes coinciding with these mounds, as though the surveyors who measured out the village communes had taken these tribal triangles as their basis. It follows that at the time of the nomads, or just at the time of the reconquest of the territory by the indigenous people, a local population already existed, which took over, by groups of villages, these tribal 'cells' left by the riders of the steppe.

In conclusion we ought to say that we have only been able to print out the theoretic schema of some typical 'models'. In reality, human social history is much more complex. Thus one should not think that before the formation of the state, the entire surface of the country had been divided up. There were mountains, and especially forests, covering whole regions, which could not be divided. It was first the clearings, the clearing work lasting for centuries, and the non-wooded zones, good for human habitation, along the rivers or in the heart of the Carpathian depressions, which were used by men. Thus these areas were the first to be divided. The village communes grew with the later possession of newly conquered areas. From the already established topographical bases, the communes could grow until they met other communal complexes which had pushed out in the same way. (Where these topographical bases were absent, villages grew by progressively clearing the land around the original clearings rather than by spreading out along pre-established lines.)

Communal villages and 'voivodal' formations

We must keep in mind two conclusions from the analysis we made of the mode of dividing up the land into village territories. First, the villages being laid out were equal in rights; and the division took place before the formation of autochthonous states. Secondly, when this egalitarian distribution of the land was made, there must have been some authority above that of the participating villages capable of performing the surveying and of imposing decisions.

This raises a very important historical problem: what were the social conditions during the centuries before the state was formed? And this brings us to the main problem of our very ancient social history.[9] We know that the Roman Empire, after conquering Dacia in 106, made it a 'province'. This does not mean that the Province of Dacia was comparable to the Province of Gaul or of Italy – far from it. Moreover, the Romans did not subjugate all of Dacia. The Province of Dacia was but a fragment of the whole of Dacia in which 'free Dacians' continued to lead their old tribal life. Even in the province, during the high point of Roman domination, the slave or colonial latifundia existed only as an exception. It is true that the Roman domination created a flourishing urban life, imposing a general cultural influence that was decisive to the local population, without, however, being able to completely transform the villages, which remained as they had been: village communities of a deeply tribal character. After the Roman army left Dacia in 271, the cities fell into decay, drowned in the anonymous rural mass.

Then, for almost a thousand years, a total silence covered the events that took place there. We know nothing except that wave upon wave of invaders – Goths, Huns, Gepids, Avars, Slavs, Bulgars, Hungarians, Petchenegs, Cumans and Tartars – swept across the region. But as soon as the first historical sources begin to appear, we find the peasantry well along the road of its social development: in each village there were *knez*

9. C. Daicoviciu, E. Petrovici, G. Ştefan, *La formation du peuple roumain et de sa langue*, Bibliótheca Historica Romaniae, *Etudes* series, no. 1, Bucharest, 1965. Also *Brève Histoire de la Transylvanie*, Bibliotheca Historia Romaniae, *Monographies* series, no. 2, Bucharest, 1965.

and there were confederations of villages under the leadership of a voivode. We may pose the following question: what were the forms of social organization that enabled the Romanians not only to survive in spite of the oppression of the migratory people, but also to evolve in such a way that there were, at the beginning of their written history, *voivodats* and then 'states'?

This is a problem of social history that could not be solved by means of the written texts alone, even if they were richer than they are. We have to call in sociological theory once again. We know that a form of social life can exist and evolve even though it is subjected to the exploitation of conquering peoples if the rulers do not expropriate the land that they exploit. This is the case of village communities. If the historical documents were completely missing, we would still be forced to admit that during the entire obscure millennium of our history the indigenous people, under the thin layer of superimposed nomads, must have had a life of communal villages which came out of an earlier tribal development.

Comparative sociology enables us to follow the main lines of such an evolution. The early tribes were organized on territorial lines at a certain stage of the development of their agricultural and pastoral technical capacities. Each part of the larger tribe took possession of a certain territory, thus forming a village. The old blood ties, real or fictitious, which held the tribes together, were replaced by the ties of neighbourhood. Spatial proximity replaced kinship as the main basis of social cohesion. This evolution was slow. Villages that were formerly a part of the tribe remained under a confederate authority which comprised a whole region. This tribal authority, having undertaken the work of partitioning the land which led to the territorialization of villages, continued to safeguard the larger group. It thus fulfilled the duties of a quasi-state: to defend the area and settle disputes between villages. By great good fortune we were able to see the historical and ethnographic vestiges of such formations in parts of Romania. In Moldavia, there are three regions which even after the birth of the Moldavian state maintained a social organization like that which must have been widespread before the formation of the state.

In his *Descriptio Moldaviae* of 1716,[10] the prince Dimitriu Cantemir does not hesitate to give these regions the name of 'Republics'. He is talking of the confederation of Cîmpulung, in Bukovina, of that of the

10. Kantemir Demetrius, *Historisch-geographische und politische Beschreibung der Moldau, nebst dem Leben des Verfassers, und einer Handcharte*, Frankfurt and Leipzig, 1771.

forests of Tigheciu, and especially of that of the Vrancea, which we have already mentioned.

Let us look at this last example, the Vrancea, which was the only one of the peasant 'republics' whose archaic forms still existed in the last decades before the Second World War and which we could study at first hand. It was a confederation of fourteen villages which shared the whole mountain area at the south-eastern bend of the Carpathian Mountains. Each village was subjected to the authority of a general village assembly. Villages situated on the same river course formed a higher level assembly at which the delegates of the individual village assemblies took part. All the villages of all the valleys in the region formed a highest assembly, 'the Great Assembly of the whole Vrancea'. This Vrancean assembly represented the villages in their dealings with Moldavia. The state dealt with it to establish the annual tribute which the republic had to pay. It was this assembly which linked the Vrancea to the Moldavian state. It had the right to send its representative to the Moldavian court; and it was this assembly which guaranteed the traditional privileges due to the region: a monopoly on salt, ecclesiastic autonomy, the fight to forbid any trespassing from the outside. Through its emissary, the 'merchant of the Vrancea', all the outside commerce of the villages was monopolized. Not until the nineteenth century did this general confederation of the Vrancea proceed to divide the mountains, an operation undertaken without state control, which lasted until the middle of the century and which is fortunately documented.

In all likelihood this confederation was a bastardized form of what all the other pre-state inter-village confederations were like. In our time, there is no trace of a 'tribal aristocracy', which is logical since this aristocracy was a warrior one and it is obvious that the state could not allow the existence of such peasant republics and allow them to have their own army.

We can find in the *voivodats* of which our eldest documents speak something in common with this true social fossil, the Vrancea. The old documents speak of the existence of *knez* and of voivodes. One can only interpret them in this way: the *knez* must have been village chiefs, or chiefs of small confederations of villages; the voivode was the chief of a whole confederated region. The terms themselves facilitate the interpretation; one finds them among the South Slavs, the Moravians, the Poles and the Russians originally meaning 'nobles' or 'chiefs' of village groups, professional warriors who had an 'army chief' or voivode at their head. The oldest mentions of such *voivodats*, if we accept those included in the anonymous chronicle of the 'Notary of King Bela' (which attests to the existence, in Transylvania before the Hungarian conquest, of the legendary *voivodats* of Menumorouth, Glad and Gelou), are those of the diploma of 1247[11] concerning a proposal made by the Hungarian to the Hospitaler Knights, to come and take possession of the Romanian *voivodats* of Litovoiu and Fărcaş and also to reconquer that of Seneslav from the Tartars. All three *voivodats* were in Wallachia. We have ample information on them: there was a flourishing economic life, there existed an aristocracy, the *maiores terrae*, who had an *apparatu bellico* at their disposal, and an obligation on the part of the population to furnish *omnium ultilitatum, redditum ac servitiorum*. This gives us a summary description of what the pre-state formations were like before the creation of the Wallachian state.

The document of 1247 dates from only a few years after the great Tartar invasion which swept through the central regions of Europe. Evidently, even under nomad domination, the indigenous social formations were able to exist and evolve up to the thirteenth century. To understand how this could happen some explanations about the conquering nomads would be useful.

Sedentary farmers and nomadic shepherds

Some social historians have postulated an inevitable law according to which the villages of peaceful sedentary farmers would necessarily be the victims of nomadic pastoral warrior tribes. The 'Iranian' would eternally be the prey of the 'Turanian'. Oppenheimer[12] invokes the tradition of Ibn Khaldun to support his theory that states can only be formed by the conquest of sedentaries by nomads. And even a Marxist like K. Kautsky[13] postulates a law of cyclical conquest where nomads become sedentarized after conquest, being conquered in their turn by other nomads, newly arrived from the steppe. He considered this fundamental to all human history before the coming of the capitalist cycle.

But to see only peaceful sedentary peoples and warlike nomads eternally in conflict is to reduce history to an excessively simplistic schema and thus to engage in bad sociology. In fact, the process is much more complex than is claimed by this theory of a wandering life across

11. Latin text published from the Vatican registers by Theiner, volume I, pp. 208–11 (*Reg. Vat.*, volume XXII, pp. 75–6).
12. Franz Oppenheimer, *Der Staat*, Frankfurt am Main, 1907
13. K. Kautsky, *Der Ursprung des Christentums, eine historische Untersuchung*, Stuttgart, 1910.

the deserts, a necessary step in the conquest of a Canaan where milk and honey flow freely. The essential problem is not that of conquest itself. It is to know in what way a feudal society is born out of, or in spite of, a nomadic conquest of a group of village communities made up of farmers and herders. To solve it, one must remember the fact that in any conquest of a people by another, two social structures meet, each with its own social history. The new situations which come out of the conquest, that is to say, out of exploitation of one people by another, are, in the last instance, determined by the social state of the conquering and conquered peoples. Every mode of exploitation must adapt itself to the modes of organization of the material to be exploited, and conversely the processes of production undergo the effects of this exploitation.

As far as the conquering nomadic peoples are concerned, they are always tribal confederations. But the peoples subjected to conquest can be at extremely varied stages of evolution, from the system of slave or colonial latifundi organized within large states, to primitive village communities which are still at the initial stage of tribal formations. The conquering peoples will thus have to solve completely different social problems, depending on the degree of development attained by the peoples they are exploiting.

Social organization of the conquering nomads

Within a pastoral tribe, a 'tribal aristocracy' can be born from the creation of a specialized warrior group that protects the tribe from livestock thefts by other tribes. Maintained in the beginning by their tribesmen, these groups of warriors receive a tithe from the common products necessary for their subsistence, profiting also by some more or less freely given labour dues. As war is their only profession, these groups grow rich from the spoils and slaves seized from neighbouring tribes. To add to their strength and undertake distant raids, they become federalized, and under the form that Marx calls *eine Reisegesell-schaft* they can gather impetus like an avalanche, growing larger as they move, crushing refractory tribes along the way, taking with them those who, whether they like it or not, enter the conquering confederation according to a certain hierarchy which can itself be called a type of 'feudalism'.

As soon as the military power of the Roman Empire ended, these confederations of tribes, conglomerates of diverse people, bearing the name of the tribal chief, flung themselves toward the Roman borders, passed them, and subjugated the abandoned provinces. The Germanic tribes were the first to invade Western Europe. Their social history is fairly well known: in Gaul as in Italy, they found a system of organization based on the great slave and colonial domains, they divided up the land among themselves and, by large territorial areas, the tribes took over the land of the provinces, massacred the former owners and took their place (as did, for example, the Franks) or else installed themselves as co-sharers (as did the Burgundians in south-east France or the Goths in Italy). Thus were feudal societies born.

It was completely different for the nomads of the Far East, who, after having conquered their immense Asiatic empires from China all across Europe, were tempted by the idea of sacking Byzantium or Rome. Clearing a route across the steppes of the Ukraine, they made their way around the Carpathians, coming out in the south on the Balkan Peninsula, or towards the north in the Panonian plain. In all of Asia and in Eastern Europe, they had to deal with and subjugate people living in free village communities.

These nomads could not possibly occupy the land as landowners. Nor did they do so. At first, they only raided and, in case of need, they made further punitive raids. They settled far from the cities and villages, preferring the steppe and pre-steppe zones, establishing their fortified camps from which they organized a system of parasitic, purely fiscal exploitation, dividing the land into large tribal areas in hierarchical relation to each other, according to the rules of 'nomad feudalism'. A network of roads dotted with customs points, watched by a perfectly organized police, controlled the country, enabling them to collect duties on all commercial transport undertaken by the indigenous peoples. A second system of exploitation was carried out in the mines and at the fairs, a third in the cities and on their artisans. A fourth was directed at the villages, which were subjected to the payment of tithes and to the transport of cereal products and livestock to the local nomad centres.

This *purely fiscal*[14] means of taking possession of a country was basically less onerous than that practised by the Romans. Under the condition

14. N. Iorga long ago recognized the 'predatory' nature of the nomadic state formations. According to him, 'The Arabs were not numerous and they brought with them no political preconceptions, nor even economic ones, which might properly be called their own. To believe that they might have destroyed a lucrative trade is to miss the point that the value of all conquest – even that of Attila the Hun which drew in the Romans of neighbouring provinces for whom he became a virtual emperor – lies in the use of those revenues which the conquerors found and which self interest makes them develop'. ('L'inter-pénétration de l'Orient et de l'Occident au moyen-âge', *Bulletin de la section historique*, Academia Română, 1929, volume XV, p. 16).

that they satisfied the demands of this fiscal arrangement, the subjugated populations were free to continue their way of life, to keep their social organizations, their customs, their religions and their languages, without, however, any possibility of evolving toward higher social forms. The 'predatory states' kept their nomadic character in the sense that they were not bound to a definite territory. Moving on to a new plunder, or chased out by new arrivals, they left their area open for replacements who settled into the empty territorial cells. The newcomers inherited their fiscal and road system as well as their customs network.

Thus, contrary to what happened in the west, where a social synthesis between the conquering and conquered populations could be made, in the eastern zones where the village communities dominated, 'predatory states' could form without creating a new synthesis. This was even true of long-term states such as the Perso-Indian Empire of the Great Moguls. Depending on the vicissitudes of history, a series of 'substitution states' succeeded each other. Many times these 'predatory states' ended by being reconquered and chased out by the indigenous peoples. This was the case in Wallachia and Moldavia (as well as Russia). The Hungarian nomads alone had a unique fate: settled in Pannonia, having given up their incursions into the west, they became Catholic and were able to create a permanent state which included Transylvania.

Romanians and peoples of the steppe

We are rather poorly informed about the first arrivals in the old Province of Dacia. Only the last waves, of the Cumans and Tartars, are better known to us. It appears that the Cumans in particular had a rather powerful influence on Wallachia. Their toponymic and onomastic traces are sufficiently strong for N. Iorga to be able to pose the problem of a 'Romanian–Cuman synthesis' in many of his works.[15] It is especially the existence of the 'bishopric of the Cumans' of Wallachia, with 'Milcovia' as its centre, which constitutes the pivot of our information. As the Cumans had become Catholic, information concerning them also comes from the west, as for example the letter of 1234 from Pope Gregory IX to King Bela of Hungary, in which he complains that

15. N. Iorga, *Histoire des Roumains et de la romanité orientale*, 9 volumes, Bucharest, 1940. See also *Istoria României* (History of Romania) published by the N. Iorga Institute of Historical Studies, 4 volumes, Bucharest, 1960–4. Also Barbu Câmpina, 'Le problème de l'apparition des Etats féodaux roumains', *Nouvelles études d'histoire*, volume I, Bucharest, 1955 (volume presented at the Xth World Congress of Historical Sciences, 1955).

in the bishopric of the Cumans there are, as we have learned, populations called Wallachians who, although they call themselves Christian, still have different rites and customs and do unnameable things. For, scorning the Roman Church, they do not receive the churchmen of our venerated brother, the bishop of the Cumans, who has his diocese in these parts, but follow pseudo-bishops of Greek rite.

The Wallachian population thus had its own ecclesiastical organization strong enough for 'pseudo-bishops' to be spoken of. This signifies the existence, at the beginning of the thirteenth century, of confederated villages living under the dominant layer of this people of the steppe, the Cumans, which brings us back again to our first conclusion: that of the possible existence of tribal forms of life of the Wallachian population before the formation of their autochthonous state. This Cuman bishop as well as all the Cuman formations were destroyed by the Tartars at the time of their great invasion of Europe, but without a doubt the local population survived. The Cumans, emigrating to Hungary, left their place free for newly arrived Tartars who thus occupied all of eastern Wallachia, which is spoken of in the documents of the fourteenth century as the 'Tartar regions'. Eastern Wallachia was only reconquered later, by the Wallachian state which succeeded the old voivodal formations situated in the west of the country and about which the diploma of 1247 gives us most useful information.

In Moldavia, the Tartar domination lasted much longer, as it was much later than in Wallachia that the Romanians of Transylvania (and not local Romanians) could reconquer a land ravaged by a war that seems to have been more severe than the one which liberated Wallachia 'down to the Great Sea and on both banks of the Danube'. But in Moldavia, too, the traces of a local Romanian population exist, under the same form of peasant communities, grouped into free confederations or united around several sometimes urban centres with an enserfed rural hinterland, the *ocoale*.

We are better informed about the Tartars[16] due to the fact that they dominated Russia over centuries, leaving enough information to tell us of their system of exploitation. It is very likely that they used the same procedures in Romania as in Russia. We know that after the break-up of the Golden Horde, the tribes of the Deşt-I-Kipciak, those 'from the corner of the Black Sea', who remained as masters in the region in which we are interested, divided up the land into great tribal areas (the tribe of Berendei, for example, owned the Dobrogea). But if the nomad domination had the same character in this country that it had in Russia,

16. B. D. Grekov and A. I. Yacubovskii, *The Golden Horde and Its Decadence*, Romanian translation from the Russian, Bucharest, 1953.

we must not lose sight of the fact that Dacia was an old Roman province and not, as in Russia, a country that Rome never conquered.

The nomads, finding themselves masters of regions where village communities abounded, imposed the payment of certain products and a corvée on the villages. In this way, they did not impose a head tax but one by village groups, the village in its entirety being responsible for the execution of its obligations. An apparatus of fiscal civil servants, the *daruga*, established by meticulous censuses what each village had to pay. Then the village chiefs had to take complete responsibility for the tax collection.[17]

The survival of the rural communities under nomad domination had the gravest social consequences. For in the free indigenous military democracies, the relations between the chief and his subjects had long kept their initial character of tribal fraternity. The tithes and corvée paid in exchange for services rendered to the collectivity and the chiefs (at first elected by popular assembly) became hereditary, but chiefs remained liable to the censure of their communities. But when the nomads used these chiefs as local agents of their service, giving them if necessary the support of arms to assure the collection of taxes and the transport of products, these indigenous chiefs could cut off the ties that bound them to their tribes, thus rising above them and growing rich at their expense. In the *Miserabile Carmen* of the monk Rogerius,[18] who describes the invasion of the Tartars into Transylvania, we can find direct confirmations of the manner in which the nomads used the *knez*, members of the 'tribal aristocracy'. A community of interests could be established between the indigenous 'tribal aristocracy' and the nomad conquerors; this was strong enough to cement a social synthesis, a synthesis not between populations but between aristocratic layers.

But the voivodes and *knez* making up a distinct class, bearing the Turanian name of 'boyars', still had a common interest with their old tribal brothers, that of independence. They thus profited from any favourable moment to reconquer and cast off the foreign yoke and establish their own states. This was possible when the power of the

17. N. Iorga, 'Les premières cristallisations d'État des Roumains', *Bulletin de la section historique*, no. 1, 1920. The Tartar Khans 'strongly felt the need to have native rulers of the same race, language, and blood as the other subjects in order to collect the tithe, collect gifts, and ultimately to perform certain tasks such as commanding the contingents of Christian Tartars of whom the Byzantine chronicles speak. This was the case in Moldavia, in the plains of the Danube, and of course in the Russian area' (p. 34).
18. *Monumenta Germaniae historica*, volume XXIX, Hanover, 1892. Latin text and Romanian translation by G. Popa-Lisseanu, *Izvoarele istoriei românilor* (Sources for the history of the Romanians), volumes V–VI, Bucharest, 1935.

Tartars began to wane. The autochthonous states which were born were themselves, in a way, 'substitution states', in the sense that the warrior class which had led the reconquest continued to fill the fiscal role which the nomads had assigned them; but this time for their own profit. They maintained the road network which led across the country between the centres of Eastern Europe and those of the Black Sea, of the South Balkans and of the Adriatic, roads sown with customs points and with *Stapelplätze*. They also maintained the network of *olac-s*, a Tartar term designating the internal road system. They continued to exploit the mines, especially the salt mines, and the great fisheries of the Danube, as well as to collect taxes from the merchants and artisans of the nascent cities. The cereal tax *iliş* kept the Turanian word *ülüs* and fiscal exemptions continued to be called by the Tartar name *tarcan*. The new autochthonous class of boyars even inherited a whole mass of gypsy slaves which the nomads left behind upon retreating.

Having posed the problem and formulated our hypotheses, we must now leave history and take up sociology. For if the whole of Romanian social history is really dominated by the presence of village communities and if such communities survived to our day, it is obviously necessary to study these survivors and, for this, there is no other means than field work. Although these communities were found only as dying survivors, they can throw light on many historical problems. And if they cannot solve the questions of their origin, at least they can illuminate the social conditions which provoked the process of decay. Thus, they can explain the latter-day forms which generally replaced them, and so guide our historical research.

Part I

The internal life of two types of contemporary village communities: 'non-genealogical' and 'genealogical'

As their right to the land is undivided, that is according to use, it is not possible to establish that someone owns such and such an area and another that other area. For if ownership is joint, it follows that each member of a village can keep for himself and for his own account as much land as he can work and clear.
    Document of 1793
Marking out the village of Soleşti, we found 411 pieces of land, each piece of land twenty steps wide, without counting the area for hay. And these pieces of land were divided by three ancestors and it was decided which part should belong to what ancestor.
    Document of 1709

3 ❧ The free communities of the 'archaic' type

Since free villages (*răzeşi* and *moşneni*) still existed between the two world wars they could be subjected to field research, undertaken as monographs between 1925 and 1946 by the School of Sociology directed by my teacher, Professor Dimitrie Gusti.

We have already had occasion to report on at least one of these villages, the most archaic one we knew, in the three volumes published in French, to which we send the reader for fuller information.[1] We will attempt in the following pages to synthesize our knowledge concerning these communities, presenting only the details which will help us understand the history. We will moreover divide this material in two, for there are two principal forms of social organization in these villages, each one helping us to analyse two distinct historical periods.

    1. Stahl, *Nerej*.

35

'Non-genealogical' archaic villages and 'genealogical' evolved villages

Without a doubt, the great majority of Romanian communal villages that we were able to study directly have a clear 'genealogical' character, not only in the sense that the inhabitants claimed that they formed a single large family lineage descended from a single ancestral hero believed to have been the founder of the village, but also because they settled their patrimonial rights in the whole of the village territory according to a family genealogy, either memorized or written. Many believed in the historical truth of this family origin of the village communities, finding it normal that family-villages could exist; for them there was no problem.

However, it is doubtful. From the outset it appears that the assertions of the peasants all have the character of legal myths that belong not to the archaic villages but to those which have already attained a higher level of evolution. In particular such myths originate when the original community begins to decay and divides its property into unequal, hereditary parts, and then into private property. Let us note first that there are some villages, particularly those in the most isolated regions of the country, which invoke no ancestral hero and only use a genealogy as a measure of hereditary rights to strips of land. Let us mention next that in many cases we have documentary proof that genealogical villages began as non-genealogical ones, the transition from one to the other having taken place in circumstances which can be analysed. We will thus study the non-genealogical villages first.

The essential traits of the village communities

From the theoretical point of view, we agree that Tschuprow[2] was not completely wrong when he defined communal villages as 'a group of households, holders of a territory, bound among themselves by relations such that the group has the right to interfere, according to precise rules, in the economic activity and in the legal rights of each particular household'. But we will add that this definition only works for the 'free' villages; for, as we will show, *in the case of a village which falls under the domination of a feudal lord, the lord takes over, by force, the old rights of 'general assemblies'* which thus lose their powers even though the village remains 'communal'.

2. Alexander A. Tschuprow, *Die Feldgemeinschaft, eine morphologische Untersuchung*, Strassburg, 1902.

Because, in fact, the village community is above all a mode of economic exploitation of a collective territory by pastoral and very rudimentary agricultural techniques. These are regulated by social relations directly derived from old tribal organizations whose traces are maintained because of the poor degree of development of the processes of production. Thus, although they are 'enserfed' in the feudal manner, these villages remain 'communal' as long as the common exploitation of the village territory is assured by the same primitive pastoral and agricultural techniques. This will remain the case as long as these communities do not make direct contact with a more developed market economy.

In any case, the analysis of the village assemblies remains the keystone of the original system. Its breakdown begins the process of enserfment. For this it is useful to study its laws.

Rights and duties of the village assemblies
Rules concerning the convocation, debates and decisions of the assemblies

The village assembly (*obştia, grămada satului*) normally holds its sessions on holidays, preferably after church, outdoors, in the shade of a tree, but also on any other day, in any place, depending on the circumstances; in case of need, such as a peasant revolt, they meet furtively, at night, in the forest, spreading word of the day, hour and place of the assembly from house to house.

In fact, the only rule is that there be a quorum. All inhabitants have equal right to participate once they have reached maturity, women as well as men. They discuss questions on the agenda and vote orally. No one presides over the sessions; no one has a right to the title of village 'chief'. He who wants to speak does so, expressing any opinion that he sees fit. Those of more stature, family heads, older people, who are termed 'good and old men', 'white beards', are, in fact, due to what jurists call a 'reverential fear', more likely to impose their will since their sons and nephews hasten to take their side. At a later time, once the patrimonial rights had ceased to be equal, the voices themselves became unequal according to wealth in property. At times youths make their rights felt in spite of the family heads, often by open revolt. Sometimes there is heated debate, degenerating into a fight, especially when it is a case of different lineages contesting their reciprocal rights. But when a majority forms, its opinion prevails.

The village, object and subject of laws

The assembly is, in fact, the nominal landholder of the territory, for if we have to admit that every territory must have an 'owner' who can manage and defend it against any other competitor, then it must be the village community that has this function. The village assembly seeks to safeguard the collective patrimony in two ways: by not allowing neighbouring villages to trespass over the inter-village boundaries and by fighting against any attempt by the feudal class to conquer the village.

In the case of conflicts between villages over the territorial boundaries surveyors are generally called in, but whether they are named by the state or privately they never proceed without the village seeing and knowing about it. The surveyors are accompanied the length of their course by a double crowd of peasants: one from the village whose territory is being measured and one from the neighbouring villages involved in the litigation. At every point, witnesses come out of the crowd, give testimony, continually watched by the two crowds which are also keeping an eye on the honesty of the surveyor. It is an unforgettable sight to see the villages carrying out such operations, accompanied by this ritual, constituting one of the most interesting chapters in the ethnography of field boundaries.

When the village has to defend its legal rights against the action of a boyar, delegates must be elected, for it is evident that the whole village cannot speak out to plead its case. But these village delegates go to the litigation accompanied by a large number of villagers, men and women. Thus a document of 1807 attests that 600 men on horseback went from the Vrancea to Jassy, where they stayed for seven weeks, in order to defend their rights. And, not many years ago, when some of these villages were being judged, the courtrooms were filled with their popular assemblies which, by gestures, murmurs and shouts, approved or disapproved of the proceedings. Cases are known where such groups, having lost their case and been declared, against all justice, liable to corvée, sought vengeance by going at night barefooted and in their nightgowns, carrying torches, to put a collective curse on the unjust boyar by putting out their torches in pitch, which was supposed to kill the boyar and his whole family without delay.

The village is in fact a subject and an object of the law, able to pass contracts by which it sells, rents or pawns itself for a loan. Villages can thus sell themselves as serfs. This constitutes the most significant phenomenon for the whole period from the end of the sixteenth century to the middle of the eighteenth. Even in 1864, at the time of the law which abolished the corvée, there were many villages which had recently sold themselves in this way, or, to put it better, had temporarily rented themselves, accepting, for a certain sum, the condition of peasants liable to corvée.

The village could also sell its territory, all or in part, specifying that the 'dry' land was for sale, 'without men'. On the other hand, the village could buy land; there are even old cases where a free village might buy a serf village.

Leasing the land, all or in part, or pawning it, was also practised communally. This patrimonial right extended not only to the property but also to its inhabitants, sometimes taking most singular aspects. There are cases, though rare, it is true, where an inhabitant who could not pay his debts was leased out by the village to his creditor as a worker or servant. Or, very frequently, where a debtor had fled, the assembly sold his patrimony to indemnify itself, for the village was bound by a collective fiscal and penal solidarity.

The collective penal and fiscal solidarity of the village

Until the middle of the last century, in penal and fiscal matters the state was only able to deal with the village community and not individually with each peasant. Serious infringements of the law, in which the state reserved the right of judgement, thus gave place to a collective penal solidarity where the village was absolved only after arresting the guilty and handing them over to the authorities. Otherwise the village had heavy fines to pay (the *duşegubina*), an unfortunate circumstance which often brought about its enserfment. The village thus had to organize a local police, supervised by the organs of the state.

The same collective responsibility[3] applied in fiscal matters. Taxes were not established 'by head' but by village, according to the fiscal rules of the *cislă*: a total sum to be paid or a quantity of products to be furnished was imposed on each village. The village assembly, once it knew the total tax, proceeded to divide the sum among all the households on the basis of an evaluation of the economic resources of each household. The quota of someone failing to pay his part had to be paid by the collectivity. Even if the state tried to introduce a head

3. D. D. Motolescu-Vădeni, *Gesamtburgschaft im rumänischen Rechte, verglichen mit anderer Rechte*, Prag-Weinberge (no date).

tax, as was done in Bucovina, the part of Moldavia that the Austrian state occupied in 1775, the assembly continued to respect the traditional rules, ready to camouflage the result to fit the Austrian fiscal rules. Let us underline the fact that the importance of this village fiscal solidarity, although very strong, must not be exaggerated to the point of making it the determining cause of the collective village formations, as some believe. For there is a mass of other social functions within the assemblies which have nothing to do with the fiscal rights of the state. Many are in direct relation to the economic system of the village.

The right to prohibit economic abuses

As we will see, all the family households making up the village had an equal right to use the common patrimony: forests, prairies, pasture land, farm land, waters, etc. But so that this right did not degenerate into anarchy private initiative was submitted to the judgement of the village public opinion and if need be, to the decision of the assembly, which had the right to prohibit an economic activity so that the essential rule of equality of rights be respected.

The rights of the assembly went as far as taking in hand, if necessary, the organization of the economic life of the village, dividing and distributing the land or setting laws to be followed concerning farming, pasture, construction and clearing. This was the law, moreover, that most easily enabled the boyars to take over full ownership of the territory. But on this subject we will have to give fuller details by analysing the economic activities of the villages, both free and serf.

Authentification and control of private contracts

To supervise better the economic life of the village, the assembly had the right to control and authenticate private contracts that the inhabitants of the village could make among themselves or with outsiders. These contracts, in order to be valid, had to be made with the consent of the assembly. If the contract was made in writing, it was necessary to have a large number of witnesses and the acknowledgement that 'the whole village, rich and poor' was in agreement. 'This document was drawn up before the whole village', 'the amount was paid in the presence of the whole village', say the documents. If it was not a written contract, the agreement of the village was manifested by public festivals (the *aldămaș*), sometimes taking place in church, with a special ritual accompanied by a secular ritual.

Moreover, it was not only the legal contracts that had this character, but all important acts in the lives of the villagers: birth, marriage, death, festivals, all had a ceremonial and public nature; they make up a very rich folklore which is based on a 'diffuse collective memory' but does not directly concern us here.

Rights of maintaining justice and of interfering in family life

Even conflicts between families and within a family fell under the assembly's jurisdiction. Not only did public opinion note the behaviour and attitudes going against law and public morality, something expressed many times by the annual ceremony of the youth who 'shouted through the village' the ironic tales of the storytellers and the village chronicle of scandals, but the assembly also had the right to judge the guilty. One went to the assembly so that it could settle the conflicts 'before the whole village'. The assembly, as arbiter, thus found a solution for the litigants, using as its guide its knowledge of the precedents, the juridical norms of the common law, and especially its good sense and feeling of justice. In penal matters, the village went further, jailing the guilty or exposing them in public in the stocks.

The village delegates with a limited mandate

If possible, the assembly itself went about executing its decisions. If not, it elected a delegate with a limited mandate, whom it could relieve at any moment and whose words and deeds were continually controlled by the presence of all the inhabitants. The most visible person was undoubtedly the tax collector who, by his contact with the state organs, was somehow endowed with a double quality. One can still find in Romanian villages the 'notched sticks' (the *răboj*) which served as accounting registers, each contributor having in his name a piece of wood cut in half, on which was marked with a knife the conventional signs showing the amounts paid in such a way that each half could serve to verify the other. The stick also had a symbolic meaning, as a sign of coercive force, for it was used to beat offenders. The state tried to transform these village delegates into state civil servants, but the village kept struggling to safeguard its right to consider them as mere representatives.

The village also had to elect or nominate certain professional people. The most important people of the village were the pastor, the miller, the potter, and the guard. It is perhaps not superfluous to insist, however, that there is no trace of a caste system in Romania; on the contrary the full equality of all constitutes the supreme law. As for the village priest, he could not be elected by the village as he had to be approved by the episcopal hierarchy. But the village could elect a candidate for priesthood, give him the means for the necessary schooling in a monastery or bishopric, and make contracts between the candidates for priesthood and the village assembly which took responsibility, with certain conditions, for 'making a priest'. Let us note that in that exceptional area, the Vrancea, the fourteen villages making up the regional confederation had economic contact with the market only through the intermediary of a 'Vrancea merchant' holding a monopoly over the 'outside' commerce of this autonomous region with the rest of the country.

However, a class of village chiefs was born, without really being an aristocracy. In our contemporary villages as soon as a social category of rich peasants was formed, they obtained a preferential position with a mostly economic base. This does not mean that, in past centuries, a tribal aristocracy of military function did not exist. But by the twentieth century these villages were only the decaying remnants of old communities, the state having captured all their common rights, leaving only the private ones. These are sufficient, however, to understand how the whole series of rights and duties of the popuar assemblies at the heart of these 'primitive democracies', whose administrative power was shared by all the group's members when they were assembled, could be transformed just as easily into the means of social oppression if a lord monopolized them in his favour.

Nominal owner of the common patrimony, responsible before the state for the collection of taxes, with the possibility of managing the economic activity of the peasant households, of prohibiting and of authorizing the deeds of the inhabitants, able to partition the land, cutting out for himself the largest part, to judge the people and apply penalties, the village chief as he became a lord, rapidly turned into an absolute master. With the help of circumstances, nothing was easier than to go from the use to the abuse of these rights.

Family organization of the 'indivisible' type
The rules of family life

Every old village contains but a few ancestral lineages, a few dozen at the most. The total population rises, at most, to a few hundred. The

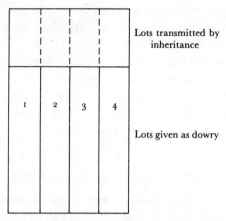

Fig. 5. Diagram of the division into lots which are given as dowry and transmitted by inheritance.

fact that they form a 'village' and hold a common territory to which they have equal right is explained by the fact that such villages derive from ancient tribal organizations. These villages form closed social groups, necessarily endogamous, for exogamous marriages would allow inhabitants from other villages into the community, thus upsetting the order that must reign from territory to territory. It is true that sometimes girls, who have no rights to the land, do marry outside the village. Their dowry may consist only of what 'can be taken away in a cart', i.e. nothing but furniture. To take a wife from a neighbouring village, which is generally poorly viewed, is accompanied by a whole ritual, simulating abduction and purchase.

Once a family group is established, by clearing or simply taking over a certain part of the territory, it grows, biologically and socially, until it forms a hamlet. According to Le Play's term these are 'stem families'. Once the sons are grown, they take wives in the village, found their own household and settle down near their parents. They clear land and build houses together, but the households live separately, as small individual families. The parents, when their sons marry, provide them with a dowry. An old man who has, for example, four sons, will divide his land in four parts, keeping for himself only a transversal zone (see fig. 5), called 'the soul piece', the only one to be inherited and not given in dowry. In addition, one of the sons, usually the youngest, will inherit the paternal house, on condition that he take care of the parents and render the multiple services, both religious and secular, deemed necessary for the peace of their souls. It is, in fact, a 'law of male ultimogeniture', a sort of effective old-age insurance. The whole cleared land area, houses and gardens will ultimately be divided by the dictates of this agnatic inheritance pattern.

Let us stress that even if at the beginning several unrelated families settle in the same hamlet, they will end, in several generations, by forming a single family group, a single 'lineage'. These hamlets of family descendants are often so isolated from other similar hamlets that they even have a private cemetery.

Genealogical joint possession of the first degree

As long as these households have plenty of room and live in peace, they need not establish their genealogy. But as soon as the descendants pass a certain limit, at the slightest conflict the households will take control of the land they hold, recalculating the previous dowries, and thus establishing a retrospective genealogy. Let us name this sort of private organization, valid for a single family line, as 'genealogical joint possession of the first degree'. In Romanian terminology there is another way to express it: we say that this group 'walks on a certain number of ancestors'. That is to say, it is organized as though a certain number of equal sub-groups, each symbolized by an 'ancestor', derived from a single original ancestor. If the territory is divided into three household groups with equal rights, we say that the hamlet 'walks on three ancestors' or 'three old men', 'walking' having the sense of 'subdividing'.

The actual situation resulting from a series of successive endowments is thus juridically camouflaged, *a posteriori*, under the form of succession. The lineage thus formed bears a name derived from the common ancestor (be he real or fictive). If the hamlet is recent, men will remember the name of the oldest family head who will be considered the ancestor, or the first arrived family chiefs, considered as 'brothers', of the lineage of a hypothetical common ancestor.

In every case, the group expresses its solidarity by invoking an ancestor, whose name, if necessary, it invents, taking it from that of the hamlet which goes from being a toponym to a socionym. If, for example, the inhabitants of the hamlet of Chiricari want to symbolize their rights by means of their ancestor, they will say that the whole lineage descends from someone named Chirică, from whom they will derive as many 'big brothers' as there are household groups equal in rights, and then a whole series of 'little brothers', representing the

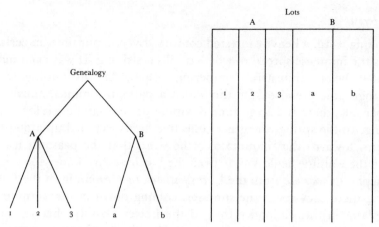

Fig. 6. Equivalence between genealogy and lots of land.

unequal branches of successive generations. Such genealogies go back only about five or six generations, although we have the certainty, sometimes the proof, that the lineages are much older.

There are cases where such genealogies are written down. If, for example, the village contests the rights of a group, a document is drawn up before witnesses comprising a genealogy which certifies that this group derives from that other group, sometimes expressed in Biblical language which is individualized: so and so is son of so and so who, himself, was the son of so and so, etc. All these genealogies have a belated character, appearing only in cases of conflict or controversy, thus at a stage of decay of the archaic village, when the population has grown to such size that the territory begins to be coveted by too many competitors.

Itinerant pastoral and agricultural techniques

What is most striking in every village of the archaic type is the extremely low level of pastoral and agricultural technology. This gives the local rural countryside such a special character that one might think oneself in some 'ethnographic reserve' that had survived miraculously until our time.

The forest

Romania is still a heavily forested country. Even in our time, in certain areas the immense spread of wooded hills is striking. It was even more wooded before industrial lumbering began. Let us outline some biogeographic premises. On the high Carpathian summits, above the timber line, there is a large zone of alpine pasture land good for sheep raising. In the spring, the great collective herds were led up along the streams towards the 'mountains' (the word that the peasants use to mean these alpine fields is *munţi* from the Latin *montes*), under the watch of shepherds (*păstori*, from the Latin *pastores*, or *păcurari*, from the Latin *pecus*); there they spent the summer, coming down in the autumn to the plains in transhumance toward the Lower Danube. Below, there is a large forest zone, first of pines, then of beech and, closest to the plain, of oak. The human habitation is mostly in the forest zone, of beech or oak, or in the vast clearings which are especially visible in the region of the sub-Carpathian depressions. Still lower down, there is the vast plain, often of an ante-steppe or steppe character. The old maps and the vestigial traces in the mountains show that large bands of tall forest came down along the rivers all the way to the banks of the Danube, dividing the plain into more or less populated compartments.

The life of the old villages was largely tied to these forests. They served as a refuge when, by lighting fires from hilltop to hilltop, the plains people made it known across the land that a horde of Tartars or Turks was coming, pillaging and massacring, forcing the villagers to flee into the forests to hide. A rich collection of legends has preserved up to our day the tradition of these unfortunate times. The boyars and sometimes the voivode's court itself took refuge there, hastily building a wooden chapel in a clearing and moving in for long months at a time. The army could make a safe retreat in the woods and by cutting trees make fairly impregnable fortification or else make the forest itself a defensive tool, piling up trees and then pushing them over on any enemy daring to come into the trap.

Gathering techniques. The peasants, however, also found in the forest a direct source of food. There they picked fruits, berries, roots and mushrooms. During dry years (as, for example, for two years immediately after the disasters of the Second World War) people resorted to a 'famine diet', which is very interesting ethnographically for it permits us to reconstitute the ancient ways of using the forest for simple gathering.[4] In addition, they hunted and fished in the rivers. A rather surprising detail is that they also harvested the hives of wild bees, who had probably 'escaped from cultivated hives', but who were to be found in rather substantial numbers. In 1911, for example, it was noticed that in a certain forest belonging to a boyar, the forester watched over more than 300 hives, spread through the forest in rotten tree trunks. In the forests of free villages, any peasant had the right to take them. But it was the wood itself that was most useful for these villages, which were still in what is called the 'civilization of woods'. It was used not only for heating but also for building houses and tools: beams, planks, posts, shingles, ploughs, forks, spades, harrows, and so on, everything was made of wood, fashioned by the peasants themselves, sometimes with exceptional artistry.

Pastoral utilization of the forest. In the heart of the forest the villages raised their animals. There they grazed the pigs, the goats and even large livestock. Eating acorns, beechnuts, leaves and grass, the herds roamed around almost wild, unfenced, always in danger of attack from wild animals, especially liking the clearings with good grass. But as these were rare, artificial clearings were made by the 'drying' technique: the bark of trees was removed, the trees dried standing and, once the sun could reach the ground, grass grew. To clear the ground better, the dried trees were burned. These clearings were called *ochi de lumină* (eye of light) or simply *lumină* from the Latin *lumen*. Or else they were called *secătură* (from the Latin verb *secare*, to cut, thus to dry), or *runc* (from the Latin verb *runcare*, to clear). Such a clearing did not last long. In a few years, the forest took over again and it had to be abandoned for other new clearings.

In our time good forestry aims to ensure the growth of the forest, a valuable commodity. But in the old villages the procedure was the opposite: peasants spent a good part of their time clearing trees. Even today, many villages consider the forest as an obstacle to struggle against, axe in hand. In the Vrancea in 1938, during the summer nights one could often see in the distance the light of forest fires. The people laughed: 'It's one of our men who started the fire, cooking his corn meal.' 'If we aren't careful, the forest will swallow us up', they said.

These clearings obtained by drying represent a primitive foresting

4. Ion Claudian, *Alimentaţia porporului român. In cadrul antropogeografiei şi istoriei economice* (The food of the Romanian people. In an anthropological-geographic and economic historical framework), Bucharest, 1939.

technique, established according to a rhythm of 'forest–grass–forest'. The forest was also useful in obtaining food for the livestock which returned to the village for winter. Even in our day, in the spring the peasants harvest leaves which they put in large reserve piles, in case there is not enough hay. If the forest was deemed to be too far from the village, they would cut the bottom branches of isolated trees. The rural Romanian landscape abounds in 'pollard trees', with only skimpy foliage at the top, a clear ethnographic sign of very active sylvo-pastoral customs. The same technique of clearing was used, always for a pastoral purpose, to obtain 'hay holes'. But to cut the grass with a scythe, the clearing had to be specially prepared. It had to be set on fire to get rid of stumps. Then the roots had to be dug out to make the area smooth. Such a 'hay hole' was thus the result of much arduous labour. This was more long lasting, although the rhythm was the same, forest–grass–forest. The 'grass' phase was divided in two periods: grass for hay and grass for pasture. Such a clearing obtained by burning carried the name *arșiță* and was generally enclosed, at least during the hay-making phase, to prevent the animals from coming in.

Technique of the beekeepers. To harvest honey and wax in a more certain fashion than can be done from wild bees, artificial clearings were made, prepared as for hay, by the foresters. Now apiculture is done scientifically, but not long ago, bees were raised in primitive hives, simple tree trunks or straw. To harvest the wax and honey, the bees had to be killed. But the number of these apiaries situated in the forest, called *prisacă*, was enormous. Honey and wax constituted one of the important sources of revenue for the state, which collected a tithe on them. At the same time, they were important commodities. One can see their importance, for example, by noting that in 1786 a fiscal exemption from the tithe was given to poor boyars and widows, valued at 67,000 hives. The boyars had such important apiaries that law suits connected to them were tried in the princely court, supported by the testimony of the metropolitan. There was a boyar, so it was told, who had 16,000 hives.

Sylvo-agricultural techniques. Agricultural terrain could also be obtained by clearing, not by systematically cutting a whole forest, but by the same procedure of enclosed artificial clearings. The forest was 'dried', burned, the roots were dug up, the terrain was worked by hoe or plough and seeds (millet, rye, buckwheat, corn) were sown in the earth mixed

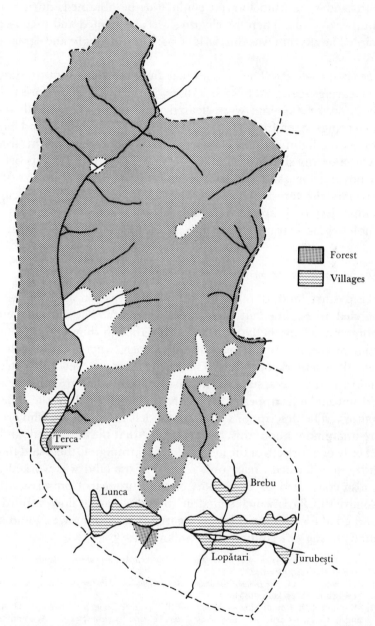

Fig. 7. Penetration into the heart of the forest by corridors and clearings. Villages in Buzău region, in the mountains to the south of Vrancea.

with cinders. A thin harvest could thus be obtained, during a short number of years. Then the clearing was abandoned and used as a 'hay hole'. The rhythm was thus as follows: forest–plough land–grass–forest.

The forest landscape. The villages take over the forest, not frontally, but by clearings scattered here and there, in the depth of the forest. To this end, gaps or openings were cleared, linking the village with the area of clearings. Seen from above, the forest is full of these round clearings of very small dimensions. Nowhere does one find clearings in 'fish-bone style', nor any sign of systematic cutting. Even in the forests belonging to boyars, the same peasant technique was used. The exception is certainly the forests which were savagely exploited by the capitalist companies; they are recognizable by such complete clearing that a whole region is transformed into a vast quasi-lunar landscape.

The pastures and the meadows

The pasture land, dominating the plains, was just as extensive as the wooded areas. The cultivated areas were rare. The old villagers were more animal raisers than farmers, even though they practised farming from prehistoric times, but for subsistence, whereas raising livestock gave them a market product. This is why there were few cultivated areas and in some places, such as the vast steppe of the Bărăgan, the plough did not make its appearance before the second half of the nineteenth century. The descriptions of Romania left by travellers who crossed it are unanimous about this. Some claimed that the cultivated land made up only one-fortieth of the land good for farming.[5] Others said that even in the best farmed areas 'only a third of the land was worked'.[6] This is also confirmed by the report of the European Commission for the Congress of Paris which stated in 1858 that 'up to now, a third of the land good for farming is barely cleared',[7] something we should keep in mind during our study of Romanian history.

5. Jean Louis Carra, *Histoire de la Moldavie et de la Valachie, avec une dissertation sur l'état actuel de ces deux provinces*, Jassy, 1777.
6 I. F. Neugebauer, *Die Donaufürstenthümer. Beschreibung der Moldau und Walachei*, volumes I–II, 2nd edition, Wrocklaw, 1854–9.
7. 'Rapport de la Commission européene de 1858 pour le Congrès de Paris', in D. A. Sturdza and C. Colescu-Vartic, *Acte şi documente relative la istoria renaşterii României* (Acts and documents about the history of the renaissance of Romania), 1889–1909, volume VI, part II.

Technique of free passage and transhumance. The plain was thus a vast pasture land on which enormous herds of horses, cattle, sheep, pigs and fowl were raised. The mountain peasants, especially those of Transylvania, spent the winters with their flocks of sheep on the banks of the Danube. In the autumn they descended to the plain, following the traditional routes marked by large stone crosses, avoiding villages, preferring to stay near the waterways and the woods. But the peasants of the hills and especially those of the Danubian plain were not transhumants, or at least their movements were local ones. They preferred to raise their herds moving freely across the pastures all around their villages, letting even the horses wander in a wild state. One traveller stated in 1834 that in Romania

the number of animals is considerable. Very few peasants have none; a rich man has up to twenty or thirty horned beasts and horses. There are even some men with hundreds. Few shelter them during the winter, under a miserable roof, for true stables do not exist... by the hundreds, sometimes by the thousands, these animals wander across the vast steppes. As with the cattle, the horses are not kept in stables but at liberty. When one wants to buy one, it must be caught and lassoed by a horseman.[8]

Likewise, in 1880, an agronomer states that in winter when 'the weather is nice, they graze the horses, who scrape away the snow with their hooves to find the grass. This freedom makes the horses of our stud farms wild: no one can approach them and to catch them one has to use a lasso. Once these horses are in the stable, they tremble when approached.'[9] This ancient state of affairs still survived in the Carpathian villages into the twentieth century. Almost all the village lands were forest and pasture. The herds of cattle and horses, even the pigs, wandered at will in the forest and around the pastures, regardless of village boundaries. Stabling and raising animals in sheds were completely unknown, as was growing fodder.

Technique of hay enclosures. Common herds were raised, watched over by shepherds. Oxen, steers, cows, horses, and pigs, after wandering all day across free common pastures from one village to another, were brought into enclosures to protect them against the rigours of climate and the attacks of wild beasts. The sheep, especially, could not be left alone in the forest and pastures as could cattle, horses and pigs. They had to be continually watched by a shepherd who brought them into an enclosure

8. Carol Freytag, *Regatul României din punctul de vedere al agriculturii sale* (The Romanian Kingdom from the point of view of its agriculture), Bucharest, 1899.
9. P. S. Aurelian, *Terra nostra, schițe economice auspra României* (Terra nostra, economic essay on Romania), Bucharest, 1880.

at night to milk them. These little round enclosures were scattered over the fields at random. After they had been used for a certain amount of time, the dung mounted up and the animals' trampling feet turned the ground into mud. The fence was then taken up and moved to another place, which is why these little enclosures are called in Romanian *mutare* (from the Latin *mutare*, to move).

The pastures. The best pasture land was reserved for hay. It was left to dry in place, before being brought into the village late in the autumn. To keep the livestock from eating it, haystacks were made in the trees, on wooden platforms or directly on the ground, when each haystack was protected by a fence. So, as the enclosures were made to keep animals from leaving, the hay enclosures were to keep them from entering.

Sometimes, when these pastures were far away from the village, the inhabitants, especially the newly married, preferred to build their house directly on the pastures so as not to have so far to go with the animals and the hay. Even those with houses in the village built themselves a hut in the pasture. In these constructions, which are called in Romanian *odai* (rooms), they made a shelter serving as stable, hay loft, and house. Young families moved in. Large families sent only a few of their members, to watch the animals during the winter. New hamlets were thus formed, sprinkled across the pasture land, giving the village a diffuse aspect, a true diaspora of houses spreading over a whole territory.

The village communities belonging to this pastoral type with a communal base are characterized by a tendency to cover the territory with multiple 'small-holdings', which form a very characteristic landscape. We find fairly old documentary testimony for this. But as common land began to grow scarce and cultivated land began to compete with pasture land, problems arose. In this situation, the state administration, for fiscal reasons, and the boyars, for economic reasons, both tried to force the houses to stay in the centre of the village near the church. The peasants, on the other hand, would try to leave the village and spread out over the fields to find free commons. Let us add that the isolated houses set near the woods were sometimes surrounded by such strong fences that they resembled small fortresses: these were the 'fortified houses', the 'walled houses' that existed in the regions most suited to the pastoral economy we have described.

The ploughlands and itinerant agriculture

Although it seems paradoxical at first, the ploughland had the same transitory character as the pastoral enclosures.[10] Agricultural technique was still in its first stages. We were able to study this in detail during our field work in 1938 in some of the Carpathian villages which still practised an itinerant agriculture, creating such a characteristic rural landscape (vast pasture land, sprinkled with enclosed islets for cereal crops among the pastoral enclosures, both periodically moved) that one could not help remembering the words of Tacitus: *arva per anno mutant et superest ager.*

The common tool was the wooden plough (without a mould-board). Sowing was primitive. The ground was neither cleared of stubble nor fertilized, nor were crops rotated. The land was cleared, the bushes, brambles and weeds pulled out and burned. The ground was ploughed twice, lengthwise and crosswise (*în lungiș și curmeziș*). If there was no plough, the earth was worked with a wooden hoe; in Romanian they say to indicate extreme poverty 'to be reduced to a wooden hoe' (*in sapă de lemn*), thus to fall back on a 'poverty technique'. Once the ground was ploughed more or less, seed was sown (millet, barley, buckwheat, corn), in spring rather than in autumn. The earth was packed with a harrow, made from thorn bushes, and a first crop grew. The second year the planting was repeated with the same crops. But this time the harvest was mediocre. The third year the ground barely produced. The ground which had become completely sterile was abandoned for a new clearing, and the cycle began again.[11] Romanian terminology has names for only the first three harvests thus obtained: the first, *în țelină*, that is, on cleared ground; the second, *în prosie*, and the third, *în răsprosie*. There is no name for a fourth harvest except for the term *samulastră*, used for any spontaneous crop of plants that are outside the cultivated area, on abandoned land.

The agriculture practised was thus itinerant, moving from place to place on the enormous pasture to profit from the abundant virgin land. Rarely, in the more densely populated villages, the same lands were returned to after a certain time and, if possible, the areas already having served as livestock enclosures, enriched with animal dung, were used.

10. P. S. Aurelian, *Exploatarea moșiilor prin meteiaj* (Exploitation of estates by share-cropping), Bucharest, 1888.
11. P. S. Aurelian, *Despre sistemele de cultura și raportul lor cu starea socială* (On systems of cultivation and their relation with the social situation), Bucharest, 1891.

Absolute joint ownership and the regime of 'holdings'

These pastoral and agricultural techniques, which presuppose the existence of an especially pastoral, not very dense, population, enjoying an abundant *terra libera*, were ruled by a system of common law which varied depending on whether it concerned relations between free villages within the village communities or between peasants and boyars in serf villages.

Let us first study the common law of free villages, of which we found the last surviving vestiges. Theoretically, every system of ownership is a system of social relations, varying with the infinite modification of ties between men in the course of their history. But all the same we must keep in mind the fact that ownership differs according to the object appropriated and the technical means of its appropriation. As long as an object exists in *practically infinite quantities*, the idea of an appropriation, that is, of monopolizing the use of it, is not possible. Thus, like air and water, the woods and fields do not constitute 'property objects' as long as, the population not being dense, they cannot be used up. The land, the woods, the pastures, the waterways belong to nobody – unless to God, as a Romanian folk song goes. The rule is thus as follows: every member of the village community has the right to use, as he deems fit, the goods of nature: 'according to his needs and his possibilities', as one of the tenets of Romanian common law affirms.

Most of these modes of using the inexhaustible goods of nature have, moreover, a *temporary nature*, leaving no trace; gathering wild berries in the forest, cutting wood, fishing or hunting, grazing animals in the pasture land, all are part of the gathering technique, which has nothing to do with an individual property right. At the most, one must grant a right to the first comer. It would be unjust for one to come and take the wood that another has cut, the game that another has hunted. Thus, a document of 1827 tells us of the fine that was applied to a peasant of the Vrancea who 'stole' a wild beehive previously marked by someone else who had found it.

There are, however, other ways of using the goods of nature which involve more human labour. To make a clearing for hay or farming in the middle of the forest is not an easy thing, and involves great effort: stripping the bark from the trees, waiting for a year while they dry, burning them, watching the fire, digging up the roots, digging the earth with a hoe and plough. This is a whole series of labours which constitute a source of rights for the man who does the work. It would

be unjust for someone to take possession of a clearing already made;
especially as nothing stops him from making his own, as many as he
likes: 'the forest is sufficient for all', 'there is room for everyone', say
the peasants to express the right which justifies these sorts of appro-
priations. A document of 1836[12] gives us a good description. It is about
a 'clearing made with an axe in the virgin forest' which was abandoned
'and the forest again took over'. A peasant invites his brothers 'to come
and clear; my brothers and nephew did not want to, saying: whoever
clears the forest owns it'. So if some of them want to claim this clearing
already made once, 'may they be cursed by the Holy Fathers of
Nicea...for I burned my eyes and my hands' making it.

These sylvo-pastoral and sylvo-pastoral-agricultural techniques give
way to a property right benefiting the man who put out the necessary
effort. The same is true for the pastoral and agricultural enclosures in
the common pasture land, even more so for the surfaces occupied by
the houses and orchards belonging to them. It would be inaccurate,
however, to apply the term 'property', or even 'possession', or any other
term from the Romanian legal repertory. In Romanian, these rights of
use, justified by work performed on collective land, are referred to by
the untranslatable term *stăpînire locurească*. One might attempt to
explain it by the rather rare French term *tènements*, which is not the
equivalent of the feudal 'tenure', for it does not refer to a land granted
by a lord, but rather to a right of *maitrise* (mastering) a piece of land
belonging to a village collectivity and which one 'holds'.

A document of 1793 attempts to define this system of Romanian
common law.

Their right to the land [*stăpînire*] being joint [*de-avalma*, in common], that is *locureşte*
by *tènements*]...it is not possible to establish, that so and so possesses so many measures
and somebody else so many. When possession is joint, by holdings, each member of the
village can hold for himself and for his own account as much land as he can occupy
and clear. And one may hold more and another less. So that there are not possessions
equal in area.[13]

Another document of 1801 confirms that

Thus we were told by several old men that in the old days the forests were not measured
or divided into strips or any other plot. Rather, anyone possessed any surface on which
he could with his own means, cut the trees and make clearings and hay and plough
fields and sites for beehives and vineyards and fruit trees or grafting wild trees; all this

12. C. D. Constantinescu-Mirceşti and H. H. Stahl, *Documente vrîncene* (Documents of the Vrancea), volume II, in manuscript. A translation of this document can be found in N. Iorga
(ed.), *Anciens documents de droit roumain*, volume I, Paris, 1930.
13. N. Iorga, *Studii şi documente* (Studies and documents), 31 volumes, Bucharest, 1901–16, volume
VI, p. 505.

area was his, none of his neighbours could take it from him. And if he sold it, he could sell it as his own belonging.[14]

As for the possibility of selling such *tènements*, it is necessary to specify that any peasant having laboured could cede his place to one of his co-villagers. In fact, it was not the land one was ceding, but rather the work furnished, given that the seller and the buyer had equal rights in the land, both being members of the same collectivity. As these holdings were, for the most part, temporary, it was not a question of a 'sale' but rather a 'leasing contract', in old Romanian *a vinde*, meaning 'to leave' as well as 'to rent' and 'to sell'. Such a legal system is very simple as long as it only has to do with temporary possessions ('ownership of the furrows' and not of the worked land). But as the peasants could use the land for planting or to construct houses on, etc., with a long-term use in mind, this sort of possession tends to be transformed into property – not yet ownership of the soil but only of the plants and constructions. A whole series of contemporary deeds, backed up by numerous documents, supports this interpretation. One reads about the 'sale', for example, of a certain number of vine plants or trees 'without the land', which continues to be the possession of the man who worked it. The buyer is considered the owner of the plants, not of the land. It is a sort of contract to lease the land forever, a 'hereditary lease', which is thus made and which is called in Romanian *besman, embatic, otaşniţă*. However, if the peasant permanently uses collective terrain which he himself cleared or burned, his right will increasingly take on a 'landed' character, although it continues to be justified by the amount of labour furnished and to remain under the control of the collectivity.

But if every inhabitant of the village had the right to use the common territory, that did not mean that he could abuse it. The rule was that one had only that which was absolutely necessary to the subsistence of the household, and the village assembly judged if the rule was respected or not. Certain customary norms were unanimously accepted, as, for example, that recognizing as legitimate only the clearings whose measured surface did not extend beyond the distance that one could throw an axe, all the way around. Likewise, if each inhabitant had the right to make enclosures anywhere, this did not mean he could make one on the route which the herds took communaly to and from the village. If poorly placed, a holding was judged antisocial and the whole village went together to destroy the fence and make the recalcitrant

14. *Ibid.*, p. 111.

peasant move, by force if necessary. Thus, for example, in 1773, a peasant

made a house where he should not, that is, on the village ploughland, without consulting anyone; the inhabitants of the village, seeing that he was building, told him several times to stop; but he did not listen and kept on building. So in the spring, when it was time for sowing, all the peasants, large and small, got together and destroyed his house.

At other times, the village would aid in moving and rebuilding fences, huts and houses on a new site that the assembly indicated was well chosen. Most often it was a question of mills, which had to be built in such a way that all those with the right could build their own mills, without anyone being able to monopolize the water course.

Technique of the 'quarters' or sections of general enclosure

As soon as communal land became scarce, hay and plough fields began to bunch up. Private enclosures became contiguous, and because of this contiguity they had to change form, from round to rectangular. Corridors were left between them to let herds pass, and a new rural landscape was born. A second chapter of the peasant agricultural system, very important from the practical and theoretical point of view, thus began with more intense agricultural and pastoral activity, brought on in part by a demographic saturation and/or by some contact with a local market. In the latter case, men wanted to grow more cereals and livestock than in the time of the subsistence economy; that is, produce began to be considered as a commodity.

It is only at this point that division of the land came in. Fundamentally, it had the same justification: equal right for all members of the community to benefit from the common lands. But as the lands were now coveted by too large a number of peasants, the rule that 'there is land for all' no longer worked. There was a double saturation: economic and demographic, which was for the time being only relative, limited to a single territory and related to the small productivity of the techniques employed. In such cases the village assembly judged it convenient, to avoid conflicts, to distribute the land equally. For this, the amount of land to be distributed was decided upon; it was cut in long parallel strips, so that all the plots were equal in surface area and in quality, and the peasants drew lots. A 'quarter' was thus formed, enclosed in a 'general enclosure' (*gardul ţarinii*), provided with a door (*porta ţarinii*) and, if necessary, it was put under the watch of a *jitar* to see that the fences were not destroyed by the herds. These 'quarters', which could be for hay or cereals, might themselves be movable, with the village changing their location from time to time.

But as there were areas of exceptional fertility, able to be cultivated for a longer period of time, with better access, and located nearer to the village centre, the quarters could be permanent and passed down from father to son. These hereditary 'quarters' constituted one of the focal points which enabled the village to transform its egalitarian system of joint ownership into joint ownership with unequal portions. Let us study these 'quarters' a little more closely, for they will give us the key to certain processes (otherwise enigmatic) leading toward the enserfment of village communities.

What we have is a rectangular piece of land, completely enclosed, cut into strips forming a bundle of parallel plots bearing the evocative name *delniţe* (from a slavic word meaning 'drawn by lot') or simply *soarte* (from the Latin term *sors*). Or else, by allusion to their shape, they are called *curea* (strip), *sfoară* (string), *blană* (plank), etc. The whole terrain, comparable in a way to a *Gewanne*, is called *raclă* or *dric* (synonyms meaning 'coffin', as if to express a piece of land buried in a vast common (i.e. jointly owned) pasture), or else *hliză*, *ţarină*, *tei*, etc. There is no possible doubt as to their origin: these quarters are the result of the egalitarian division of an old common piece of land. Not only do ethnographic proofs abound, but we also have documents, both old and recent, as witness to the fact that the quarters were born thus.

It is evident that in agricultural quarters of a permanent nature, a collective system of rules was indispensable. In working the fields, the ploughs had to follow a common direction. The paths for going and coming and for bringing in the harvest had to be laid the length of the plots and between the plots of different peasants. If the road had to cross a plot, it went at a right angle so as to do as little damage as possible, which gives the total scene an easily recognizable design. And the peasants do not forget that these fields, subjected to partitioning, were originally common territory. Thus, as soon as the harvest is completed, the hay or cereals brought in, the land lies fallow and the animals take over their rights. Common land is thus the dominant rule in these quarters. Only the right of gleaning is not known in Romania. The common land imposes in its turn another rule, obliging the peasants to sow the same cereals. This is what the Germans call the *Flurzwang*, the 'constraint of the fields', which comes from the fact that if one of the peasants (partitioners) sows a cereal with a different period of maturation, longer than the others, the animals loosed in the fields will soon have trampled the late harvest. Thus the same grains have to be sown at the same period and the harvest must be done together so that the fields become common again at the same time.

Vineyards and enclosed gardens

There are certain agricultural occupations which necessitate more continuous land use. Vineyards, for example, that are well tended can last an infinite amount of time. And, as not all terrain is good for vineyards, there will be competition to acquire it. This makes for a division of the vineyards into large quarters, with a general enclosure not to be used as commons or for the *Flurzwang*. On the contrary, each vinegrower will be obliged to fence in his lots, which will have the same oblong form. But vineyards can be planted individually on terrain chosen by the free initiative of the vinegrower and also be fenced in. The case of orchards, garden plots or terrain used for the specialized growing of flax and hemp is the same.

In this type of village, many kinds of enclosed fields can thus be born. For example, there can be two quarters on which a biannual agriculture is practised, along with *Flurzwang* and commons; or there can be several quarters of vineyards. It is a fact that all these 'quarters' take up very little area and the total territory remains joint property, cultivated according to the old technique of itinerant enclosures, held according to the legal system of absolute joint ownership and *ténements*. There are thus, in the same village territory, two distinct territorial zones: zone I of absolute joint ownership and *ténements* and zone II, split up into parallel plots.

The archaic rural landscape

To illustrate the territorial structure of such a village of the free, archaic, pastoral and forest type, we will use the example of the village of Nerej, one of the most characteristic we have known. Fig. 8 shows that, in this territory, zone I (forest and pasture) by far dominates. Islets of private enclosures are found scattered through the forest and pastures; these are the pastoral and agricultural areas of a non-permanent nature. Zone II is constituted by two quarters cut into strips; these are hay fields. Agricultural quarters are totally absent. In reality this sketch of the Nerej territory underwent continual changes. We were always surprised,

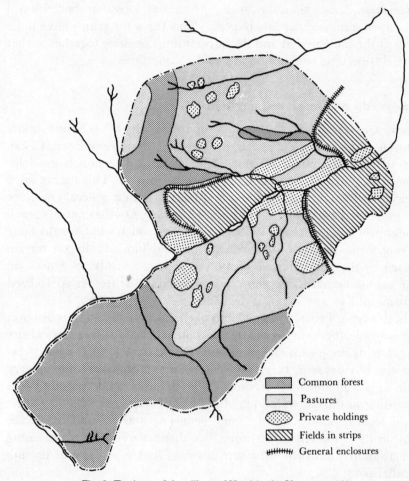

Common forest
Pastures
Private holdings
Fields in strips
General enclosures

Fig. 8. Territory of the village of Nerej in the Vrancea (1938).

even in 1938, to see that new enclosures had been made on the simple initiative of the peasants. From one day to the next, on the pasture land, enclosures for animals, for a hay harvest, for a few thin crops, appeared and disappeared, in a continual play which was supervised only by village public opinion.

Let us point out the original character of this rural landscape. Undoubtedly, rare quarters, cut in strips, were to be found, but one must not confuse them with the *mansus* or the *hufen* of the west. In Western Europe, from the time of the late middle ages, they practised what physiocrats continued to call 'large-scale agriculture', that is, they practised a three-field rotation, the *Dreifelderwirtschaft*. This describes an

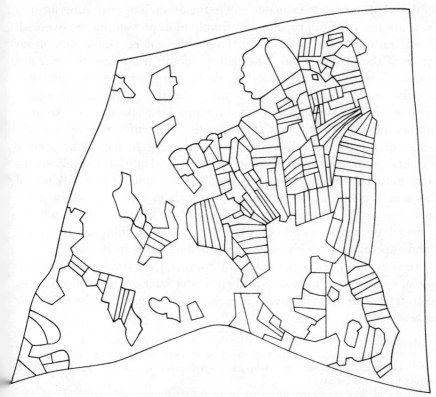

Fig. 9. *Tenements* (holdings) scattered through the pastures. Taken from a cadastral register.

agricultural system in which each peasant must have plots in each one of the fields. In the system of itinerant cultivation, there is no need to regulate any definite plot allotment; each peasant uses only temporary plots that are periodically moved. It was only exceptionally, and only from the time of the quarters of general enclosures, that plots had to be allotted, but in the beginning these rare plots were not very important and were themselves periodically created and destroyed, by always dividing up new lands. It was not until the archaic village passed to a new stage of evolution that a system of stable quarters was established and that plots resembling real farms became usual.

In general, the archaic villages are characterized by a landscape resembling an 'open field' of the western type, although not identical to it. For it is not the necessity of keeping a third of the land fallow and managing the commons which dominates the Romanian 'open field', but rather the fact that it is the pasture land which constitutes the basis of the whole territory, from one end to the other. The enclosures located in it are not signs of property but simple tools preventing the livestock from trampling the plots which have different economic aims from those of the pasture land. The fences, rebuilt from year to year, are moved from one place to another. As for the general enclosures, they are the work of the whole community, collective in their origin and in their goal. If, exceptionally, a man wants his enclosure to take on a private character, as a sign of ownership, he reenforces it by a whole series of rituals. Ritualistic magic is necessary to legitimize private ownership since traditional opinion has it that private land is malevolent, and only charms can rid such land of evil spirits. The folklore of boundary magic is, incidentally, very rich in Romania. At a more advanced stage, internal boundaries will be born and trees will be planted on them as a sign of duration. However, nothing like the *bocage* landscape of small fields enclosed by hedges exists in Romania.

In conclusion, let us put down the characteristic traits of this archaic social system, so as to recognize them better later on, in the documents concerning the serf villages. It is important to remember the following aspects:

(1) dominant forests, characterized by the right to cut firewood freely;
(2) dominant pasture land, across which herds have the right to roam freely;
(3) itinerant agriculture and temporary agricultural fenced enclosures, scattered across fields and forests;
(4) mobile hay enclosures sprinkled across the territory;
(5) houses and hamlets, spread out also without rules;
(6) system of *tènements* on cleared lands in the forest or burned on the plain;
(7) plots within 'quarters' of 'general enclosures'.

4 ❧ Free evolved communities

The great majority of the village communities that we studied directly had already passed the archaic stage and attained the evolved 'genealogical' form of unequal portions; the old full equality of the rights of use of all the members of the commune was thus replaced by an economic and legal inequality. The mass of the population found themselves split into 'large peasants', 'comfortable peasants' and 'poor' whose social struggle was hard, especially because of the struggle against the 'foreign' invaders in the village, large and small boyars, merchants, and city dwellers who attempted to penetrate the community and exploit it.

By the end of the last century this process had taken on a special aspect, under the influence of direct attacks from the big timber companies that succeeded in monopolozing the wooded mountainsides of the communes, thus putting an end to their history.

Egalitarian limited joint ownership

The communes began to give up the full equality of the rights of use in favour of unequal portions in several steps and in different ways under the influence of many social conditions. Studying them will help us to understand how and when the decay of these archaic communal forms took place.

One cannot neglect the influence of demographic pressure on the process of decay. In any case, the demographic saturation was only relative, taking place only in the more sought-after areas of the village. We have seen that the solution in these cases was the egalitarian partitioning of a 'quarter'. But another form of demographic saturation is much more important. It, too, is only relative, and is brought on by the transition from the subsistence to another economy.

There was a time when families had only the *use* of the common

63

patrimony, just enough for the subsistence of the group. The peasants knew all the techniques necessary for their subsistence; they built their houses, made their own tools, wove their own cloth, tanned hides, etc., using the wood, skins, and plants furnished by nature. A rich set of technical procedures was used, according to ancestral tradition, some of which are of surprising ingenuity, such as the turbine mills, examples of which are the glory of the ethnographic museums. Artistic techniques in painting, weaving, sculpting in wood, making musical instruments, and even pharmacopoeia must not be forgotten.

This does not mean that commercial exchanges did not exist. On the contrary, there was a peasant commerce having mainly to do with the production of wax and honey, with the potassium extracted from wood, with the skins of wild animals, and especially with domestic animals and even cereal crops. Exchange between villages of different geographic regions, specializing in certain products, was practised. Some commodities even had the role of money, for example, horses. Money properly speaking was not absent either, existing as much as a standard of value as actual cash. But the basis of economic life remained just the same that of the *Naturalwirtschaft*.

More and more, villages moved into a monetary economy with the internal and external markets gaining in importance. The village families ceased to aspire merely to the usufruct of the common patrimony in order to create some 'revenue'. Goods for immediate use were transformed into commodities and inequalities in living standards began to be felt among the peasants. Certain families grew rich from commerce and from a more systematic exploitation of the common patrimony. The land had always been at the disposal of each, 'according to his needs and his means'. As soon as the peasant began to aim at producing market goods, the 'needs' no longer had a limit and the means for working were multiplied by the use of a labour force other than members of the family. The few families that grew rich thus tried to graze a larger number of animals on the common pasture land, to submit to the system of *ténements* larger areas, to cut more wood in the forest, not only for heating but also to sell as boards, beams, shingles, barrells, ship's masts, etc.

The attitude of these local merchants finally began to bother the mass of the population, which saw the land areas more and more reduced. The means of defence that the village assembly could take as long as the majority was still made up of poor peasants was to impose a limit to the rights of use, thus replacing absolute joint ownership with a 'limited' joint ownership, by proclaiming that no one had the right to graze more than a certain number of animals, to cut more than a certain quantity of wood, or to occupy more than a certain area of land.

As the population increased and the social struggles for land grew more serious, the villages even passed to an 'egalitarian' system of joint ownership, egalitarian in the sense that each member of the community received as his portion an equal area of land, an equal quantity of wood, an equal amount of the common revenues, which meant that the assembly's rights to supervise became more and more rights to direct administration. We were able to follow at first hand the manner in which the rich peasants tried to defraud the others in this process in Nerej, putting up stockades around vast areas of common land during the night, the fences no longer serving as a 'tool' but as a sign of ownership. We also saw how the peasants went *en masse* to tear down the fences, pillage and burn the houses of the rich, taking up arms against the police who came to put an end to these 'revolts'.

Against this background of commercial possibilities offered to the big peasants, a disintegration of infinite variety begins to take place. In order to assure the production of market goods the rich peasants will struggle against the old legal rule of absolute joint ownership and of limited and egalitarian joint ownership in favour of a system of rights of unequal joint ownership and, in the end, for private property; the poor, on the other hand, will struggle for maintaining the traditional rules and will fight for this to the end. This history is better known to us because of surveys made in contemporary villages. We will schematically retrace the main steps.

'Possession by number of lengths'

The quarters divided into lots, although set up to ensure the equality of the rights of use, nevertheless end up as the keystone of the new system of common law of unequal portions. This not only helps in understanding the genealogical villages but also in understanding one of the paths of reduction to feudal serfdom in the past.

At the time of a partitioning, the collectivity allows as beneficiaries only those families belonging to the lineage whose descent in the village is perfectly clear. This is done by eliminating the intruders. *Thus to hold a plot of land in a quarter is proof that the village recognizes you as a member of the collectivity*, fully enjoying the common rights: participation with voting rights in the assembly, unlimited rights to use the forest, the pasture land, and the plough fields. The simple fact that such a proof of lineage is judged necessary constitutes a first symptom of the birth of new conditions imposed on the village group which finds itself menaced by the intrusion of outsiders against whom it must take defensive measures.

To hold any kind of *ténement* does not mean that one is a member of the village, for such a site may be bought or rented. However, to hold a plot in a quarter means to have a right 'of everywhere', according to the Romanian idiom (*de pretutindeni*). The appearance of this proof is in itself a sign of fairly advanced disintegration of the primitive community. Also, given the narrow relation between the possession of a 'part' and the right 'of everywhere', understanding the effort of the feudal lords of the sixteenth century to break the tie between the peasant and his 'part' (*delniță*) will help us understand a double reality: on the one hand, the communal character of the serf village, and on the other hand, the mechanism which enabled the boyar to reduce the formerly free peasants to serfdom. To understand the social mechanism of the 'part' or share giving the right 'of everywhere', one must first understand the surveying techniques which are used at the time of partitioning and at the time of calculating the hereditary shares which, equal in the beginning, become more and more unequal with passing generations.

The free villages fortunately furnish us with the details of this social mechanism, which, if we had only the old documents and their enigmatic formulas, would be unknown to us. The procedure is as follows: to begin with the land to be partitioned takes as nearly as possible the form of a rectangle. One starts, at any rate, from three parallel base lines: the bottom line, the middle one, and the upper one (*cele trei trăsuri*); this constitutes, incidentally, the rule for all Romanian peasant field measurements.

Let us take the example of a simplified schema. Let us assume that there is a terrain with the form and dimensions pictured on fig. 10. Let us say, to simplify the calculations, that there are only four households with a right to the partitioning. Plots could be made for them by cutting each of the 'three lines' in four equal slices which would form the boundaries of the four plots. These lots being hereditary, each one would be divided for the second generation into the same number of sub-lots as there were inheritors. Let us assume that family A has four inheritors; family B, three; family C, one, and family D, two. This can be expressed by the peasant formula in two ways: genealogically and in portions by 'number of lengths' (fig. 11).

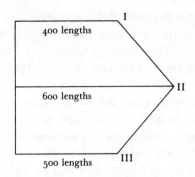

Fig. 10. Technique of 'the three lines'.

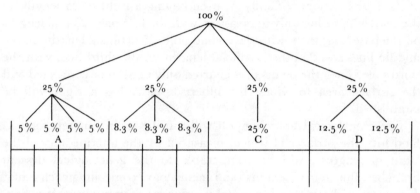

Fig. 11. Division of lots by genealogies and by 'sums of lengths'.

We can thus see that the lots A, B, C, and D are equal. But the sub-lots are no longer equal, except within their own group and depending on the chances of unequal descendancy from one group to the next. How can one now pass to the actual distribution of land? Our peasants proceeded thus: they took as the basis of their calculation one of these three 'lines' (for example, the one of 400 lengths), which they considered to express symbolically the whole of the quarter. They gave the following formula: the quarter 'walks on 400 lengths'. Each one of the four families had a right to '100 lengths out of the total 400'. But one of the four inheritors of the family A will only have a right to '25 lengths of the 400', less, then, than the inheritors of B who each will have 33.3 lengths, the inheritor of C who will have 100 lengths, and the inheritors of D who will each have 50. Thus calculations are neither in surface areas nor in percentages but in 'number of lengths'. To trace these lengths on the line chosen as base is easy: one has only to divide this line into lengths and distribute to each inheritor the number of lengths due to him from the total 400. Next one moves to the second line, that measuring 600 lengths, and cuts it into 400 pieces, which will each measure 1.5 lengths. The same operation is repeated on the third line, that of 500 lengths, where each one of the 400 pieces this time measures 1.25 lengths.

Then three units of measure are made, three poles of unequal length; one, that of a real length, will be used to measure on the base line; another, of 1.5 lengths, will be used to measure on the line of 600 lengths, and a third, of 1.25 will measure on the third line, that of 500 lengths. Thus there will be a real length and two artificial lengths. With these three poles, when the surveyor wants, for example, to measure the lot of the four interiors of family A, each having a right to 25 lengths of the total 400, he has only to measure, with the first pole, 25 real lengths on the base line; then, with the second pole, 25 artificial lengths on the middle line, and 25 other artificial lengths on the third line, with the third pole. Then the points thus charted only need to be connected and the surface area to which the inheritor of A has a right will be established.

The genealogical branching off will thus be set in concrete form in land lots, the surfaces of which, measured by the intermediary of the 'sum of lengths', will be comparable to the genealogical descent branches, the 'sum of lengths' and 'genealogy' controlling each other. A quarter laid out thus is a social instrument of many uses. It is first, as we have said, a register of citizenship; it is next a means of controlling the successional rights of each family, by genealogies made concrete in land lots.

The system of 'sums of lengths' also allows another means of calculating, much more subtle, even surprising if one keeps in mind the fact that it is a matter of an oral village tradition, which one would not have thought capable of such high mathematics. In fact, if the terrain does not lend itself to a regular geometric division on all of its surface, there is another means of making concrete the rights of each, by resorting to a calculation of the arithmetic mid-point. For this one adds the total number of lengths of the three lines $(400 + 600 + 500 = 1,500)$, and divides them by three $(1,500 \div 3 = 500)$. The 500 lengths thus obtained are called 'overall lengths'. The quarter can thus be expressed by a synthetic formula, saying that it 'walks on 500 overall lengths'. The partitioning can thus proceed, this time not by measuring successively and by means of the poles the lengths of three lines, but by a mental calculation of the arithmetic mean. Any given line is divided into 500 equal lengths. Then, the 500 'overall lengths' are divided by four, each of the four families thus having a right to 125 overall lengths out of a total of 500 overall lengths. This will allow a lot of any form, allowing for the unevenness of the terrain, and knowing that one's three lines give the mean of the lengths to which each of the co-dividers has a right. This system of the 'sums of lengths' soon lent itself to even more curious uses than those having to do with dividing a single quarter, for it was this system which was used to establish a joint ownership of unequal portions of a genealogical character, valid for the whole village. This brings us back to the beginning: what are the relations between family lineages and the total life of the village?

Genealogical joint ownership of the second type

We have seen how and why a 'genealogical' joint ownership could be born with a family line. But this first type of genealogical joint ownership had only a strictly private character, of interest only to the family in question. As soon as possession by sum of lengths is introduced into a divided quarter, we come to a stage where the village in its entirety must take genealogy into account. To explain this system of possession by sums of lengths, we have used, for the sake of simplicity, the terminology and the genealogical way of thinking of the peasants, assuming that families A, B, C and D made up a first generation to which the inheritors were then added. In fact, such cases are rare. Most of the time, the procedure is different for establishing which families have a right to the distribution. First, people are grouped by large family units by referring to the first degree genealogies already existing in the hamlets. The terrain is divided with reference to these family lines, each lineage continuing to divide the lot which it receives according to its own genealogy. The result is the following situation: the land is subdivided according to the indications of the family trees, as if it had been subjected for several generations to a hereditary transfer, although in fact it is a single direct division, profiting the present generation. As the lots of the different family lines are equal, there is nothing more normal than to consider them 'brothers', as if all the family lines derived from a single ancestor even if there was no real common ancestor. A system of *second degree genealogical joint ownership* is thus born, *valid for all the lineages in the village, but its validity is limited to the possession of the quarters of a general enclosure*; the rest of the territory is still part of zone I and remains at the stage of absolute joint ownership and of *ténements* with no other rule than the private initiative of each inhabitant.

Let us add that even in the archaic villages where this second degree genealogy is found, very few conflicts between families concerning the lots in the quarters of general enclosure are resolved by referring to the genealogy of the whole quarter. Most of them involve only a partial confrontation of the genealogies of the neighbouring families who have a part in the litigation.

Social struggles between rich and poor peasants, between natives and outsiders

The peasants of the archaic collectivities formed, as we have seen, a single homogeneous, endogamous and xenophobic group, not tolerating entrance by outsiders. The village family members were perpetuated, from one generation to the next, only by internal proliferation. It could happen that one of these families, though it had daughters, might not have a son; the parents were in danger of not being able to carry on from lack of manpower. They could resort to a subterfuge, to a juridical *pia fraus*: they would declare that one of the daughters was a son. She received an inheritance as if she were a boy, and she took as husband a member of the village who settled down in her parents' household and received the customary status of in-law. In Romanian there are two locutions to express marriage: a woman *se mărită*, whereas a man *se însoară*. The son-in-law who comes to live at the woman's house is considered to 'have been married' and not to 'have married'. He thus loses his name and takes on his wife's, or rather the name of the family group making up the household into which he has been married. The customary legal expression for this exceptional situation is 'to enter as son-in-law in the household courtyard'. Every person carries the name of the household where he lives. If, for example, a widow continues as head of the household of her deceased spouse, she bears his name. When she remarries, if her new husband comes to live with her, since he 'is married' he takes his wife's name, the name of her first husband. Even his children will bear the name of the household they belong to, thus of the first husband.

Sometimes another procedure was used, that of 'fraternization'. When it was desired that a son-in-law be allowed to live with his parents-in-law, even though there were real sons, he was declared 'brother' of his brothers-in-law. If this son-in-law was an outsider, fraternization was always resorted to, even though this was viewed with disapproval by the village. The fate of these outsiders admitted into families, it must be added, was not enviable, for the village continued to look on them as second degree members, simply tolerated, and their opinion was not taken seriously. There were even cases where these 'brothers' were obliged to accept the role of humble servants of the lineage and the village which accepted them, to receive orders docilely, with no pretension to the public goods but limited to what was granted them. It is only after several generations that the successors of such outsiders begin to be considered as members with equal rights, in spite of the fact that their surnames recall to all that they are mere outsiders.

We find ourselves here at the point of transformation of the *pia fraus*, properly speaking, into outright fraud. According to the old custom, the peasants practised fraternizations of a special type, making two men, strangers to each other, into 'blood brothers', in a ceremony of ritual acts and gestures, before witnesses, and in the old days with a church ritual besides. The important fact is that these blood brothers gave each other gifts. If one wanted to defraud and introduce an outsider into one's lineage, giving him the right of an indigenous person, one had only to resort to fraternization.[1] Thus to sell a right of indigenous citizenship became possible; the peasant gave as his 'share' a quarter lot, receiving in exchange, always in the form of a gift, a sum of money. A sale was thus camouflaged under the form of fraternization.

The collectivity continued to have the right to control all private contracts made between indigenous villagers or between indigenous villagers and outsiders. Every villager also had a right of pre-emption, allowing him to 'throw the money' in the face of the outside buyer, thus annulling his ill-acquired rights. But by the semblance of fraternization this right of withdrawal was annulled, for to introduce someone into one's family line by fraternization interested, at least on the surface, only the family concerned. Thus having obtained by fraud a right of indigenous citizenship, the buyer, a merchant with a lot of money at his disposal, or even more likely a boyar, could continue to buy all the land he desired within the village that he coveted. Lending money at interest, practising fraud, even using violence if necessary, he appropriated the village patrimony to raise herds of livestock, to rent pasture land to outsiders, to subject his co-villagers to a tithe and to corvée. He could capture the rights of the assembly which he succeeded in terrorizing with his men, his debtors, the whole clique he managed to create. Between these monopolists and the villagers a bitter struggle was born.

1. Marcel Emerit, *L'adoption fraternelle en Valachie et son influence sur la formation de la propriété collective*, Bucharest, 1928.

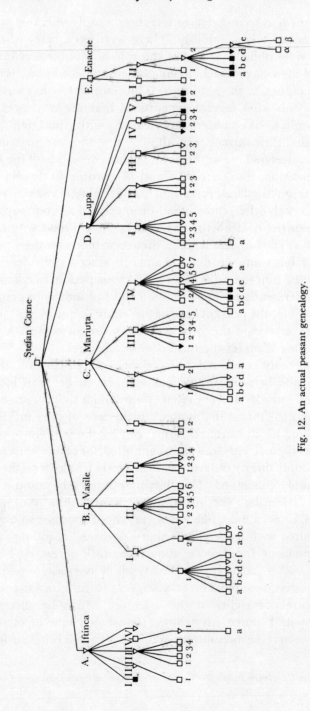

Fig. 12. An actual peasant genealogy.

The third type of genealogical joint ownership

To deal with these fraudulent acts, made possible by the villagers' lack, of vigilance or the weakness of a family, the other families had but a single means to protect their patrimonies: to proceed to a sort of total joint ownership, dividing all the village territory according to the same rules used for dividing the 'quarters'.

Thus, the existing 'lineages' are numbered, using those who already figure in the partitioned quarters, or if there are no lots or if they are contested, a social struggle begins among the inhabitants to determine the number of social groups with a right to equal parts. Each lineage being symbolized by its ancestral eponym, the debate consists of deciding into how many 'ancestors' the village must be divided; or, according to the Romanian expression, 'on how many ancestors the village must walk'. They discuss, argue, fight, and end by agreeing on a compromise in which certain unfavoured groups receive only 'half an old man', or a 'quarter'. The mythical ancestral hero supposed to bind together all the lineages thus loses all veracity. The institution shows its true legal face, which is that of a simple means of disguising in the genealogies the calculations of shares.

It has even happened, right into the nineteenth century, that towns, such as the Wallachian Cîmpulung, debated, with modern legal terminology and the Napoleonic code, the number of 'eponymal ancestors'. Those with the case before the court paid their lawyers not in money but in 'ancestors'.

As soon as an agreement is reached concerning the number of eponymal ancestors who have a right to the division, the land is partitioned according to the technique of the 'three lines', just as for a quarter, this time cutting the whole territory into equal lots and calculating the lengths by the number of ancestors, each lineage then dividing its own ancestor into as many sub-lots as there are sub-groups.

Due to this kind of joint ownership, to receive an outsider in one's family or to sell or give him a lot of land has now only a limited effect in the social group of the 'ancestor' whose members sold to, adopted, or fraternized with the outsider. For all the other 'ancestors' outside communal ownership he continues to remain an 'outsider'.

As any partitioning into lots dividing the whole territory from one end to another is but a belated operation, carried out on land already sprinkled with *tènements* on which orchards have been planted and houses built, it follows that *tènements* belonging to some can 'fall' into

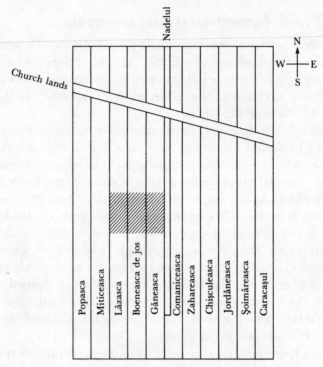

Fig. 13. Village with eleven 'ancestors'.

lots belonging to other family lines. These pieces of land enclosed within the land of others are called *în fundătură*, enclaves with no exit, located 'at the depth' of strangers' lands, which gives the rural landscape a particular aspect, so meaningful that, as soon as one notices it, one knows that it is a territory that has gone from the phase of absolute communal ownership and *tènements* to that of a division by lines, according to the *third type of genealogical joint ownership*, that is, by large plots dividing the whole territory.

The fourth type of genealogical joint ownership

Once the outsiders penetrate the village by means of fraternization, once a category of rich peasants forms, their purchases will grow at the expense of the poor. There is selling, pawning and hoarding of the 'lots' in the quarters, of the *tènements*, the enclosures already made, and the inequality between the rich and the poor grows. Each sale is camouflaged by the introduction of the buyer into the genealogy of the seller. The genealogy ends by no longer having any biological significance, transformed into a mere land register. From being manifest as it was in the beginning, the genealogy becomes latent, giving way more and more to a calculation by lengths. In the end, the genealogy is no longer even referred to, blood brothers being transformed into 'plot brothers', with the term 'brother' now empty of meaning, simply a terminological survivor from the times when lineage truly constituted the heart of the social organization. Step by step, ties of consanguinity are replaced by 'proximity'; even so the land lots continue to be considered as forming a 'lineage', this time of a purely landed character. The rich possessor could thus take over, as a single individual, a whole 'lineage' of lots, which would continue to bear the name of the 'ancestor', or of several 'ancestors', or even of the fragments, halves or quarters, of 'ancestors'.

These rich owners soon began to act as if the rights to the benefits resulting from the exploitation of the village territory were proportionate to the surface areas held by each. For example, he who held a larger number of lots in a quarter claimed a larger area of the common pastures, by grazing a larger number of animals than his poor fellow villagers or by leasing his portion of the pastures to merchants who raised livestock. This led to numerous quarrels, which were ended only with a ruling determining, for good, the shares of each peasant family. Let us say that on a village pasture there was room for only a thousand cows. If the village was divided into five 'ancestors', each 'ancestor' could have 200 cows. The village 'walked on 1,000 cows, by five ancestors, each with 200 cows'. But, as with succession and purchases, the portions became more and more unequal; some could have dozens of 'cows', others less than one 'cow', which was expressed by 'feet', a 'foot' being one-fourth of the unit 'cow'. The result was a very picturesque way of expressing shares, still encountered quite recently in certain pastoral villages where one could find peasants having only 'three feet' or a single 'half-foot of a cow'. 'Sheep' were also used as a subdivision of cows, four sheep being considered the equivalent of a cow.

In other cases, it was not a question of grazing herds in the first struggle for establishing shares, but of the renting of alpine meadows to outside shepherds. These shepherds paid in cheese, weighed according to the local measure called *dram*. If, when the first calculation was made, the shepherds furnished a total quantity of 400 *drams*, the village 'walked on 400 drams', and from then on the shares due to each family line, to each family and to each individual, were calculated in *drams* even if it concerned the rights to a common sum to be divided, the number of animals one could graze, or even the right, which became unequal, to vote in the general assemblies.

There were other cases where the 'ancestors' were calculated in money. Taxes were paid by the inhabitants according to their economic capacity. The rule that each should contribute according to his patrimonial means became reversed, so that each had patrimonial rights proportionate to the amount of money paid in taxes. Likewise, the sums paid during village trials constituted a source of unequal rights among villagers. The 'overall lengths' were also used sometimes. Nothing is more curious than the example of a village which, in recent times, was calculating and distributing its royalties on oil wells by 'overall lengths'.

Little by little the distance between the calculation by 'ancestors' and that done on a purely economic basis grew and the systems of calculation by unequal shares rapidly lost any genealogical character. This system of joint property of unequal shares, bearing on the totality of the common revenues, can be called the *fourth type of joint ownership*.

Let us stress the fact that in this social system, to know that a peasant has a right to a certain number of lengths, cows, *drams*, or lei in a certain village is meaningless to us if we do not know what the sum totals are in the village. The length, for example, has as subdivisions 'steps', 'hands' and 'fingers'. If, then, a new or old document tells us that so and so holds, for example 'three steps', we cannot know what the total surface area is nor appreciate the value of the rights of use concerning the village territory, 'step' or 'strip' in a tiny territory not having the same value as a 'step' or 'strip' in an immense territory.

The initial lot cut in a divided quarter often bears the name of 'ground' (*pămînt*). We are also baffled when an old document tells us about a right to 'four grounds', for the documents never tell us the total number of 'grounds' in the village concerned nor the total surface of the territory. 'Lengths', 'steps', 'hands', 'fingers', or 'grounds', 'parts', 'strips', 'boards', 'straps' and *delniţe*, *jireabii* and other untranslatable terms, form a whole gamut of synonyms used to represent the same system of communal shares that we have described. In any case, these types of joint or communal ownership are the result of a belated social process. We have direct proof in numerous documents.

Let us take the case of the town of Cîmpulung in Wallachia, which is known to us from recent documentary evidence and observation. According to the forestry law of 1910, this town put in writing the rules of its organization, establishing also a nominal register of all the members of the community as well as their rights. At that time, the existence of a system of communal ownership with unequal shares, measured according to an apparently genealogical criterion, was noted. This town 'walked' on forty-four 'ancestors' with equal rights, each one sub-divided into 400 *drams* of a total value of one *oca*. Thus, the community had at its disposal forty-four *oca* or 17,600 *drams*.

How did these *drams* serve? For example, during the year 1942, the Administrative Council stated that a profit of 2,021,484 lei had been made, 1,657,775 of which was distributed to the members. Each *dram* received 100 lei, and since the members had only 16,577.75 *drams*, the balance belonged to the community represented by its Administrative Council. This decision was taken in the course of a long meeting of the general assembly, ratified by the local justice of the peace. Each member had a vote proportionate to the number of *drams* he had. These individual rights were very varied, going from 612 *drams* to half of a single *dram*.

If instead of 'community' one had said 'corporation' and instead of *dram*, 'share of stock', we would be tempted to believe that we are dealing with a form of organization following the rules of modern corporations; which, by the way, the sylvicultural code of 1910 attempted to do, while respecting as its means of calculation the hereditary shares and popular genealogical nomenclature. But we must not be too hasty in our conclusions, for the town of Cîmpulung knew a time, not too long ago, when the inhabitants, all 'urban', practised agriculture, animal raising and wood-cutting in the forests. By a lucky chance for our research, the struggle between members of the community, the rich and the poor, had already begun long before, leaving written records. Newcomers, bold merchants, slipping into local families by marriage, adoption, or fraternization, exploited the common property. There was an attempt to regulate the situation and, in 1846, a first ruling was published, an important document as it is one of the rare ones setting down the rules of common law. This ruling is absolutely clear: in 1846 the town of Cîmpulung did not yet have communal ownership with unequal, hereditary shares but rather the archaic form of absolute communal ownership and of *tènements* obtained by private initiative.

There is no mention of 'ancestors' or of *drams*; instead, article 19 specifies that, 'according to the rules of the present system, all management of the common property and revenue is under the guidance and administration of the council, all members of the collectivity being from now on prohibited from using the common goods for his own profit'. And article 21 adds: 'The administrators have the right to prohibit the actions of those, who, by their own force, make enclosures in the common pasture, anywhere, to plant their own orchards.' The rights to cut firewood are also prohibited if they are used with marketing in mind.

However, this did not stop the members of the community from continuing to use the common land as they had in the past. We have proof in the documents of 1915 which reveal that, to put a halt to the abuses, it was decided that it was better to divide the land, giving the right to enclose up to a maximum of 150 hectares for each *dram*. These *drams* had therefore come into use in recent times. Thus it was to be 'determined, as soon as the surveyors had completed their work, the share to be allocated of rights to revenues, the basis of and rights to the vote' by use of a cadastral register. But the assembly recognized that it was not a question of *pia desideria*, as the private enclosures continued to multiply in the old manner.

As for the forty-four 'ancestors', their history is even more eloquent. In 1846 the register published records of the existence of thirty-three groups given the name of lineages (*neamuri*). The thirty-three lineages were obtained by arbitrarily grouping several families so that all these thirty-three lineages were approximately equal numerically. We thus have:

$$
\begin{array}{rcr}
9 \text{ lineages of 1 family} & = & 9 \\
12 \text{ lineages of 2 families} & = & 24 \\
8 \text{ lineages of 3 families} & = & 24 \\
3 \text{ lineages of 4 families} & = & 12 \\
\hline
32 & & 69
\end{array}
$$

In addition, the families of the two town priests were considered to make up the thirty-third lineage! The term *neam* (lineage) had thus become a conventional term, no longer having anything to do with a family phenomenon. This solution gave way to some new trials and, by judicial decision, a thirty-fourth group was admitted as a 'lineage', the lawyers! A thirty-fifth group, at first omitted, was able to win recognition as another 'lineage'. These court trials continued, and nine other 'ancestors', as a block, were admitted, raising the total number to forty-four. This example, to which other similar ones could be added, shows us how a community with the archaic, non-genealogical type of communal ownership can experience a process of division into unequal shares, camouflaged under the form of genealogical communal ownership.

Let us add that, towards the end of the last century, this system became extraordinarily extended, at the time when the forest ceased to furnish wood merely for peasant household needs and for a meagre local market to become the prey of large timber industries. This gave some trouble to the magistrates who, according to the forestry law of 1910, had to calculate and register in writing the shares of all those belonging to the village communities so that the timber corporations could know what it was they were buying before beginning operations. As, at the time, there were still regions where the archaic type of communal ownership with equal rights of use existed, the corporations profited by buying the rights of certain peasants under the terms of the civil code. They then used the rule of common law, 'according to needs and possibilities'. For them this meant according to the needs of the international market and by means of a railroad, funiculars, power sawmills, etc. This led to a frightful deforesting, which transformed entire regions, formerly pastoral and well off, into vast deserts and areas of famine.

Recent forms of the conquest of free villages

Let us move back a little to an historical period which is not so far removed from us, to establish in what manner these free communities were reduced to serfdom by the conquest of unjust boyars. To succeed, the boyars had first to penetrate the village system, which could be managed in a way we have already analysed: simulated fraternization and the donation of a lot. This practice was so current and excessive that the state took measures. Thus, in 1785,[2] a decree specified that:

Often, when the small and poor make gifts to the rich and powerful, without any family relationship that binds them, it is discovered that these gifts are without basis and purely fictitious. These gifts have as their aim stopping neighbours and relatives from exercising their right of pre-emption. In reality, they are sales, the price of which is sometimes higher than the value of what is being sold. What sum will a rich man not spend to buy land so that he can slip into the patrimony of others, hoping that soon he can enlarge his domain at will? But then, so many quarrels, complaints, curses and imprecations from the inheritors! This is seen every day.

So it was ordered that such donations be made from then on only between people of the same standard of living, by the rich to the poor or by anybody to monasteries. 'And if some dare, after our decision,

2. T. Codrescu, *Uricariul*, 25 volumes, Jassy, 1871–95, volume IV, p. 31.

to give such fraudulent gifts, as soon as they are caught and proved guilty, the two parties will be penalized with the loss of both the object and the price [sale money] which will be given to their lineage or co-dividers.' There is no clearer description than this of one of the classic means used by the boyars to take over villages. This order was soon annulled because the boyars were so forceful and tenacious that nothing could stop this veritable mass expropriation of the free villages. Their actions justified their reputation as 'eaters of free peasants'. They did not hesitate to use force, administrative abuse, bargaining, money lending and especially legal decisions taken by dishonest collaborators.

Let us cite, for example, the complaint made in 1857[3] during the debates of the 'Divan Ad Hoc' of Moldavia, by the delegates of the free peasants:

We could see litigations invoked where there were none; we saw the most evident topometric signs annulled, hillocks transformed into simple mounds of earth, rivers diverted from their course, plateaux made into valleys and plains raised to the crest of hills and mountains. We have seen complaints because the domain of so and so went a little over a boundary at the expense of another domain and the court ordered the whole domain to be given to the one who only claimed a piece.

Given this state of affairs, the few domains of the *razechi* [free peasants] still in existence have nearly been destroyed. In some places they have been limited to only the centre of the village; pressed on all sides, with their roads and access to drinking water and watering areas for the animals cut, many of these unfortunate free peasants have had to abandon their ancestral homes and flee into the world or else submit to their neighbours, undergo corvée, attaining peace only in this manner. Many among them have only their old documents left, as proofs crying for justice to heaven, saying that the land they now work with the sweat of their brow was once conquered by the blood of their ancestors, who defended it against foreign enemies, land that their descendants have not been able to defend against their enemies from within their own country.

The great Romanian historian, N. Bălcescu,[4] claims that

small property was a quarry for the princes, boyars and even monks. Nothing was spared in plundering the peasant; the clergy and religious communities lent the laymen a hand. The castle and the church organized the hunt of the *moşneni* [free peasants]; they refused no means: open violence, iniquitous trials, injustice, falsification and theft of documents, everything was done; the dispossession of the *moşnean* was erected into a governmental system and pursued with a vigour, a harshness which would make history difficult to believe if this steeplechase on the peasant lands did not continue into our own time by the same means and by virtue of the same traditional system.

The great number of 'mixed villages' is explained by this violent infiltration of the boyars into free village communities by a conquest which they had not been able to carry to a total submission of the

3. Sturdza and Colescu-Vartic, *Acte şi documente*, volume IV, part I.
4. N. Bălcescu, *Question économique des Principautés danubiennes*, Paris, 1850.

village. Let us stress that, according to the degree of internal evolution in a village, the boyars' purchases could be made lot by lot, by a series of individual contracts, or by large strips, thus lineage by lineage or by purchasing the patrimony of a whole village sub-collectivity. We will find traces of this going back to the sixteenth century.

The rural landscape of villages with unequal shares

As opposed to the territory of the archaic villages, the territories 'walking by ancestors' are characterized by a division into large strips, going from one end of the territory to the other, themselves cut into long, thin 'strings', sometimes of a length that can be measured in kilometres with a width of a few metres. Jokingly, the peasants say that if you sleep crosswise over your land one neighbour could steal your boots, the other your hat. These long strips cross parallel economic zones: forest, pasture land, ploughland, the village centre. They are bordered by trees, brambles, or piles of stone, as are the interior strings. Enclosures do not exist. It is more like an 'open field', sprinkled here and there with small enclosed lots, sheepfolds, vineyards, fields for special crops (flax, hemp).

Recognizable by sight and especially so on aerial photographs, these villages are easily distinguishable from the archaic villages as well as from those of the old serfs, the great latifundia. However, this system of large strips (not that of the thin interior strings) was also practised by the small boyars who jointly possessed serf villages, as we will have a chance to show. Such territories seem to us most characteristic of this type of Romanian village community.

In conclusion let us name the specific traits of the villages having already attained the stage of joint ownership of unequal shares, of manifest or latent genealogies.

1. Village territories cut into large strips going from one end of the territory to the other, subdivided into thin strings.
2. Existence of enclave *tènements* in strips belong to others.
3. Use of genealogical calculations by 'ancestors', valid for the whole territory.
4. Existence of a system of unequal joint ownership proved by calculations 'by total' (of lengths, parts, *drams*, etc.).
5. Utilization of lots of land within quarters as a proof of indigenous citizenship.
6. Utilization of the same lots as a measure of the unequal rights of use.
7. Inequality of economic levels attained by rich, comfortable and poor peasants.
8. Appearance of fictitious fraternizations, camouflaging sales.
9. Social struggles against invaders, indigenous or foreign to the village, who take over the common land.

As to the interpretation of the old documents, our conclusion is as follows: as soon as the documents give us proof that a village 'walks' according to a system of division by unequal shares, as soon as the existence of 'strips', 'parts', 'lengths' or any other means of calculation 'by sum' is shown, or else as soon as there is proof that the peasants no longer have the same standard of living, but some are richer, some poorer, as soon as fraternizations appear, we will have indirect proof that the village of the archaic type has ceased to exist and that already a certain level of disintegration of the primitive community has taken place, under the effect of a more and more powerful penetration of the system by the market economy.

5 ✥ The former serf villages

We must not consider the forms of the social life of the free village communities, which we have described, as characteristics of the old serf Romanian villages, as these had, in the twentieth century, a completely different form of social organization. There is, however, a problem: to know whether these villages, long ago, did or did not have characteristics similar to those that we have found in the free villages. In other words, did these villages once have forms of communal ownership?

We will proceed to study them, beginning with the period between the rural reform of 1864 and the year 1944, the date at which we were able to make our last study of a village dominated by a large landowner. Will it be possible to find traces, however belated, of an earlier period, which will recall the characteristics that we were able to study due to their survival in the free village communities? Let us first briefly glance at the old serf villages at the time of the Rural Law of 1864 as well as at this law itself.

Analysis of the Law of 1864
Absence of a 'seigniorial reserve' before the Law of 1864

Let us first note that the peasants, even in our times, continue to refer to this Law by the name *delimitare* (setting of boundaries), considering its main effect to be the appearance of a demarcation line cutting off at a single stroke a third of the village territory for the profit of the boyars and separated from the two-thirds which remained in peasant hands. This 'third' is also called, incidentally, *delimitare*.

The peasants have reasons for interpreting this Law thus, for only after 1864[1] did the boyar succeed in becoming owner of a terrain, formerly common, by taking away any right of use from the local population. This proves that before 1864 such a 'seigniorial reserve' did

1. Georges Moroianu, *La Loi Agraire de 1864 et l'état du paysan en Roumanie*, Stuttgart, 1898.

not exist, the purpose of the law actually being to form one. We have written confirmation of this fact. Thus, in the course of the debate preceding the Law of 1864, a boyar complained that 'the principal owner' (such was the opinion of the conservative party, which was struggling to have the boyar recognized, at least, as the principal owner, if not given the full rights of the bourgeois code) 'does not know definitely to what part he has an exclusive property right; the peasants, on their side, do not know to what they have a right; both live in a kind of perpetual common ownership and, in a sense, one can say that they are joint owners.'[2]

Furthermore, the conservative leader, one of the biggest boyars, did not hesitate to recognize that

the land that the boyar leases to the peasants [this author held the thesis that the boyar was the only landowner, leasing land lots to the peasants which he was not legally obliged to do] and that which the owner works on his own account is not constantly at his [the boyar's] disposal; on the contrary, it changes practically every year, according to changing circumstances and the necessities of each, passing from the hands of the owner into the peasant's, and from his hands back to the owner's.[3]

We will note this fact later when making an historical analysis of the serf villages, for it is unlikely that the boyar had, at an earlier period, a true seigniorial reserve that he then lost, only to regain it in 1864.

The details of the Law of 1864 and of the code of rules that followed it prove that, until this Law, the village lands formed a single land unit in which peasants and boyars had mixed their rights of use, under different titles, the boyars as masters, the peasants as serfs. As for the two-thirds going to the peasants, it is true that in 1864 there was no partition. To be sure, there were special commissions to determine, in each village, what was the total area of the two-thirds. There was even a written list of the names of the peasants, formerly liable to corvée, who had a right to the land, with a mention of how much land was due to each, according to the number of livestock he had. But the fact that it was the livestock which determined the extent of land to which the peasant had a right gives proof that this peasant did not have land belonging to him personally. Thus we do not find the feudal system of the 'serf manors', owned hereditarily; the basis of the peasant rights was not of a landowning nature but resided in the capacity, greater or lesser, to use the common land (hence the importance of counting animals). In addition, the Law of 1864 granted land to the peasants

2. S. Golescu, *De l'abolition du servage dans les Principautés Danubiennes*, Paris, 1856.
3. B. Boeresco, *La Roumanie après le Traité de Paris, du 30 mars 1856*, Paris, 1856. Katargiu Barbu, *De la propriete en Moldo-Valachie*, 2nd edition, Bucharest, 1857.

only up to the maximum of two-thirds of the total (forests not included) of village lands. If the village was overpopulated, the extra peasants, though they had the necessary livestock, did not have a right to use the land. Thus, it was not individuals who were dealt with but the village, considered as a community; the litigating parties were, on one side, the boyar with a right to a third and, on the other side, the village community with a right to two-thirds.

Without a doubt, the Law had foreseen that cadastral engineers would come to divide up the land, giving each peasant ownership of a plot. But this operation was never performed. The peasants divided, for better or for worse, by themselves, the two-thirds of the territory, which, in some cases, remained communal. In 1920, at the time of the second reform, the administration was often surprised to discover that many peasants still held certain areas of their land in common.

Absence of a multi-field rotation system

Did these villages practice the agricultural technique of three- or at least two-field rotation? According to the laws of rotation, each peasant, whether owner or user of the land, was supposed to have lots in each one of the rotation areas, the same from one year to the next, regardless of his livestock. Likewise, the boyar was to have lots in all the existing areas. For a boyar to acquire a demesne constituted clearly, in a formal legal way, it was necessary to undertake a whole series of operations which characterize, for example, the reforms made in the last century in the region east of the Elbe: an inventory of the plots, a marking out and identification of lots, etc. The fact that the partitioning could be done by tracing a simple line diagonally cutting the whole territory is proof that this territory, in 1864, was still communal land, at the communal disposal of its users, boyars as well as peasants, practising a different agricultural system from that of a two- or three-field rotation system. The technique implied by this state of affairs could be none other than that which we have already encounterd in our study of the free peasants, that is, the raising of herds on common pasture land and itinerant agriculture. Neither the two- or three-field system existed before 1864.

Presence of old peasant 'tènements'

There is but one exception to be remembered: the Law of 1864 considers as individual peasant property only house sites and the few acres in gardens and orchards surrounding them. These were considered separately, just as in the free village system of *tènements*. However, the Law granted a right to the new 'owner' to bring these lots of land into his 'third', with the responsibility of giving in exchange other lots, situated in other places. This led to so many abuses that they can be considered as another manifestation of the disintegration of traditional social forms at a period in which control over well-established peasant farms that were tightly tied to particular lots of hereditary land did not yet exist.

Degree of disintegration of the peasant class

Another fact to remember, in concluding the studies on the Law of 1864, is that the peasant class, liable to corvée, which was 'liberated' by the Law was not homogeneous. Rich, comfortable, and poor peasants formed the three legal categories according to which the area to be distributed was determined. This is an evident sign of a capitalist penetration that had taken place in the village communities reduced to serfdom by diversifying the work capacities of the households. This could not have happened except as a result of a peasant commerce which enriched some at the expense of others, the rich being able to work and sow a greater area of the common land.

To assess this process of social differentiation better and to understand its history, it is interesting to keep in mind the situation existing at the time of the Law of 1864. At the time the proportion of large, middle and small peasants was as follows:

'Rich' peasants (with four oxen)	70,999	17.67%
'Comfortable' peasants (with two oxen)	198,882	49.49%
'Poor' peasants (without livestock)	132,022	32.85%
Total	401,903	100.0%

How were these categories of peasants distributed throughout the country? Figs. 14 and 15 clearly show that the large peasant was dominant in the newly cleared lands, such as the Bărăgan, as well as near the Danubian ports where the transportation and sale of grain was easier.

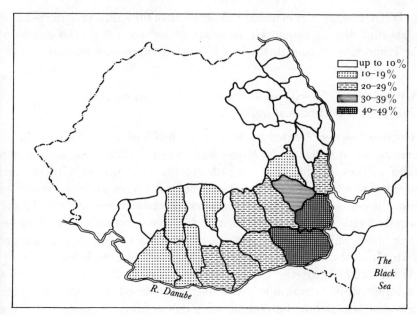

Fig. 14. Percentage of peasants who were 'rich', by county.

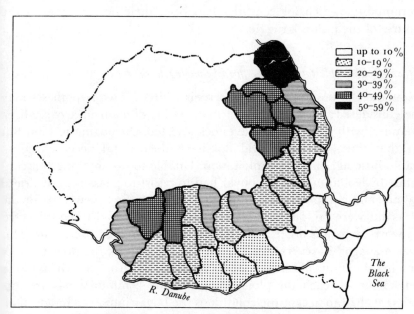

Fig. 15. Percentage of peasants who were 'poor', by county.

It is necessary to remember this problem of the splitting of the peasant class into diverse categories, in order to see when this class ceased to be homogeneous and thus when a peasant commerce was born.

Situation of the villages after the Reform of 1864

Transition to a contractual regime

The new 'owner' created by the Law of 1864 had succeeded in securing certain advantages: he no longer had to cede to the peasants as much land as they needed, the peasants having to make do with the lots granted to them by the Law. These peasants were no longer liable to him for corvée. The relations between the two classes were no longer legally fixed, but had to be decided by 'free contracts'. And, what is even more important, the peasant community ceased to have a legal status, the boyar now having only private relations with each peasant. As replacement for the village assembly, the Law created a modern 'administrative commune' with elected council and mayor which received land from the communal territory. But because of this the peasants were disarmed, no longer able to use as such the peasant community, which for centuries had been their best weapon in the course of their class struggle.

Quasi-feudal exploitation of the third belonging to the boyar

How did the boyar intend to work his 'third'? Two hypotheses may be considered: the boyar could manage his domain in a capitalistic manner, with hired labour, livestock and tools belonging to him. But at that time, the boyar did not have the capital necessary for a capitalistic agricultural exploitation. Unable to do anything but continue by feudal means, the boyar had to resort to peasant agricultural labour and equipment. But this had to be done in a new way for the peasants were no longer liable to a corvée. They had to be subjected to work by means other than those of para-economic constraint. This was managed in several ways. First, the boyar took the precaution of tracing the limits of his domain so that the exits from the village were cut. Thus to reach the ploughland and the communal pasture, the peasants had to accept the conditions the boyar imposed. In addition the plots accorded to the middle and poor peasants were so small that a single family could not subsist on them. The peasant thus has to beg from the owner lots within the 'third'. Leaving the village was not possible, as the Rural Law had declared the peasant lots inalienable. The owner thus had full latitude to impose on the peasants the conditions he wanted.

The village community, although no longer having any legal foundation, continued to survive in fact, at least on the agricultural level. The boyar dealt with the village, proclaiming the conditions under which he would consent to rights of passage and of labour within his domain. The peasants deliberated among themselves and through their delegates arranged individual 'contracts' with the boyar. These 'agricultural contracts' rapidly took on all the characteristics of a feudal regime, though camouflaged under the forms of the Napoleonic civil code that had just been introduced in the country. That is to say, the boyar's third was divided into 'tithe lands' which were given to the peasants who were responsible for paying the 'tithe' in produce (not a tenth, as in the old days, but a half) and into 'corvée lands' that the boyar reserved for his own account and which were worked, sown, and harvested by the peasants. The contracts also involved all sorts of supplementary obligations, transportation corvées, tithes on fowl, etc., reproducing to the letter and stiffening the feudal conditions. These contracts were also usurious in the sense that the boyar established them during the winter, lending the peasants the corn they needed so as not to fall victim to famine, while specifying amounts of work not possible in the course of a single year.

As the peasants were recalcitrant, in 1866, two years after the reform, a 'Law of Agricultural Contracts' was established, giving the boyar the right to use the armed force of the police to oblige *manu militari* the contracting parties to furnish the remaining corvées. This led to a monstrous regime, the consequence of which was the misery of the peasant class and the revolts of 1888–9 and especially of 1907.

The analysis of these aspects of the peasant problem does not enter into our study. We will, however, remember the fact that this quasi-feudal regime was in fact the continuation of an old regime which formerly had the run of the whole village territory and which, restricted to a single third of the territory, continued in some areas until 1945. To study what went on in this third, the feudal survivals after the reform of 1864, will be useful to us in understanding the situation before this date. If one had to choose the most significant aspect of this period, one should stress the fact that the owner himself divided each year the lots he granted to the peasants. We will reproduce a page by a contemporary observer,[4] who described the situation in 1905 thus:

He who has travelled at the beginning of spring across the plains of our countries has certainly seen dozens of peasants going through the fields after an agent of the owner or his farmer and he must have understood that *they were dividing the land among the peasants*. These simple words, which have no meaning for most people, break the heart of the peasant, make him tremble from head to toe. For he knows that, at the time of the distribution of lots, they can let him starve to death; he knows that the agent desires his daughter or his wife; he knows that at the surveying he will be the last to receive his lot; he knows that the lots are not sufficient for all; he knows that he will be horribly beaten if he dares to say that in his opinion there are so many lengths to a hectare; he knows that, among the hundreds of people present, none will dare defend him; he knows all that and much more, that one must keep quiet; he knows that by the time he is given a lot, the time for barley will be passed, the month of March will be over and when finally he begins to plough, the agent of the owner will come to requisition him to do his corvée. He will only be able to work slowly, for on the lot of the boyar one unit makes up five quarters, and he cannot flinch because otherwise the next year they wil not give him any more lots. He will be fortunate if he can escape at this price. Is there in our countries a single peasant who has been allowed to cultivate, on the boyar's land, the same lot several years in a row? Never. The peasant would never dare utter such a request.

Nevertheless, this vivid picture of the agrarian realities after 1864 must not be taken as the faithful copy of an earlier regime. For a long time it was believed that the boyar had from time immemorial the rights and powers of dividing the peasant lots and of directing agriculture according to his own plans. In fact, after 1864, there was a catastrophic worsening of agrarian relations due to the fact that the boyar had become 'owner' with full rights, especially since the village community had been killed, as much legally as in fact. The peasant class, split in 1864, as we have seen, continued to divide into rich and poor peasants. The rich peasants themselves became at this time merciless exploiters of their co-villagers, using the same means as the boyar, though even more severely.

In 1944, we were still able to see these disastrous social realities in a village which can serve us as example.[5] There were in this village 265 plots of less than 5 hectares (the average being 2.8 hectares) and twenty-six plots of more than 5 hectares (with an everage of 28.4 hectares), of which there were two of more than 100 hectares. The owners with more than 5 hectares held 63.7% of the land, the two

4. I. Voiculescu, *Scurtă ochire asupra învoielilor agricole* (Brief review of agricultural contracts) Bucharest, 1905.
5. H. H. Stahl and G. Filip, Învoielile agricole din jud. Vlaşca (Agricultural contracts from the county of Vlaşca) in *Caminul Cultural*, nos. 1–2, Bucharest, 1945; *Idem*, Loturi şi haturi ţărăneşt (Peasant lots and border markers) in *Caminul Cultural*, nos. 3–4, Bucharest, 1945.

large boyars alone holding 41% of the total. But what must be remembered is the fact that the owners of more than 5 hectares had neither farm implements nor livestock. To cultivate 738.58 hectares this group had only eleven carts, fifteen ploughs, fourteen weeders and thirty-four head of livestock, whereas the group of poor peasants who had only 478.17 hectares had 149 carts, 178 ploughs, 175 weeders and 309 head of livestock. Two peasants with no land did have carts, ploughs and livestock whereas the two large owners of latifundia had but one plough, one weeder and seven animals. The land was in fact worked by the mass of poor peasants. The tithe and corvée contracts were still the rule in spite of the fact that article 3 of the law of 1910 formally prohibited such corvée contracts containing 'the peasant's obligation to cultivate, in exchange for a personal lot, another lot for the owner or his farmer'.

The picture of this retarded village was not rare. One of the great property owners, an historian and theoretician on the agrarian question, author of the Reform of 1920, does not hesitate to acknowlege that the whole inventory of a boyar landowner consisted of a wagon and the necessary harness to pull it in order to inspect his domain.[6] Another theoretician, studying the setting of prices of agricultural domains, recognized that it was neither the extent nor the quality of land that was principally considered, but rather the number of peasants and the content of the usurious 'agricultural contracts', involving a number of years to come.[7]

Agricultural technique of the 'latifundia fallow field'

During the second half of the nineteenth century a large latifundium was formed by the accumulation under one owner of a large number of villages long ago reduced to serfdom. There were even leasing 'trusts'. This, by the way, brings up the very interesting subject of the penetration of finance capital into the exploitation of the old serf villages. What interests us for the time being, however, is establishing what exactly was the level of agricultural techniques attained on these large domains.

The boyars always had a tendency to confuse 'large landowners' and

6. C. Garoflid, *Agricultura Veche* (Traditional agriculture), Bucharest, 1943.
7 C. D. Creangă, *Die Bodenbesitzungsverteilung und die Bauernfrage in Rumanien*, Leipzig, 1907; *Idem*, *Considerațiuni asupra reformelor agrare și asupra exproprierii* (General considerations on the agrarian reforms and expropriation), Bucharest, 1913. Michael Şerban, *Rumaniens Agrarverhältnisse, wirtschafts- und sozialpolitische Untersuchung*, Berlin, 1914.

'large agriculturists', considering them synonymous, so as to invoke the advantages of a big exploitation in favour of the large landowners of the latifundia. The reality was completely different: every large latifundium was worked by a crowd of small peasants with the peasant livestock and implements, with primitive techniques that our agronomists baptized with the name of 'latifundia fallow field', which is nothing but the growth to gigantic proportions of the procedures of itinerant peasant agriculture which we have already described, with the single difference that, once the harvest was finished, the land was ploughed. Moving to a single cereal agriculture, the system was repeated to the saturation point on still virgin land until complete exhaustion of the soil resulted. Then new areas were cultivated. This practice was continued as long as there was land in sufficient quantity.

This technique of the 'latifundia fallow field' itself constitutes an historical document not to be ignored, for this savage exploitation of the natural qualities of virgin soil could not have been introduced and spread if the stage of itinerant agriculture had been passed. For example, if Romania had practised the system of three-field rotation, the 'latifundia fallow field' could not have been born and a system of *Koppelwirtschaft* would have emerged, as in Prussia. This enables us to state that, given the existence of these primitive techniques up to the nineteenth century, it is impossible to say that in previous centuries techniques of a higher level could have been practised. It is thus legitimate to project this quasi-contemporary data as an illumination of all our history before the nineteenth century.

The rural village landscape after the Law of 1864

The cutting out of a third of the territory for the boyar resulted in giving the countryside a distinctive look. This 'third', bare plain, without trees, without enclosures, was an 'open field', part pasture, part subjected to cereal mono-agriculture. The peasants' 'two-thirds' was, on the contrary, cut up into little lots, in chaotic fashion, by thin strips of land, separated by a thin growth of brambles and little bushes. In a few generations, these lots of land were crushed into tiny plots, economically unfeasible. A varied subsistence cultivation was practised, giving to the peasants fields the look of a multi-coloured tapestry. In all, a territory divided according to the Law of 1864 was chaotic, resembling neither the archaic village territories nor those 'going by ancestors' which we described in chapter 2.

Our attempts to reconstitute the existing state of affairs before 1864 in these former serf villages never succeeded in finding traces of a division into lots going from one end of the territory to the other; on the contrary, everything seemed to fit with the norms existing in the archaic communities, which raises a question we must explain. Unfortunately, this kind of archaeological reconstitution was very difficult to make. We could use aerial photographs only rarely. Now it is too late, as the mechanical means used in our modern agriculture have erased the traces of these plots which dated back more than a century. In any case, after having discovered, by direct field work, a base of data concerning the village communities, free as well as serf, it is time to return to a slightly more distant period: that which immediately preceded the social crisis of 1864. We know this period fairly well as there is sufficient documentary information.

Part II

The village communities of the peasants liable to corvée (eighteenth and nineteenth centuries)

By calling for individual liberty for the peasants, the large landowners had in mind freeing their property from the obligation of ceding more land to the peasants than the two-thirds of the arable land of their total property.
Report of the European Commission for the Congress of Paris, 1858

6 ❧ The communities of corvée peasants

General characteristics of the period of the corvée communities

We will first consider, in our trip back to the historical origins of the serf village communities, the period between the 'abolition' of serfdom and the act of 'dividing into thirds' of 1864. In 1746 in Wallachia and in 1749 in Moldavia the voivode Constantine Mavrocordat declared the entire peasantry 'free' from serfdom in the sense that their masters no longer had any right over them as human beings. Formerly, the serfs had lived within the peasant communities, having at their disposal, as members of the commune, the collective patrimony of the village territories. Now they were but simple 'inhabitants' of a 'domain' which no longer belonged to them, having to purchase their rights to use the land through a tithe and corvée, according to the rates established by the state: the 'urbariums'.

Socially, the state was confused, as the communal forms of the villages were mixed with the forms of private property which took shape by degrees, as the boyars went from exploiting the agricultural production of the peasants by tithes to directly exploiting the land with corvée labour. The final result of this social process was the eventual breakdown of the village communities brought about in 1864 by the formula of dividing into thirds, which we have already described.

Historians[1] consider for the most part that the year 1829 marks the most important turning point for this period, for it was at this date that the Treaty of Adrianople forced Turkey to open navigation on the Danube and Black Sea, thus opening wide the doors of western commerce, obliging the Sublime Porte to renounce his monopoly on the commerce in livestock and grain of the Danubian countries and inciting the boyars to become grain producers and exporters. However, the economic and social importance of this treaty must not be exaggerated, for the historical workings that we are going to analyse and which ended in the 'transaction' imposed by the Law of 1864 had begun long before. Already, at the Treaty of Kutchuk-Kainardji of 1774, imposed by Russia on the Ottoman Empire, the Black Sea had become partially open to western commerce. In addition, even before the Treaty of Kutchuk-Kainardji and the Treaty of Adrianople, an important trade in livestock and grain had already taken hold in Romania, not only in spite of the Turkish monopoly, but also because of it; for if the Turkish trade was onerous, it also produced effects. The Treaty of Adrianople, however, raised Romanian commerce to a higher level and essentially transformed it. On the one hand, from the time of this treaty it was no longer a question of exchanges made under a regime of fiscal exploitation imposed by a sovereign state on a vassal state, but rather of a free trade, according to classical capitalist rules. Also, it was no longer a question of clandestine trade, carried on with other countries in defiance of the Turkish monopoly, but of an official international trade. And, what seems to us of the highest importance, this trade ceased to be primarily in livestock and became a trade in grain.

In fact, after 1829, the Romanian economy changed rapidly from

1. N. Iorga, *Développement de la question rurale en Roumanie. Une contribution*, Jassy, 1917; *Idem*, *Evolution de la question rurale en Roumanie, jusqu'à la réforme agraire*, presented at the 14th International Congress on Agriculture, Bucharest, 1929; Marcel Emerit, *Les Paysans roumains depuis le Traité d'Andrinople jusqu'à la libération des terres (1829–1864)*. *Etude d'histoire sociale*, Paris, 1937; A. Oţetea, 'Consideraţii asupra trecerii de la feudalism la capitalism în Moldova şi Ţara Românească' (Considerations on the passage from feudalism to capitalism in Moldavia and Wallachia), in *Studii şi materiale de istorie medie* (Studies and materials for medieval history), volume IV, Bucharest, 1960; Şerban Papacostea, 'Contribuţie la problema relaţiilor agrare în Ţara Românească în prima júmătate a veacului al XVIII-lea' (Contribution to the question of agrarian relations in Wallachia during the first half of the eighteenth century), *Studii si materiale*, volume III, Bucharest, 1959.

animal raising to wheat growing. Instead of the immense herds of horses, cattle, sheep, and pigs, exported overland, providing animals for Constantinople to the south and for the European cities to the north, via Transylvania and Poland, the transport of grain by boat along the Danube was developed. Modern Danubian ports were hastily constructed (Turnu-Severin, Calafat, Corabia, Turnu-Măgurele, Zimnicea, Giurgiu, Călăraşi, Brăila, Galaţi). With the whole economic axis of the country thus displaced, with land routes replaced by river and maritime routes, wheat became the main export merchandise. Pasture land underwent massive clearing. In 1837 in the Danubian principalities, Moldavia and Wallachia, the area sown with wheat amounted to only 249,102 hectares. The number of hectares of wheat had grown to 697,220 by 1886, to 1,509,683 by 1890, and to 1,931,147 by 1916. During the same period the total area under cultivation went from 1,048,600 hectares to more then 6,000,000.

Pasture land was disappearing and there was a catastrophic decrease in the number of animals raised, all the more painful to the peasants as a real demographic explosion was taking place at the same time, with the population of Wallachia and Moldavia increasing from less than two million at the beginning of the century to 3,917,541 in 1860. One can get an idea of the process, although there are insufficient statistical data, by looking at the fiscal criteria of the period, which in certain regions of Moldavia in 1805 considered a peasant 'rich' if he had eighteen head of cattle, 'comfortable' if he had twelve, and 'poor' if he only had six. In 1864, the 'rich' man had only four, the 'comfortable' man two, and the 'poor' man none. There is no better description of the economic disaster which befell the peasant class, nor of the state of deep poverty into which it had fallen by the end of the nineteenth century. One must remember that the boyar class held a quasi-monopoly over the growing and trading of grain.

A bitter struggle was the logical outcome of this radical transformation in the economic and social life of Romania. Let us note, however, that it was a struggle begun long before and only aggravated at the time of this true collision between two worlds which occurred in the nineteenth century: that of the old feudal order, on the one hand, and that of the new order, powerfully influenced by capitalism, on the other hand. But from the perspective of the social struggles between the peasants and the boyars, 1832 is the most important date to remember, for it was then that the 'Organic Regulations' of Wallachia and Moldavia benefited the boyars by declaring them 'owners' of the village territories and by imposing the principle of 'thirds' for regulating the reciprocal rights of the peasants and their masters in the entire country.

The stakes of the social struggle between boyars and peasants

The struggle for control over the land, which had changed from pasture to farm land, was led by the boyars with incredible vigour. The appeal of the big profits obtainable on the world wheat market incited them to undo as much as possible of the old social system of the village communities and to restrict to a minimum the peasants rights to use the land. To this end, they wanted to be recognized as modern 'landowners' and not just 'feudal landowners', and thereby have the right to cultivate as much land as they wanted, diminishing the 'tithe land' belonging to the peasants, in favour of the 'corvée land' belonging to them. These boyars did not nor could not intend to introduce an agriculture of a higher technical level. At most, they wanted to perfect the technique of the 'fallow field latifundia' which we have already described as typical of the second half of the nineteenth century, an agricultural system which, as we have shown, is none other than the extension of itinerant agriculture, so pastoral in character.

To attain this end, the boyars had first to end the peasants' right to choose for themselves what land to cultivate, to prohibit the 'scattering' of lots, to separate the tithe lands from the corvée lands, thus to replace the 'freely chosen land' with land 'distributed' by them, and to avoid mixing the two. To clear the way for this new manner of cultivating, the boyars had to find the solution to a contradiction: to hold the greatest amount of land possible yet at the same time to have a sufficient amount of corvée labour. They thus had to continue allowing the peasants to feed themselves from the village territory, but to reduce them to the extreme limit of poverty, barely allowing them to survive. The tithes they received from the peasants no longer interested them very much, and the corvée became their principal means of becoming wealthy. By raising the corvée rates, they could reduce the number of inhabitants necessary to work for them. The right to use the land now could become a salary, paid in kind as the cost of the corvée labour.

Thus there developed a 'relative' demographic saturation: as soon as the number of peasants exceeded the strict needs of the boyar's exploitation, the boyar maintained that the village had become 'narrow', unable to feed everybody. The peasants' rights to use the land were allowed up to a certain limit, varying with a household's capacity to work, which was calculated according to the number of working animals it had. In other words, the calculation was based not on the household's needs but on its corvée value, on its capacity to furnish corvée days. The peasants only had the right to use land that went up to the limit of two-thirds of the territory. Any surplus of peasants not able to satisfy themselves within these two-thirds had to get along as best it could, for better or for worse, by leaving to look for under-populated villages.

The boyars thus went, during this period, from being 'feudal masters', to being 'legitimate masters', then to 'perpetual masters' and finally to being recognized by the Organic Regulations as 'landowners'. On their part, the peasants, relying on the ancient custom, claimed their right to cultivate as much land as they needed, with the boyars, as lord of the village, only having a right to a tithe.

As for the problem of 'property', the peasants had no idea what it was all about. There is nothing more sadly picturesque, for example, than to see the manner in which the debates between peasants and boyars took place at the time of the revolution in 1848, within the 'Commission for Property' instituted at that time to settle the 'peasant question'. The revolutionary boyars, imbued with progressive ideas from the west, would have liked the meetings to begin with the formality of solemnly recognizing the abstract principle of the 'sacred right of property', along with the 'sacred right of liberty'. They thus gave an inflammatory discourse and presented a motion that would have recognized the 'sacred right of property' in order to later pass another motion on the 'sacred right of liberty'. The peasants were suspicious. They asked: 'If we pay a tithe, is that not sufficient sanctification?' Trying to understand better what was meant by 'property', they all said in chorus: 'Speak to us in Romanian so that we can understand.' Once they had understood that what the boyars wanted would in fact deny them the right to use the land, declaring them 'free' like the birds in the sky, without any patrimonial right, they said, 'We will sanctify property if we get our share, if not then we will not.'

Even in 1864, administrative leaflets had to be distributed in the villages to try and make the peasants understand that they were 'landowners' and explain to them what that meant. It was thus in a purely verbal fashion that the Regulations gave the boyars the title of 'landowners', for the regime of landownership that they were instituting had nothing in common with what the bourgeois code understood by it. The village communities were much too strong for such a revolution in social relations to occur without difficulty. The Regulations could only bring forth a hybrid that the people of the period themselves did not understand. They would ask, 'What is the Romanian peasant? Is he a free man? Is he a serf, a long-term leaser, a tenant, a co-landowner, a user, a settler? The question is difficult to resolve. He is all of these and one of them. He is a mixed abstraction created by the Regulations.'[2]

The same statement was made by the 1858 European Commission for Peace:

It would be difficult to establish whether, from the beginning, landed property in the Principalities has been constituted on the basis of the same principles as in the west, for the relations and the reciprocal rights of the lords and peasants were so little defined that it would be almost impossible to analyse them today from the European point of view of property rights.[3]

This struggle ended nevertheless in the triumph of the boyars; but at the price of a long effort which lasted more than a century and which was only ended by the Law of 1864, which divided the pie by giving the peasants two-thirds of the village.

Given the special theoretical goal we are pursuing, the analysis of a problem of social morphogenesis, we will try to describe the long history of the corvée villages from the standpoint of the village community, checking to see whether the symptoms we have identified as being characteristic of the communal village are also found in the corvée villages, despite the dominating presence of the boyar. Let us pursue the same themes as we did when analysing the free contemporary villages, pointing out the similarities and the differences.

Substitution of the boyars in the rights of the village assemblies

The serf village, is, in a way, a reverse image of the free villages. As long as a community has no lord, the plenary council of the population is considered 'owner', at least nominally, of the territory and has a right to supervise the administration of any activity of the families making up the local population. In a serf village, the feudal lord of the village, substituted for the council, has a legal status which is almost the exact copy of the council's. But by the very fact of this transfer of powers, the

2. Boeresco, *La Roumanie après le Traité de Paris*.
3. Rapport de la Commission européenne, in Sturdza and Colescu-Vartic, *Acte și documente*.

whole series of rules which formerly acted to preserve liberty and the population's rights to use the land becomes just as many means for breaking up the community, to subject and reduce it to serfdom.

Going through the rights of the council, as we have described them, gives us the inventory of the lord's rights and explanation of the means by which he transformed his 'chieftainship' into ownership.

The boyar begins by being nominal landowner of the village. With numerous opportunities to appear before the judges or the chancellery of the voivode concerning the affairs of his village, or to be responsible for tax collecting, the feudal lord appears as leader and emissary for the collectivity, as if he had been elected by the council, though in fact he is a hereditary chief accountable to no one and with a right to the final decision in all matters.

Rights of interference in the economic activities of the peasants. As master of the village, the boyar replaces the council in its rights to intervene in the economic affairs of the peasants. In a free village, the aim of this right was to maintain full equality among all the members of the community, with regard to the rights to use the land – clearing, cultivating, gathering, fishing, etc. – in order to put an end to any individual abuse. The boyar, along with this obligation to insure the effective administration of the life of the village, had in addition an interest in supervising agriculture, the pasture land and all other sources of revenue, to ensure his right of withholding a tithe of all the produce. He had thus not only to administer but also to supervise his peasants so that nothing might escape him. The best means for achieving this was to make his authorization necessary prior to any private initiative. The councils had also acted thus in the cases where there was competition over highly coveted land. The boyar applied the same rule, but to safeguard his own interests. So, for a peasant to be able to clear the forest or to cultivate cleared land, he needed the permission of the boyar and had to submit to his right of control, as the only guarantee for maintaining the tithes.

Rights of local justice. It was normal for the boyar, as village chief, to be present at the assemblies which litigated between peasants, softening the conflicts and watching over, as chief of the local police, the conduct of the villagers. But more and more he began to monopolize the right to bring the guilty to judgement, which permitted him also to judge and penalize the peasants who did not submit to his orders and did not fulfil their tithe and corvée obligations. It was still possible at the beginning of this century to see such judgements, not only by the local boyar but also by his administrators. The right to judge had become synonymous with the boyar's property right.

Let us underline the fact that the rights of local justice had also become an important source of revenue. The voivodes who wished to give favours to monasteries or boyars gave them the right to petty and even high justice; the fines were given to the village lords, with the state judicial apparatus gradually being replaced by the judicial apparatus of the local lords.

Rights to obtain corvée labour. At certain times, the villages furnished communal labour to ensure the common interests or to render service to those who needed it. The work, done in common by large groups, is called in Romanian *clacă*, a name which ultimately came to designate corvée labour. The village council could thus impose the carrying out of such work to establish the general enclosures, to construct ponds, to build roads and bridges and wells, but also to help the priest in his harvest, to ensure the livelihood of widows or old people and even to pay the guardians of the fields, the potters and other artisans of the village. This was still common practice a few decades ago. The village chief thus also had a right to communal works. But as he was the one controlling the village administration, it was easy for him to transform this help into a duty and to impose ever heavier corvée labour.

The 'non-genealogical' character of the corvée villages

Let us recall that in a village of free peasants with a common territory to which no boyar had a right, the local population was stable, kept in place by its very possession of the soil, which gave it not only life but also liberty. The local demographic group was thus naturally an endogamous and xenophobic one. The simple fact that a human group lives long generations in the social conditions of demographic isolation is sufficient for lineages to form, with the whole group, tied by blood, becoming one big 'family', within which relationships are intermixed in a single inextricable network. If there develops a demographic saturation with the number of inhabitants exceeding the capacity of the land to feed everyone (the technical level remaining the same), the only solution is to better the techniques or to have the surplus emigrate. But a demographic saturation can also take place in a purely relative fashion, for example, within a single quarter, which, as we have shown, transforms the village from an 'archaic' one into a 'genealogical' one by using the lineages as a system of ownership with unequal shares.

Nothing of this can be found in the villages of corvée peasants. The fact of having been liberated from serfdom allowed them to flee their village, no longer retained legally by anything but their fiscal obligations, which were one of the reasons for their flight. They could thus look and hope for better new conditions. There took place then one of the most impressive demographic movements, with enormous masses of peasants finding themselves in perpetual flight, from one end of the country to the other as well as from one country to another, not only between Moldavia, Wallachia and Transylvania but also beyond the Danube toward the Balkans or the Ukrainian steppes, from which big waves of other immigrants were arriving. Varying with the hazards of fiscal and economic crises, grasshopper scourges, wars, plagues and cholera epidemics, there were periodic increases and decreases in population in the Romanian countries. We do not of course have the precise statistics necessary and the information furnished by people of the period is open to doubt. Can one safely rely on the statement of a foreigner, General Bauer,[4] travelling in Moldavia, who tells us that there were 147,000 tax-paying peasants in 1744, that in 1745 there were but 70,000 and a few years later only 35,000? At any rate, even though the numbers are not reliable, it is certain that a massive depopulation did take place around the time of the reforms of Mavrocordat which freed the serfs.

To bring home those who had fled, to encourage foreign immigration and thus repopulate the country, to be able to face the injunctions of the Turks who looked unfavourably upon the administrators of countries undergoing depopulation, as their capacity for economic exploitation was reduced, the voivodes resorted to a policy of 'saved' people, among whom the new arrivals enjoyed a favoured position: temporary fiscal exemption, number of corvée days reduced to six, and so on. From 1628 these decrees concerning escaped persons begin to appear, but they become more important with time, as, for example, the decree of 1756. The reforms of Mavrocordat precipitated large demographic shifts as peasants fled in order to benefit from the advantages given them when they returned. Even voluntarily, the boyars whose villages had become deserted or badly depopulated had an interest in temporarily relieving

4. F. G. Bauer, *Mémoires historiques et géographiques sur la Valachie*, Frankfurt–Leipzig, 1778.

immigrants of their feudal obligations in order to draw in more men.

This continual peasant migration had important social consequences. In the first place, any traditional tie between the peasants and the land of their native village was broken. Renewed by this coming and going, the population of a village lost all homogeneity and large lineages could no longer form. Not tied by consanguinity, the inhabitants of the artificially repopulated villages were in a way strangers to each other and without traditional ties to the land. Thus nothing of the 'genealogical' forms of possession of the land can be found in the corvée villages.

Genealogical joint ownership of the small boyars

The above is true only for the peasants. The boyars often formed family collectives in which the mode of social organization and the judicial form of their property rights were in all aspects similar to what we know as having been characteristic of the free peasants in the evolved communal villages. It is difficult and sometimes impossible to conclude from the isolated written documents whether it is a peasant collectivity calculating its shares by 'ancestors' or a boyar family enumerating its family lines, by naming either living people or ancestors. Their mode of ownership, like that of the peasants, bears the common name of *de-a valma* and the technical details as well as the whole corresponding terminology are the same: the two types of collectivities are said to 'walk on a certain number of ancestors', calculated 'by number of lengths', 'strips', etc.

Nevertheless, in spite of the identical forms of these two types of collectivities, the two phenomena should not be confused. As far as the boyars are concerned, their family joint ownership is real. Under each 'ancestor's' name, one does not find made up 'lineages', large collective groups of a para-familial form, but rather a restricted number of descendants whose genealogy is not fictitious but real. In addition, the object of ownership that the boyars have in mind is not the soil, as a direct means of labour, but rather a right to exploit the serf villages by tithes and corvée labour.

We will have a chance to note that in the first centuries following the formation of the autochthonous states, the peculiar character of the social system consisted in the fact that the communal villages were reduced to serfdom by communities of boyars. In the centuries studied

in this chapter, these boyar collectivities were only a vanishing phenomenon, large latifundia having appeared in the meantime, monopolized by a small number of families. It was now only the small boyars
who still held their villages jointly. And this joint ownership had many
forms. There are cases where a small family, which had not given up
joint ownership, continued to possess *de-a valma* (jointly). There are
also cases of complex joint ownership between groups of boyars and
groups of free peasants, between boyars and monasteries. As the
statistics of the time are very imprecise, simple analysis cannot reveal
what kind of joint ownership is in question. But this is a completely
different problem which we only mention in passing.

Flight from the village

We know that a mixed pastoral and agricultural economy made up of
big collective herds which wander over open pasture land and of
isolated mobile enclosures for agriculture and for growing hay results
in a certain rural landscape, characterized by the scattering of houses
and areas for cutivation. Any newcomer in a corvée village, in spite of
the presence of the boyar, could, by clearing, burning, or by simply
taking possession, settle where he wanted. It was in the boyar's interest
to make the peasants settle in the centre of the village, around the church
which served as a gathering point. But it was in the peasant's interest
not to settle there. They attempted, on the contrary, to settle secretly
in the farthest corners of the territory, even in the forest, to escape the
fiscal and feudal exactions. At least they were safe for a while until they
were discovered.

A long series of documents from the eighteenth century until the
beginning of the nineteenth record the complaints of the boyars against
these peasants who set up house without permission, living in the forests
or settling in the very middle of agricultural land, thus upsetting the
effective administration of the domain while in addition forcefully
resisting payment of the tithe and corvée labour. Here are a few
examples: in 1702, complaints were laid against the peasants who
settled in a clearing for beehives, demolished the fences and began to
clear the forest. They were ordered to rebuild their thatched huts
elsewhere. But a later document, from 1740 states that they had not yet
moved; this time their houses were destroyed. The procedures are the
same in a great many cases in which people 'settle where there was
never any village' (1756), 'people who have come and who, without

our knowledge, build their houses right in the cultivated fields' (1759) or 'spread out, build their house in the middle of plough and hay land, very far from each other' (1793). They were ordered to move, their houses were burned and destroyed. An edict proclaimed that 'it cannot be tolerated that any settle so far away, building their village with no order, needlessly encroaching upon good land; they must be ordered to move their houses from areas that can serve for agriculture and hay and to build their houses next to each other so that the village will be apart from the cultivated lands' (1793).

This was not always easy to accomplish *manu militari*, as the peasants actively resisted. A chronicler of the period complains of this, when informing us that

> the voivode had spread the slogan that there should be no more serfs in Moldavia and had given orders to all the districts that the boyars and the peasants come and debate before him the question of serfdom. And the serfs from everywhere came together, to the Divan, impertinently, for Constantin voivode had led them to respect no one any longer.

Thus, for example, the abbot of a monastery tells them to go away but the peasants 'jeer, letting loose a stream of profane epithets', not wishing to settle down near the church. If the village lord names guardians of the fields, the latter 'are captured during the night by masked men, wearing hoods, who dumped them in the pond and beat them, wanting to drown them and warning them that they had better not find any more field guardians near the pond or they will be killed', all of which is judged to be of 'criminal impertinence'.

But the voivode of the country did not always agree with these strong solutions, despite the complaints of the boyars. So in 1768 the great boyar council delivered a memoir to the voivode to let him know 'the peasants are in the habit of fleeing their villages where they used to live, settling by two and threes in the hay clearings', and thereby spoiling them. From a fiscal point of view, this situation was considered intolerable because 'the tax collectors have a lot of trouble finding them, one after another, in the forest where they are scattered'. A request was made that they be forced to return to the village. But the voivode believed that 'if they have been settled for two or three years, then they should be left alone and not forced to move', or else they should be allowed a grace period. Thus, in 1776 a monastery complained that 'during the upheavals of war, the inhabitants began to move uphill amongst the vineyards'. The voivode gave orders, once winter had passed, to 'bring the peasants back into the valley by force, to settle in the village; but not now in the middle of the winter'.

The reaction was harsher in Oltenia, after 1728, under the Austrian occupation; since the inhabitants had fled into the forest, the administrators of the province, in order to collect the taxes, organized a manhunt across the fields and woods to find the inhabitants and force them 'to come back to the village'.

The more the boyars wielded their power, the more they forced the formation of villages. At the time of the Organic Regulations they decided that no peasant should have a right to more than 400 lengths in the plain, and 300 in the mountains, to build his house and plan his vegetable garden. 'These lots will be connected to each other in a certain part of the domain designated by the landowner'. But like so many of the other articles of this law, it remained a dead letter, for the peasants continued to settle anywhere. It was only by the Law of 1864 that a certain order was established, by the creation of the modern type of 'administrative commune', which is a more centralized kind of village. The rural landscape, however, even in our time, contains quite a number of villages whose houses are scattered over the entire territory without any recognizable 'centre'.

Surviving communal forms

Even though these corvée villages could not rely on consanguinity and had nothing of the familial respect so characteristic of the free villages, they did form 'communities' by virtue of a set of local and historical conditions. In the first place, the pastoral and agricultural techniques, imposing on the village the regulation of common pasture and the moving of ploughland, implied the adoption of the community system. Next, a strong tradition made it impossible for the people even to conceive of a form of village other than the communal one, the only one besides, which ensured the state of the collection of taxes, by putting it under the supervision of the council, which was collectively responsible to the treasury. Moreover, the massive presence of free communities furnished a permanent model for that kind of social organization. Even in the case where completely new villages were formed, peopled with foreign immigrants and treated with favour by the state as *slobozii* (freed), the only form of village organization conceivable was that of the communal villages, fashioned after the free villages, a phenomenon which we will study more closely in another chapter.

Thus, whether they were indigenous or newly arrived immigrants, as corvée labourers they were organized into communities. The boyar had certainly seized most of the important rights of the village councils, and as we have shown, he was the landowner, at least nominally, of the village territory, defending it against outside atttack; he was the one to represent the village before the organs of state; he was the one to manage the economic administration, supervising the lots of land to be cultivated every year; and he was always the one to act as local police, to judge conflicts and especially to bring in the taxes. But this boyar, nevertheless, was dealing with a 'village', not a mass of individual landholders. To defend their rights, the corvée labourers had no other means than the popular assembly of old common tradition, effective enough as a weapon of social struggle for the boyars to consider it their main enemy, the first one to overcome.

This was no easy task. The Organic Regulations, granting the boyar title of 'landowner', cannot deny either that the 'village' exists; or that if forms an *obştie*, a *grămadă*, that is to say a collectivity, the inhabitants being *cetaşi*, members of a *ceată* – the terminology is the same as that used to refer to the peasants of free communities. As for the rights that had to be recognized as belonging to these peasant collectivities, it goes without saying that the boyars granted them only in self-defense, just enough to ensure the effective management of the local administrative life. But this minimum was nonetheless sufficient to keep the village councils alive. Thus the Organic Regulations contained a set of articles that could only be put into effect by the intermediary of the village general assemblies.

For example, the village had the duty to put at the disposal of the landowner 4% of its able-bodied men to act as his servants. However, it was not the boyar who chose them, but the peasant assembly, through the procedure of the *cislă* as it was also practised in the free communities: the text reads, 'so that there may be no injustice in performing the *cislă*, each year, the whole village, unanimously or as a majority, will choose four men for each hundred inhabitants, making sure of a rotation so that no person will be wronged'.

These assemblies of corvée labourers were given the right to participate in the judgement of small local conflicts, instituting for this task 'juries' made up of the village priest, assisted by three 'sworn' men who were elected by the assembly, with the village lord having the right to sit in. One of these three 'sworn' men had to belong to each of the three peasant classes: rich, comfortable and poor. The jury had to meet every Sunday and holiday, after church, at the priest's house.

The fiscal duties of the assemblies were themselves upheld. They had to carry out fiscal censuses every seven years in Moldavia and every

five in Wallachia. These were carried out by the landowners with the
help of the priest and six peasants elected by the village. A copy of the
fiscal obligations of the villagers had to be left with the 'village', which
remained wholly responsible, 'one for another', for the collection of
taxes. As tax collector, the 'inhabitants, farmers and labourers of each
village had to elect every year a *pîrcălab*' who would record the
payments on his *răboj*, which we described for the free villages. The
village collectivity was, in addition, wholly fiscally responsible for the
inhabitants who fled. Likewise, each village had to name each year six
inhabitants to care for the management of the amounts collected.

We can only conjecture the exact extent of the rights of these
assemblies; only by chance do we have certain details. Thus it should
be kept in mind, first, that in all the documents from the eighteenth
and nineteenth centuries, all references are to 'villages' and 'inhabitants' as the collectivities which were the contracting parties and not
to individuals. And, as in the free villages, these corvée villages entered
into contract always by the intermediary of their delegates. Their
documents bear the formulas which we already know, affirming that
they were made 'in the name of the whole village', according to one
of the most interesting formulas. Here is an example:

that is to say we, the village of Ioneşti [thus the 'socionym' of the collectivity of the
lineages of Ioneşti], who sign below, give our true word to his holiness the father
superior of the Monastery of Motru to announce that, having been summoned to fulfil
twelve days of corvée at the blessed monastery, we have knelt in prayer so that they
may take pity on us and so out of charity we will have to pay only two zlotzi per house
and two days of collective labour in addition to the corn ploughing and harvest...And
so that we may be believed, we have signed below to be believed...April 18, 1783.

Then come the signatures of the delegates, among whom are 'I,
Gheorghe, *pîrcălab*', and 'I, Constantin, shepherd' 'with the whole
village'.[5]

Even the custom of accompanying the delegates when they met the
authorities is recorded. For example, in 1783, the villagers of Ploieşti
– which at that time was not yet the city that it is today but a simple
village – brought a case before the court of the voivode concerning their
territory. The voivode said, in his order of convocation

And as they demand a trial...tell them to elect three or four, at most five delegates
for all concerned and to come before me in five to six days. And do not allow them
to come with the whole crowd, as is their awful wont, but as we order you, that at most
five come, as there is no need of their presence.

5. *Documente privind relaţiile agrare în veacul al XVIII* (Documents concerning agrarian relations in
the eighteenth century), volume I, *Ţara Românească* (Wallachia), Bucharest, 1961, p. 693.

This did not prevent the villagers from coming to Bucharest with their women and children, thereby alerting the authorities to their demanding attitude. Of course, neither the laws nor the private documents ever acknowledged the fact that these serf collectivities formed a sort of 'moral person' (a notion foreign to the ancient law). But in fact, was it not recognizing the village to make contracts with delegates from the assembly and to give the serfs the right of pre-emption in case the boyar wanted to lease out the village? In 1792, the voivode Michael C. Soutzo of Wallachia decreed that 'only the inhabitants with domiciles on the domain have this right of pre-emption', specifying that 'the leasing out of the domains will begin on the first of March, the peasants having the right to pre-emption according to the Law and the custom of the country will not be able to exercise it after May 1'. This was to avoid the serfs' habit of seeing first if the year was good or bad, in order to annul the lease made to an outsider if they felt like it.

Thus, in 1801, a monastery leased its domain for the sum of 1,200 thalers. The peasants would have liked to rent the land, but did not believe that the monastery had been offered that much for it. The monastery swore that such was the price, so the peasant delegates gave up their rights to the lease, in writing, as the price seemed too high. It was not before 1815 in Moldavia and 1818 in Wallachia that this right of pre-emption was annulled: 'from now on such a right is absolutely prohibited and each lord is free to sell the revenue of his domain as he wishes and to whom he wishes'.[6]

6. Valentin A. Georgescu, *Preempţiunea în istoria dreptului românesc. Dreptul de protimisis în Tara Romanească şi Moldova* (Pre-emption in the history of Romanian law. The law of the right of withdrawal in Wallachia and Moldavia), Bucharest, 1965.

7 ↦ The economic life of the corvée villages

The forestry techniques and the rights of the peasants to cut wood

It must be remembered that the boyars did not become full landowners until the Law of 1864, which, though its avowed aim was to establish a peasant ownership, resulted paradoxically, among other things, in the expropriation of the ancient rights of the peasants to cut wood in the forests. In fact, article 9 of this law specified that the rights of the peasants to use the forest would be upheld for fifteen more years; the boyar would then have the right to deprive the peasants, either directly or through judicial channels, of their rights over the forest, thus permitting the boyars to include the forests in their patrimony without further trial. Until this late date, therefore, the forest was not a part of the exclusive patrimony of the boyar. The idea that the forest cannot belong to anyone was so commonly admitted that the boyars had much trouble imposing on the peasants a gradual limitation of their free rights to use it. The boyars' struggle to take over the forest was lengthy and they resorted to several methods.

At first they struggled to have the peasants accept that certain small forests would be 'kept' privately and thus not subject to the peasants' right to use them. In Romanian, these forests are called *braniște* (from a Slavic word meaning 'prohibited', 'not allowed'). It was not at all a case of seigniorial forests, of huge feudal domains for hunting, but rather a simple means of imposing on those using the woods the obligation to pay a tithe. These 'kept' forests, furthermore, were for the most part very small. In 1756, a document specifies the surface area in the following way: 'That the forest to be kept around the monastery measures on all sides the length of shooting an arrow five times. Beyond that, one is free to cut wood.' There were, most likely, larger *braniști*;

111

but they were rare, belonging to the princes of the country or to large princely monasteries. Such a forest, once prohibited, gave the local lord the right to demand a tithe.

To maintain his rights to tithes was a relatively easy task for the boyar with regard to the ploughed fields, where the sown areas were visible and easily identifiable. But the forest could be used clandestinely without leaving any traces. To prevent such a thing, the boyars had to claim any unauthorized use of the woods as an infraction. But to have a forest declared *braniște*, it was necessary to have the consent of the state and a special decree. The oldest documents of this kind belong to a much earlier period. For example, from 1490 we have a princely decree giving the right to a monastery to 'fish there and graze its livestock; with no one else allowed, without the abbey's permission, to fish in that *braniște* or to graze its livestock or anything else there'. Other documents refer to the prohibition of hunting, of woodcutting, of clearing, of gathering hops, etc. From the sixteenth century, the penal character of this rare right to the woods continued to grow, involving arbitrary punishment from a fine to the confiscation of the peasant's cart, oxen, and axe, 'leaving him naked'. At times this went as far as mutilating the hand.

These documents remain rare, and even in the seventeenth century they appear only occasionally. They do not become frequent until the eighteenth and nineteenth centuries when the 'kept forests' become more and more numerous and the struggle against the rights of the peasants harsher. Nevertheless, in the beginning only these 'kept' forests were involved, and not all or most forests. The documents do not cease to mention the problem: in 1785, a princely order declared that 'the small forests were from time immemorial defended and guarded by their masters so that no one would cut wood without their permission. But within the black forests [virgin forests] wherever they may be found, they are not guarded so that anyone may cut wood in them.' And in 1786, the voivode of Moldavia decided that 'the lords of the domains do not have the right to ask for money nor to prohibit woodcutting for heating, or for beams, even that with commerce in mind. For the large forests were never defended at any time. In short, there must not be any more talk of taxing people for the right to cut wood', only the small forests being exempted from this right. This decision had to be taken to all the villages so that all might learn of its contents, a proof that the problem of woodcutting was already a general one throughout the country.

To struggle to win a tithe, however, continued to be one of the goals of the boyar class. They won their point gradually, starting with the *branişte*. The old formula continued to be used: 'that the monastery defend its *branişte* all around itself from other people's herds and from neighbours and that no one dare bring his livestock into the woods or cut wood, thereby crushing the nuts, or fish or hunt there'. As all these prohibitions continued to have as their aim the winning of a tithe, they were accompanied, in a long series of documents which became very common in the eighteenth century, by the stereotyped formula: 'without the previous permission of the lord'.

This 'previous permission' guaranteed the rights to the tithe in certain 'kept' forests, but then spread to all the forests. It was first applied to the peasants not residing in the domain of the landowner. It was then applied to the use of the forest for commercial purposes, for wood for heating, for building, and for implements. Finally, it was made absolute and general in 1864. This process lasted a whole century. One can follow the development, rather confused and often contradictory, through the documents, administrative decisions and law texts.

The result is two incontestable facts of importance. In the first place, there is the slow suppression of the rights of the peasants to use the forest; in the second place, there is the existence of the same sylvo-pastoral and sylvo-agricultural techniques which we were able to study directly in the contemporary free communal villages. These two facts are interdependent; as long as these techniques remain as they always were, prohibiting the peasants from using the forest would mean starving them. It was only by moving to a cereal economy and to commerce in wood, both created by the new, growing merchant economy, that the boyars could become masters of the forests.

It was in the forests that livestock was raised, especially pigs, an export merchandise even more desirable as the Turks did not want it. So the code of Ypsilanti in 1780 announced that

the inhabitants owe nothing to the lord of the domain for the pigs they graze in the forest; but they ought not to have the audacity to bring them into the kept forests, that is, those the lords reserve to be leased out. It is preferable for the peasants to arrange amicably with their lord master to be able to use the forest. And those daring to go there without the lord's permission will have to pay the sum that could have been obtained from other potential renters.

This proves that at this period enclosing the oak and beech forests had become common enough to have a commercial value attached to it.

Concerning the sylvo-pastoral and sylvo-agricultural techniques, the Law of Moruzi stated in 1792 that 'the inhabitants who are near the forests do not take care to prepare in time, during the summer, the hay they will need, but spend the winter with their livestock living off the woods, cutting leaves. These pollard trees bear no fruit for twenty to thirty years, and the sheep and pigs no longer have nuts to eat'; the lords suffered a loss, no longer able to enclose the forests for the raisers and sellers of livestock. Finally, 'many inhabitants continue to clear the forest for agricultural and pasture land, cutting down the trees of the virgin woods to transform them into fields, thus destroying the forest, for the only reason that they do not want to go down into the plain is because of the long distance to cover.'

The conclusion is clearly that the techniques we have found in the archaic villages of the twentieth century were also commonly practised by the serf villages.

As for the peasants' rights to the forest, they were limited more and more by the forestry laws. Thus in 1785 in Wallachia an edict proclaimed,

If it is a question of small kept forests, they must, according to custom, be defended, the inhabitants forbidden the right to cut wood; likewise if it is a question of a forests plentiful in nuts, except for dead wood and fallen branches, which are only useful for heating. And if it is a question of a forest without nuts or of very small forests, the inhabitants settled on the domain must have the right to take wood for heating that they need in their household, as it is for that they do corvée labour. But if they want to cut planks and beams or any wood meant for business, they must reach an agreement with the lord of the domain and must pay a tithe allowing them to cut wood.

The Law of Moruzi of 1792 foresaw already a true forestry code. The 'abuses' of the peasants which result in the destruction of the forests are described at length. Several types of forests are delineated. First, the small ones and, secondly, those that are growing, which must be defended, no one having the right to use them without the lord's permission. For 'just as the lords of the domains collect a tithe from the produce of the fields, it is just that the lords of the forest collect one too... Those near the Prut and Seret rivers, which have been practically destroyed, must be put off limits so that they will not be ruined, as is the wont of the rural folk', who from now on can only take the dead trees, the beeches being an exception as they are considered to be without value. As for the virgin forests, they must be supervised, the inhabitants only being permitted to use wood to build their houses.

If the peasants' rights to use the forests were deeply entrenched and difficult to prohibit, the commercial exploitation of wood was, on the contrary, easier to subject to a tithe. Thus, from 1757, a monastery received the right to collect a tenth of the ships' masts the peasants cut to sell. Likewise, it received a tenth of the boards coming out of their saw mill, as well as a tenth of the beams, barrels, kegs, spoons, boats, and all sorts of objects manufactured for trade.

But despite a virtual avalanche of official decisions on the part of the state, declaring such and such a forest 'forbidden', and making the payment of tithes obligatory, another mass of documents proves that it was more a case of fictitious politics than real ones, as the peasants continued to act on the basis of their ancient woodcutting rights, behaving as 'rebels', 'troublemakers', and 'shameless bare-footed wretches', who had to be overcome by force.

The common pasture and the right of the herds to graze freely

As long as animal raising was the main economic activity of the country, the technique of letting herds wander freely across the immense pasture land of the country was common. It was only from the time of the great social crisis of the transformation to a cereal economy that the problem of animal raising came up. As pasture land grew scarce, boyars and peasants found themselves in conflict, the outcome of which was fatal for the peasants. The boyars, in addition to taking over the agricultural lands, wanted to control the pasture land. The presence of the peasants as competitors seemed odious to them. Many times they used force to gain a monopoly over the pastures still open to use.

One boyar of more liberal views complained, in 1805, to the Metropolitan of Wallachia of the fact that 'the villagers are chased from one domain to another as the lords of these domains consider it more economical to graze their livestock there than to feed the peasants'. But the peasants intended to continue animal raising just as they had in the past. As they saw the vast common prairies becoming restricted, they would have liked to reserve at least the territory of their village as pasture, and to cultivate on the land of neighbouring villages. This calculation was justified not only from the point of view of their pastoral economy but also from the point of view of their social condition. If they cultivated within their village, they had not only to pay a tithe but also to furnish corvée labour; whereas, if they worked on outside land, they could obtain, through agreement, more advantageous conditions from a boyar for whom they were not serfs. Here are a few examples.

In 1793, a boyar complains that the peasants of his village, Cătinele, are moving and settling at Spanţov, 'for the only reason of letting

the village of Cătinele fall to ruins and become simply pasture land'.
The same year, another complaint, concerning the village Axintele,
denounces the fact that the peasants 'do not want to labour on this
domain where they are subject to corvée, and go off to labour on outside
lands, using their own only as pasture'. In 1801, as the village of
Călineanca had become depopulated, 'inhabitants of nearby villages
come to settle in it, each where he likes and not in the centre of the
village. There are thus forty houses scattered over the whole territory,
for the simple reason that they intend to keep the land as pasture; not
wanting to cultivate it, they labour on land belong to neighbouring
villages.'

But this was not the only procedure. As long as the pasture lands still
existed in an area, the peasants resorted to their right of free crossing,
without paying any attention to the boundaries between villages. The
boyars protested and their complaints grew: 'They are holding my
domain by force to graze their animals. I cannot cultivate, because the
peasants wander over my three domains' (1783); 'because of them, one
no longer dares to plough and sow, for even if one does, they and their
livestock crush the seeds underfoot and all is lost' (1785).

This technique of animal raising was so common that the state did
not even think to forbid it. At most, it tried to impose a tax on any
pasture used. Thus, in 1804, the state noted that 'it is public knowledge
that the inhabitants, taking their animals to market, must cross many
domains, as they cannot go by air! They cannot go except by land. It
follows thus that we must oblige the peasant to pay a tax of one "para"
for each domain he crosses.' It was not until 1805 that the Law of
Moruzi benefited the boyars in Moldavia at least partly, by giving them
the right to prohibit peasant pasture land on three-quarters of their
domains, a preliminary version of the formula of 'dividing into thirds',
but only concerning the pasture land and not the entire territory as was
the case later on.

Itinerant pastoral agriculture and the right to ploughland and meadows

A conflict just as serious developed between the boyars and peasants
over the ploughlands. The problem was caused by the change from an
itinerant agricultural technique to a new one, allowing a larger
agricultural production.

Let us not forget that before 1864 the boyar did not have a so-called 'reserve', but his lots were still mixed among those of the peasants, moved from one year to the next, and the procedures of itinerant agriculture were still so alive that our agronomists claim it was widespread until the second half of the nineteenth century. Thus George Maior[1] describes to us what is popularly called *moină*:

when land is used successively for the production of grains and grass. Cleared in the autumn, the agricultural land could last for two, four or six years for growing grain, especially that sown in the spring with neither manure nor rest; afterwards, when infertile, lands were left fallow for ten, fifteen, twenty years and even longer, and used as pasture or meadow. These *moină* are found in almost all the villages of the Carpathians.

And, 'We can assume that this system was the one generally used long after the unification of the Principalities', thus after 1859.

Another agronomist, P. S. Aurelian,[2] is of the same opinion:

the mixed pastoral agriculture consists of the alternation, either irregular or regular, of cultivating cereals or other crops and letting the field lie fallow; the terrain, after having grown cereals for several years, then lies fallow, used partly as pasture, partly as meadow. After four to five years or even more, it is cultivated once again...In Romania this system is used in all the regions, in the mountains as well as on the plain.

This agricultural-pastoral system, which we found in our free archaic contemporary villages and which our agronomists speak of as being widespread even in the second half of the nineteenth century, must have been even more common in the period we are now studying. The peasants, with huge stretches of prairie land available, did not hesitate to clear where and when they wanted. Going from one village to the next, settling where they felt like it, they grew their crops despite the presence of village lords, ready to pay them the traditional tithe. This was common in the eighteenth century, when the peasants, profiting from the fact that they were no longer bound to the soil, wandered over the countryside looking for good land. They especially like the lands outside domains, as there they did not have to do corvée labour, which was the obligation of those residing in the village.

In this fashion, the peasants were only following the ancient right to use the land, without the village lord interfering in their agricultural activity, except indirectly by demanding a tithe. Concerning this ancient peasant right the texts are clear. Thus in 1725 there was a rule obliging the lord 'to permit everyone to cultivate and grow hay where he wants. And may no one prohibit anyone from so doing', evidently

1. George Maior, *Politica agrară la Români* (Agrarian politics of the Romanians), Bucharest, 1906.
2. P. S. Aurelian, *România agricolă. Studiu economic* (Agricultural Romania. An economic study), Bucharest, 1911.

on condition that the tithe be paid. In 1768, the *urbarium* of the voivode Calimacus[3] proclaimed that 'the inhabitants of any domain, having decided to live there, have the right to provide for themselves and cannot be prevented from doing so by their lords'. Likewise, the *urbarium* of Michael Soutzo stated in 1794 that 'all inhabitants of villages, there where they live, may plough and sow and grow the hay that they need'. But the right to sow on other domains in the event that their village is 'wide' is forbidden them. Only if the village is 'narrow', with not enough land for everyone, are the neighbouring boyars obliged to give them enough land for their crops and their hay, under the condition that they pay a tithe, but not the corvée. The same *urbarium* proclaimed in addition that the peasants were obliged to cultivate next to each other and not be spread out over the land. Certain measures were provided against neighbouring boyars who might be recalcitrant: 'And if a lord proves recalcitrant and does not want to give land to the peasants for their crops, though they do no damage, it must not be tolerated, even from a lord, and he must understand that he has to give pasture and ploughland.'

As the boyars were already closing their domains to outsiders, the *urbarium* of Calimacus provided that in case 'lords lease out their domains, that in that year they lease them with the stipulation that the inhabitants of the village have the right to provide for themselves, without being prevented from doing so by the renter, and that the inhabitants will pay the customary tithe'. But the boyars began to protest more and more strongly against these agricultural customs as their own agriculture expanded. They began by complaining about the right of the peasants not living on their domains to come and work there, this right having become burdensome not only to the boyar but also to the inhabitants of the village who felt their space grow tighter and tighter.

In 1784 came the first complaint, from a boyar protesting the fact that, as his village was 'narrow', he did not even have sufficient space for his own needs and for those of his peasants, so he must be protected against the invasion of his territory by the neighbouring peasants. But the voivode told him that the peasants had the right to labour on neighbouring land. In 1785 there was another protest against the

3. *Codul Calimachi* (The code of Calimachus), Bucharest, annotated edition of the Romanian Academy, 1958 (text in Greek and Romanian). See also N. Iorga, *Anciens documents de droit roumain, avec une préface contenant l'histoire du droit coutumier roumain*, volumes I–II, Paris, 1930; Georges Fontino, *Contribution à l'étude des origines de l'ancien droit roumain*, Paris, 1930.

'outsiders who come and take over the land by force, spoiling it with their livestock and crops. They rose up with thirty carts and, invading the domain, began to plough, one after another, wherever they wanted.' A request was made for permission to stop them, with the boyar promising at the same time to give them sufficient land to provide for themselves, but only where he thought best. The voivode decided to carry out an investigation, and if truly 'they are spoiling the domain, by scattering all over to grow their crops, then they may be restricted to a corner of the domain'.

In 1792 there came another complaint against 'insubordinate peasants who cultivate where they want and as much as they want and do the same with their hay raising, without wanting to acknowledge me as lord of the domain'. 'They cultivate wherever they please on scattered lots, without any order', said another boyar. In 1800, there was still another complaint on the part of a boyar and his peasants against the 'neighbours who leave their own village, going to work on the neighbouring domain, occupying the land they want, some for food, others to do business. And the agricultural land right around them they leave, turning it into pasture, not wanting to graze their animals where there is free land on the prairies.' Thus there is proof that much of the land was still communal.

The boyars resisted by force, but without yet having the right. Thus, in 1731, a boyar set fire to his serfs' haystacks on the pretext that they had grown their hay on land belong to him. This was declared illegal. In 1776, a district administrator wrote to a boyar that he did not have the right to take the prairies that the peasants had held for several years. The administrator threatened him. If he did not give back the hay, 'I, myself, will take to my horse, arouse the neighbouring villages, come and take the hay and restore it to the peasants. For, by the grace of God, the country has a master and we are not here to let each do his will.' In 1775, some inhabitants made hay without prior permission. Their lords, monks from a monastery, set fire to the haystacks; they were obliged to restore the damage.

But alongside these peasant rights to the land, the boyars' rights became more and more extensive. Thus in 1780, the Code of Ypsilanti gave the right to 'the village lord to choose the best lands for himself'. In 1794 the *urbarium* of Michael Soutzo gave orders that 'as the village lord has realized the fact [that the peasants want to cultivate] the peasants will be given a place apart, sufficient for their needs, where they will not cause any damage to the master's domain. And they will have to cultivate next to each other, and not scattered about.' Likewise, in 1805, the *urbarium* of Moruzi proclaimed: 'As concerns ploughing and sowing, the inhabitants do not have the right to work scattered about...but, with sufficient space, they must cultivate next to each other in a single corner of the domain.' In 1816, the law was even more specific:

when the lord wishes to limit [we have come to the point where 'limiting' appears in its first form without yet applying the principle of dividing into thirds] the ploughlands and prairies of the peasants from his own, he will have the right to give them, all on the same domain, other lands of equal value both in number and quality, and the peasants will not have the right to resist him in any way, so that the lord of the domain can have his lands safely apart.

This Law of Moruzi also provided for a maximum area of meadow land for the peasants, varying according to geographic region. On the average, the areas were as follows:

Peasants with 16 head of livestock	8 *fălci*
Peasants with 12 head of livestock	6 *fălci*
Peasants with 6 head of livestock	3 *fălci*

[One *falce* was 1.4321 hectares)

Even the obligation of lords to give peasants sufficient ploughland was then restricted, at least in the case where the inhabitants of a village were too numerous. The Moldavian Ruling of Ioniţă Sturdza in 1828 obliged the lord to give peasants 'the land for cultivation necessary for them to provide for themselves, according to the number of mouths to feed'. But this is only true for the 'wide' villages.

As for the narrow villages, which do not have enough land to give to all the peasants, as has been said, and so that the perpetual lord of the domain will not be lacking in the agricultural and meadow land he needs, the domain will be divided into three parts, both agricultural and meadow land (the clearings made in the forest also count); two-thirds of the agricultural and meadow land will go to the peasants and the remaining third will go, in any event, to the perpetual lord.

The principle of 'dividing into thirds' itself thus appears, but only as a means of limiting the peasants' right to use the land, not as a general rule of territorial distribution and only in the event that there are too many peasants to receive 'sufficient' land. At any rate, the boyar is guaranteed at least a third of the land. It is thus not the same division into thirds that we have seen taking place in 1864. The boyar did not cut up the domain into three parts, did not grant two-thirds to the peasants for good. And, in addition, this sort of dividing into thirds was resorted to only in the overpopulated villages, while the others were still at the stage where they could have as much land 'as they needed'. Thus it was a question of dividing the land into thirds in order to manage the feudal relations in over-populated villages and not, as in 1864, a question of dividing the land into thirds in order to end all the existing feudal relations.

In 1832 the Organic Regulations, again taking up this idea of division into thirds, generalized it in two ways: by imposing it not only on the pasture land but on the whole territory, and by applying it to the two Romanian countries. It was explicitly stated that the boyar had the right to hold, in any event, a third of the territory for his own use, the land that he gave to the peasants was not allowed to surpass two-thirds of the domain. The amount given to each peasant was no longer, as before, 'as much as they need' nor according to the 'mouths to feed', but, as we have already noted, according to the new criterion of his economic capacity to utilize his land and thus be of use to the lord by the tithes and corvée he could render.

But, as a new principle, the norm was no longer defined by three categories of peasants but by a single one, considered as the average, that of peasants with four pulling animals (oxen, water buffaloes, horses) plus one cow. This peasant received one *falce* and a half of pasture, the same amount of meadow, and the same of ploughland. In all, he received four and a half *fălci*. The pastoral lands thus continued to dominate, amounting to double the ploughlands. Compared to what a peasant with four animals had in 1805, one finds that now he was getting less in total than he then had in pasture land alone. During this quarter of a century, the peasants' situation has thus substantially deteriorated. As for the two other peasant categories, their situation was managed as follows: those with fewer animals received land proportionately. And, what is an extremely important detail, if they had more they had to arrive at an 'amicable' agreement with the boyar as to the conditions to fulfil for obtaining surplus land which the law did not guarantee.

The peasant delegates who took part in the debates of 1848 as members of the Commission for Property were thus perfectly right when they declared the Organic Regulations to be an iniquitous attack on their ancient rights: 'Before the Organic Regulations', they said, 'we had a right to as much land as we could work'; which, in this time of military operation, was even recognized by the Russian representative, Prince Kisselev, who administered Moldavia and Wallachia.

In the same vein, during the debates of the Divan Ad Hoc of Moldavia in 1857, the peasants affirmed that since the days of our fathers and ancestors, we have had the right to work the land necessary to feed both ourselves and our animals, without anyone being able to stop us. All the documents, all our institutions, old and new, sanctify this right, even that of giving our children land, up to the limit of two-thirds. And before the Organic Regulations, we had the right to work as much land as we could.

The absence of quarters within general enclosures

Any 'quarter' laid out in bundles of contiguous parallel lots surrounded by general enclosures was, in the free villages, the result of a definitive, initially egalitarian, partitioning of the land. It is thus logical that in the corvée villages such quarters appear only if the lord of the village deemed it necessary himself to partition for good a certain area of the territory for the benefit of the serfs. It is possible but doubtful that he could in any way benefit from this. In the free villages, these land distributions of an egalitarian nature characteristically gave rise to a long-term ownership under the laws of inheritance. This meant that in several generations the lots became unequal and the quarter was laid out by 'sum of lengths', with the 'part', the 'strip', becoming proof and measure of the right to shares in other parts of the as yet undivided village territory. In a serf village, the lord of the domain had no interest in giving his serfs 'shares' of this kind. At the most he might distribute lots annually from the time when he could prohibit the right to choose lots freely.

At the time of the Organic Regulations the boyar, having already been declared landowner, had the right to supervise and administer the parcelling of the land into three thirds, two of which went to the peasants. Nevertheless, there is no mention made, *expressis verbis*, of periodic partitioning, with a few exceptions, which are interesting as they clarify this poorly understood though highly significant question. The first point is the provision made by the Regulations for a 'reserve depot' in each village where everyone had to deposit a certain amount of grain for the lean years. The grain put in the reserve had to be distributed to the peasants in proportion to the number of mouths to feed in each household. It was thus a common harvest that was put in these collective depots.

The Regulations say that, apart from the lots of land he must give to each particular peasant, the 'landowner' must give to the village another terrain, calculated according to the number of households in the village (which in Moldavia was one *falce* for each ten families in the plain and one and a half *fălci* in the hilly region) for the growing of corn (and in Wallachia millet, considered the usual food and easier to preserve than corn). The boyar took his customary tithe from this harvest, and the rest was put into the communal depots built by the peasants. The boyar thus granted a 'reserve quarter' (*ţarină a rezervei; holdă de reservă* in Wallachia) where 'all the villagers, without exception, will have to plough, sow and harvest'. The Regulations do not tell us the details of this operation. But the nature of the work done communally implies that the reserve land was a single holding. The names *ţarină* and *holdă* indicate the same thing; and usually any *ţarină* was surrounded by a *gardul ţarinii*, that is to say, by an enclosure. Every three years there was a distribution to the peasant population of a third of the reserve grain. Did this reserve land remain the same or did the boyar designate another reserve area every year? We do not know, but it is more than likely that this quarter was moved, just as the other ploughlands were.

As for the distributions of the tithe and corvée lots, the Regulations granted the boyar the favour of being able to distribute the lots by his own arbitrary decision, with the right to group them in a single block; 'that these lands be bound to each other and set in a certain part of the territory designated by the landowner'.

The names of *ţarină* and *holdă* are no longer used and there is no mention of the obligation of any communal labour. It is thus unlikely that these were enclosed 'quarters'. Let us look at those that survived into the twentieth century when the annual distribution of land which we have mentioned was regularly undertaken according to a technique we know in detail. Here is a contemporary description:

As soon as the agricultural contracts were concluded, the lots established on paper had to be drawn up on the land. For this, the domain had to be cut into 'lines' of 'fields'. Each 'line' had a width of 400–600 meters, the length being calculated in such a way that the total area was 50–100 pogons. The 'lines' were, as far as possible, rectangular. To obtain them, the straightest side of the domain was measured first and so on to the other end. As the borders of the domain were never parallel all the way across, the areas were of varied shapes. They were called *clinuri*. The 'lines' were bordered by paths. And these paths still exist.

In the spring, when it was time to sow, all the men came out to the fields. Over the whole plain large groups of men could be seen walking after the boyars' agents who distributed the lots. It was customary for the lots to be drawn to know which villager would be first. When the land was too good or too bad, the division was made 'by brothers', each party taking only a 'pogon' or half a 'pogon' in each 'line'. Once the land was distributed, the peasants aligned their lots, putting at the end mounds of earth, a stick with a hat at one end, and from the opposite end, pulling the oxen after them on a rope, they drew a furrow as straight as a string.

In our opinion, a similar land distribution is referred to in a much older text, of 1638, which is located in a travel journal of the Italian Nicolas Berni who tells us that

no one, neither inhabitants of the towns nor villagers, can say: this is my lot, and that is yours. For only at the time of sowing do all the people go out onto the fields and the *şoltuz* [term derived from the German *Schultheis*] and the *pîrgari* [derived from *Bürger*] show the lots.

According to the number of members in each household, a proportionate number of 'fields' is given. If there are, for example, eight men in a family, it is given eight 'fields'. If there are ten, they receive ten. The 'fields' are so numerous that all of them can never be worked; but for two years they sow in one place and the following two in another.

Between these records, one being absolutely general for all the latifundia of the twentieth century, the other referring to a distribution made to townspeople in the seventeenth century, one must interpret the whole intermediary period as being itself at an intermediate phase; but only from the time the boyar succeeded in replacing the free choosing of land with a distribution made by himself. The absence of permanent quarters does, however, indicate the absence of general enclosures. These did exist, though in the corvée villages their only role was that of placing a divider between two common lands, pasture or ploughland, or between neighbouring villages.

Another traveller, the Count D'Hauterive, who left an excellent description of the state of Romania around 1787, cites such general enclosure as an argument to support his thesis that the Romanian peasant is not, by nature, lazy, as many said (inevitable laziness in any 'despairing country' where one knows that it is useless to have anything over the poverty level, as any surplus would immediately be confiscated by the tax collector and the boyar). D'Hauterive tells us: 'if two villages have a difference over the pasture boundaries, they draw a line and in less than four days the two communes are separated by a hedge a league and a half long.'

A Romanian saying affirms, even today: 'the enclosure of the fields has nothing to do with the payment of the taxes', in the sense that to participate in the building of enclosures was a duty, but completely different from that of paying one's taxes (today, in the sense that one must not confuse two things that have nothing to do with each other). This locution also proves that 'to build enclosures' was so common a custom that it is remembered despite the centuries that have passed. As for the small enclosures built around hay stacks, pieces of ploughed land, vineyards, and houses, they are so common that the documents refer to them in great numbers. In all, this must have given the rural landscape of the period a look almost identical to that which we found on the territories of the free, archaic undivided villages which did not yet have a real enclosed general quarter.

The regime of tènements belonging to the corvée serfs

In a free village land that was cleared and ploughed gave the right of possession to the man who performed this labour. This right existed for a varying length of time, and could even become hereditary. In a free village divided into long lots, to work a terrain on another's lot involved paying a tithe. If the dividing into lots took place after the creation of these holdings, it resulted in 'buried' lots, or 'enclave' lots.

In a serf village all the land was considered as belonging to the boyar to whom one thus had to pay the tithe. No holding was exempt from the tithe, which was logical, as they were 'enclaves' within the domain. There is an altogether different problem: if the serfs had to provide labour to make a piece of land worthwhile, did the boyar have the right to take it back?

At the period we are studying clearing and cultivating virgin land was the customary work of all. The texts speak of it constantly, as something to be taken for granted. For the clearings made in the woods, the problem was evident. The work was so hard that no peasant would do it if he knew that the boyar could take the land back. Likewise, he would not plant vineyards or orchards. The rule was thus that the boyar could not confiscate these kinds of holdings. If the use of them became permanent, as was the case with the vineyards and orchards, the boyar could do nothing more than demand a regular tithe. But if the peasant gave up working a vineyard for a period of years, the boyar would take back his rights and give the vineyard to another, so as to continue collecting a tithe. This kind of right of pre-emption was called, as we have already seen, *otaşniţă* or *embatic* and continued to be a general phenomenon until the twentieth century. This gave rise to all sorts of law suits, raising most interesting problems of common law. However, it was not clearly understood by jurists that the 'land customs' cannot be comprehended without prior knowledge of the communal villages.

These kinds of holdings were so anchored in custom that the peasants claimed the right to sell them as being their own. In 1761, we thus have the complaint of a monastery against the inhabitants 'who have taken the habit of planting gardens and of selling them to others as if they were their patrimony. And other outsiders have adopted the habit of taking over the gardens of our serfs by way of the serfs' daughters [by marriage] or their nephews [by sale or fraternal adoption]'. The monastery affirms that according to ancient custom, the serfs could hold these lands only during their lifetime, as inhabitants of the domain and by providing corvée labour. But they could not sell them, give them in dowry or exchange them.

The serfs referred to had deserted the village and sold their holdings.

Not content with the fact that, by the Grace of God, the voivode has liberated them from being bound to the soil, they now wanted to be landowners, like the monastery, of the gardens planted by their ancestors and of the clearings made by their ancestors, which is not just. Thus, may those who have like holdings inherited from their parents keep them, but they may not have the right to sell or exchange them. And if they flee from the village, may the trees planted belong to the one who owns the land and may it be the lord of the village who owns them,

with, however, the understanding that if they return they may reclaim their rights. It was not until 1817 that the Code of Caragea defined the rule that 'the corvée labourer cannot make his clearing by cutting trees in the forest without the written permission of his lord, specifying where and how much he will clear. Otherwise he will lose his labour and the lord will take over the clearing.' There is a provision, however that inherited lands cannot be taken over by the boyar.

There was, in addition, another category of 'holdings', of much less duration, that of the agricultural lands. The work furnished to cultivate them was also very hard. One must remember that it was virgin land, covered with a real forest of weeds which were often high enough, say the texts, to hide a man standing in them. Clearing them, burning the weeds, and ploughing was a great deal of work. But as this land was rather rapidly exhausted, the peasant himself abandoned it after a certain amount of time. But before the time was up, it would be unjust for the boyar to take over this 'ready-made' land.

The texts are categorical: in 1780 the Code of Ypsilanti said that the boyar 'does not have the right to take the land that the peasant clears to sow or grow hay or plant'. In 1794, the *urbarium* of Michael Soutzo also recognized the right of the peasants to their temporary holdings: 'the lands worked by the peasants on the domain where they live as well as those given them on neighbouring domains, with the condition that they pay the tithe, cannot be taken away from them by the lords as long as the peasants do not abandon them themselves as no longer useful'. Likewise, in 1805, Alexander Moruzi confirmed this: 'the old lands held by the inhabitants may not be confiscated by the lords of the domain as long as they do not abandon them themselves as no longer useful'. This is also an excellent confirmation of the itinerant character of the agriculture of this period.

Conclusions

It would be a false image of reality to believe that the serf village communities always looked as we have described them. Let us not forget that, within the village communities of the corvée peasants, the boyar had already succeeded in going from 'perpetual lord' to 'landowner', and that the peasants were reduced to being mere 'inhabitants' of a domain on which they only had rights to use the land, rights which were themselves contested. But earlier, these peasants had been 'bound to the soil', the property of the boyar who could buy and sell them like work animals.

However, the land rights on the village territory of these old quasi-slaves were much clearer than those of the corvée labourers who only had rights to use the land. Thus, the old documents specify that the serf is sold 'with all his patrimony', with his *delniţa* (his 'share') 'and all that follows', 'everywhere', 'in the fields, the pastures, the forest, on the water, on the clearings he has made', 'the gardens he owns', etc.

Thus, where on the one hand the corvée village has a striking resemblance to the free, archaic villages, with simple, equal rights of use, on the other hand these much older serf villages had more resemblance to the free communal villages of unequal shares, with the system of the 'share' giving the right 'to everywhere' evidently as a fragment of the social mechanism we know already through direct field work. How can we explain this contradictory situation? And how can we understand the development of a social order in which an *adscriptus glebae* was owner of a share whereas the corvée labourer no longer was? There is but one possible explanation: it was a case of ancient free village communities falling under the feudal domination of a class of boyars who progressively nullified them by social laws that we will have to specify.

Being bound to the soil was just one step in a long social process. The first signs appeared in Romania only towards the end of the sixteenth century, not to disappear until the second half of the eighteenth century. There were thus anterior phases which were a premonition of the great social crisis of serfdom, just as there were several phases of this crisis itself, as well as belated forms and sequels to this order, a whole series of social conditions having first made serfdom inevitable, then causing its transformation into a 'corvée' regime and finally causing it to vanish.

Nevertheless, the study of the regime of corvée villages is what gives us the necessary key for understanding the history of being bound to the soil, as the documents of the sixteenth and seventeenth centuries are much too laconic, insufficient in number and could be very enigmatic if we did not first have a knowledge of the social situations of the eighteenth and nineteenth centuries. There is one lesson to be remembered from the analysis we have made of the 'corvée' regime: the understanding of more recent centuries forces us to project onto the earlier centuries the beginnings of all the social phenomena which did not emerge in a recent period, but must have been the prolongation of an older history, Thus, for example, the debris of the communal organization of the corvée villages could not have sprung up in the eighteenth and nineteenth centuries. This was the period of their disintegration, under the effect of deliberate action on the part of the boyar class. One must conclude that, in the earlier centuries, these village communities must have had a much more vital character and it would thus not surprise us if earlier the serfs had lived in village communities even stronger than those of the 'corvée' period.

Likewise, one cannot suppose that social phenomena, hardly nascent at the time of the corvée regime, could have existed in earlier centuries at a higher level of development. Thus, for example, if the 'itinerant' pastoral and agricultural technique was really still general throughout the nineteenth century, we cannot say that in earlier centuries the agriculture was at a superior technical level. And if it was only in the nineteenth century that the boyars could cut out for themselves a third of the village territory as personal 'reserve', free from any right of use on the part of the peasants, we cannot believe in the existence of such a 'reserve' in earlier centuries. As in the nineteenth century, until the Law of 1864, the lots cultivated directly by the boyars were mixed in with the peasants' lots, tithe lands and corvée lands periodically moving, just as peasants' lands must have been mixed in earlier times.

Briefly, the picture we have made of the serf village communities in their corvée form can give us a starting point for the interpretation of the process of being bound to the soil, a spider's thread which will help us to find the way back from the little known to that which we know better.

Part III

The first forms of tributary exploitation of the village communities

It is a general law of history that subjected peoples...once they are liberated, enter the skin of their former master.
    N. Iorga

8 ✤ Prior considerations on the problem of the feudal conquest of the villages

The first distinguishing characteristic of the social period preceding that which we have studied is that the peasants were bound to the soil; the physical person of these peasants was considered as an object of ownership. There was no way to escape except by repurchase or, according to the custom of the country, to be taken slave by the Tartars or the Turks, to have fled and returned to the country. The serfs were thus *Leibeigene* – to use the more precise German term – treated as quasi-slaves liable to as much corvée as their master wished to impose. They were sold, used as collateral, exchanged, inherited, made part of dowries, and forced to move from one village to another according to the will of their master, and they were prohibited from fleeing from the village.

How was this serfdom born, considering that it concerned peasants living in village collectivities? Our past historians believed that serfdom was introduced into Wallachia following an edict of Michael the Brave, the text of which has not been preserved but which is frequently mentioned by later documents under the name of the 'Bond of Michael'. According to the opinion of N. Bălescu, upheld by N. Iorga, until the promulgation of this 'Bond', that is until towards the end of the sixteenth century, the peasants were free.

This is not the opinion of C. Giurescu,[1] who, in 1914, produced the thesis that the peasants had always been serfs and that the Bond of Michael only bound them to the soil for fiscal reasons. In the course of this voivode's reign (1593–1601) Wallachia underwent one of the most disastrous occupations of the country, that of Sinan Pacha, which provoked, among other things, a general flight on the part of the peasants and a depopulating of the country. The Turks took large numbers of peasants into slavery, and those who could hide abandoned the devastated areas to take refuge in more sheltered villages. According to the fiscal regime of the *cislă*, which we have already described, the state collected taxes not by heads but by village collectivities, each village having to pay the share of any refractory peasants. Given the enormous demographic movement which had taken place, applying this measure would have resulted in the breakdown of all the half-empty villages and would thus have blocked the collection of taxes. Michael, short of money, opted for a transitional solution which kept sight of the real state of affairs, decreeing that each peasant must pay the tax in the village he was in, which is reasonable, but in addition, that he would be considered from then on as a serf bound forever to the site of the village he was presently living in. This was no longer merely a fiscal measure.

The date of 1596 seems acceptable to Giurescu as the year when this decision must have been implemented. Thus, in his opinion, the result of this fiscal measure was not to introduce the regime of the *adscriptis glebae* but, on the contrary, to forbid the boyars from exercising their old right to go after runaways and to bring them back by force to their original village. Every serf thus continued to be a serf, bound to the land, as before, though not residing in his original village but rather in the village where he was affected by the Bond. The boyars then continued as usual to exercise this fiscal right over the redistributed serfs who had come into being through the Bond of Michael.

The importance of the state's fiscal needs with respect to the peasants right of movement certainly cannot be denied; 'tax collecting' and 'place of obligatory residence' are two aspects of a single problem for all tax systems based on the fiscal solidarity of the village collectivities. The proof is that in Moldavia, where the attachment to the soil did not have the extreme character it had in Wallachia, moving was forbidden only during the interval between two fiscal censuses. Nevertheless, being

1. Constantin Giurescu, *Studii de istorie socială* (Studies in social history), 2nd edition edited by C. C. Giurescu, Bucharest, 1943.

bound to the soil is a social phenomenon much too complex to explain by simple fiscal reasoning.

Upholding a completely different thesis, but giving the same importance to the Bond of Michael, P. P. Panaitescu[2] brings up the fact that no document before the reign of Michael the Brave proves that the boyars had the right to pursue peasants who had fled and bring them back by force. On the contrary, we have the proof that the peasant could leave his village on the condition that he paid a *găleată*, that is, a 'bushel'. This probably meant a fixed quantity of cereals, or an equivalent value. After the reign of Michael the Brave, such a right no longer existed and any peasant living in a village, whether he belonged to the royal domain, to the boyars, or to the monasteries, was declared a serf bound to the soil of the village where he had taken up residence. The effect of the Bond of Michael was thus to transform all the peasants, serf or free, who were domiciled in and worked the land of a village not belonging to them, into *adscripti glebae*. Michael's decree (dated by the author as 1594) was temporarily revoked at the time of the voivode Radu Şerban (1602–11) who even accorded a general moratorium. But after 1613, Michael's law was once again applied.

It is difficult to resolve, through a thorough study of the documents, this controversy[3] which, besides, does not seem essential to us. It is not so much a matter of the peasant's right to flee as of knowing when, why, and in what conditions the physical person of the peasant had become an object of ownership. Panaitescu seems nearer to the heart of the problem when he states that, before Michael the Brave, the serf peasant depended on his boyar without being his *Leibeigene*. This 'dependence' was characterized by the simpe recognition of the lord's right to demand tithes and corvées; whereas, after the reign of Michael the Brave, the peasant's very person had become a piece of property. The peasants no longer 'submitted' (*închinare* is the Romanian term) but were actually 'sold'. But such a social phenomenon cannot be explained as being the result of a law which supposedly had the power to transform peasants, who had up until then been free, into quasi-slaves.

The fundamental question is different and consists of knowing when and why the social order in which the boyar, though not a landowner,

2. P. P. Panaitescu, 'Dreptul de strămutare în Ţările Române', (The right of departure in the Romanian countries), in *Studii şi materiale*, volume I, Bucharest, 1956.
3. V. Costăchel, P. P. Panaitescu, A. Cazacu, *Viaţa feudală în Ţara Românească şi Moldova (sec.* XIV–XVII) (Feudal life in Wallachia and Moldavia in the fourteenth to seventeenth centuries), Bucharest, 1957; H. H. Stahl, *Controverse de istorie socială românească* (Controversies in Romanian social history), Bucharest, 1969.

could collect tithes, was transformed into an order where the boyar was a feudal landowner, not only of the land but also of the men who worked it. Bound or not to the village, the essential fact is that the members of the peasant communities ceased to own their territories. The boyars split up the collectivities, broke the ancient ties which held the peasants together within large family lineages, and seized the population of whole villages, thus gaining the right to use the whole territory.

This is the problem, social and not legalistic, which needs to be elucidated. It is a question of checking whether there actually was a time when the boyars were simply chiefs of their village with a right only to the tithes and to some corvée labour, and if then they succeeded in becoming landowners in a feudal sense. The true problem is thus the transformation of the social system of fiscal exploitation of the village communities by a 'tributary' regime to a regime of 'feudal dues' of a landed nature. Such a social process cannot be accurately dated. Great social changes are never, exclusively, the result of measures taken by the state at such and such a date. The laws and the executive apparatus of a state do not have the power to bring about overnight the total transformation of the social structure of a country. In fact, we are concerned with a social development that had begun long before the reign of Michael the Brave and which continued long after him, in which the Bond of Michael was only a moment of extreme crisis in a social drama lasting many centuries.

Let us try to find its traces and interpret them. This time we will have to make a chronological sketch covering a longer period, back to the centuries for which we lack direct information, which will oblige us to look for tentative hypotheses. We will build these, however, by drawing on all the facts we have already analysed so that, as we have already said, this reconstruction of a distant past will be intelligible in the light of what we know about social life in the historical and contemporary period which is more familiar.

9 ✤ First forms of the seizure of the village communities

Wallachia and Moldavia

Given the particular circumstances which characterized the period of reconquest of the land from the Tartars, might the communal villages, which had undoubtedly contributed with their armed forces to the liberation of these territories, have been comparable to the serf villages of the late middle ages in the west? Could the villagers have been serfs bound to the soil, liable to a tithe and a corvée which were set by the will of their lords? Were their lords part of a feudal class of the classical type, with hereditary 'domains' enjoying immunities,[1] ruling small states within large states more or less independently, like those of the period following Charlemagne? This seems to us most unlikely. The local historical conditions were so unlike those of the west that, to explain these ancient social structures, it is better to renounce any of the theoretical schemas established for analysing western feudalism, and not to be tempted into error by the few rare documents seeming to justify the similarities which were actually only superficial.

We will formulate our hypotheses thus: in Wallachia, the boyar class came out of ancient communal village 'local chieftainships'. The state they succeeded in forming, as soon as they could reconquer their country by war with the Tartars, contained a mass of free villages. By 'free' we mean that it was a question of village communities set up in the classical way, with full possession of their territory. Their only obligations were to supply the Cumans, then the Tartars, and after that members of the autochthonous class which created the Wallachian state, with limited tithes and services. There were no 'feudal dues' involved. The duties were not based on the right of landownership on the part

1. See also Marcel Emerit, 'La question des monopoles seigneuriaux dans l'ancienne Roumanie', in *Mélanges offerts à M. N. Iorga par ses amis de France et des pays de langues française*, Paris, 1933; *Idem*, 'Reflexions sur le régime seigneurial en Roumaine', *Revue Historique du Sud-Est Européen*, nos. 4–6, Bucharest, 1938.

of the boyars, but rather on a simple right to collect tribute. By 'tribute' we mean any services or tithes demanded by the state. Management of the tribute was handled by the class of lords. This 'tribute' was actually of the nature of a tax. A long period elapsed before it became 'dues', and the boyars were transformed from village 'chiefs' into 'feudal landowners'. The Wallachian state thus did not have to turn the class of boyars into possessors of the villages as they were already village 'chiefs'.

In *Moldavia*, the class of boyars who created the state did not come from local chieftainships. The Moldavian villages, under the Tartar domination, had had, just as in Wallachia, a local *knez*. But it was Romanian voivodes from Maramuresh in Transylvania who reconquered the country. The local *knez* disappeared from sight, and their existence was thereafter only rarely recorded through the custom of identifying villages by the following formula: 'the village where so and so was *knez*'. Due to the wars against the Tartars, the country had been serious depopulated. Very many villages are described as being 'deserted', the population having disappeared for so long that even the names of the villages were forgotten. Statistics which we have gathered on the Moldavian villages show that between the years 1392 and 1499, of a total of 1,916 villages 455 did not have a name. Sometimes these were identified only by a former *knez* (in fifteen cases), by another known person of the period, or by simple geographic description.

The Moldavian voivode thus gave to the boyars the right to repopulate the villages. This was accomplished, as we know from written documents, according to a classical style of colonization. Often the number of 'houses' was planned. Villages so planned could have from ten to sixty 'houses'. The boyar who 'took in hand' such a 'desert' had to do the work necessary for founding a village. So, in 1439, the voivode confirmed a boyar's ownership of a village 'where his house is, on the Racova river, where he created a village all alone, in the desert and the forest, clearing the forest to create a village with its mills'. In 1429, the three sons of a large boyar received confirmation of their patrimonies: thirty-seven villages, of which twenty-three were either newly created or whose creation had just been authorized.

There were even boyars who specialized in the systematic clearing of the forests in order to make villages. Thus, even as late at 1617, Nădăbaico, a former grand *vornic* (a title of nobility signifying 'governor'), obtained confirmation from the voivode for 790 of his clearings 'all made in the virgin forest, with his men, with the help of corvées

TABLE 5. *Number of documents concerning village ownership in Wallachia and Moldavia, 1350–1449*

	Wallachia		Moldavia	
	Monasteries	Boyars	Monasteries	Boyars
1350–9	1	0	0	0
1360–9	0	0	0	0
1370–9	1	1	0	0
1380–9	5	2	0	0
1390–9	2	1	1	6
1400–9	8	4	4	6
1410–19	2	4	6	14
1420–9	6	5	4	43
1430–9	7	10	13	86
1440–9	5	3	6	58
Total	37	30	34	213

and with his serfs and his gypsy slaves and hired labour, in any way he could, with what he owned and by paying cash'.

It goes without saying that the Moldavian voivode who granted lordship over this sort of newly created village, imbued with Transylvanean feudal customs, considered the whole Moldavian territory as belonging to him and any boyar occupying the soil without his written permission as an interloper. 'On these areas of patrimony there was no one with princely documents so that they were declared to belong to us, as a princely right' (1560). All land needed 'princely legitimacy from the time of the founding of the state', declared a document of 1575.

Such relations between boyars and voivodes were not found in Wallachia. This comes out clearly from examining the statistical data found in the documents concerning village ownership. The number of documents having to do with granting ownership, recognition of ownership and of fiscal exemptions of villages are much more numerous in Moldavia than in Wallachia. And, what is even more important, in Moldavia, these documents were made especially for the benefit of the boyars, whereas, in Wallachia, they mostly concern the monasteries. The numerical situation is shown in table 5.

What was most important, then, in Wallachia, was the formation of an ecclesiastical nobility, for there were very few cases in which it was necessary to grant the boyars ownership of villages, with the exception of those in Transylvania in the area of Făgăraş. The number of villages held by these Wallachian boyars was small at this time (at the most ten). The large domains were to form much later, at a totally different period from that of the beginnings of the state.

Though an ecclesiastical nobility was also formed in Moldavia, here the primary task was the setting-up of vast domains for the boyars, domains which sometimes numbered fifty villages. In addition the decrees authorizing the colonization of new villages were frequent, whereas in Wallachia they were rare. The relations between boyars and peasants were also quite different in Moldavia, for, needless to say, the peasants who settled in the villages created by colonization could not have the rights of peasants who legitimately owned their territory since ancient times, as was characteristic in Wallachia.

The Moldavian boyars nevertheless gave to their villages, those conquered or created by repopulating, the same communal character as in Wallachia, for at that time this communal form was not only the only conceivable social model they could use, but also the only one corresponding to the level of pastoral and agricultural technical development. However, these Moldavian peasant communities did not enjoy as many rights and as much liberty as did the Wallachian peasants. From the start the Moldavian boyars had a right of ownership much closer to what would become feudal ownership than their Wallachian brothers, who had to reduce their villages to serfdom by degrees and with continual struggle. We will thus have to study the village communities of Wallachia and Moldavia by analysing them together when their fate was a common one (and there was ultimately a general convergence in the creation of serfdom and then in the process of capitalist penetration); but we must also study them separately and parallel to each other, for there were local differences.

The fiscal rights of the state

For the Wallachian boyars, barely removed from being mere local chiefs, existing in a proto-state with its voivodes and *knezi* who were the liberators of their country, there was no question of being recognized or of imposing themselves as landowners. The most they could do was to continue practising, for their own profit, the system of fiscal exploitation inherited from the nomads. There was only one way to do this: to organize a centralized state in the form of a *Domnie* (from the Latin *dominus*), in which the chief of state, continuing to bear the name 'voivode' ('army chief'), held, in addition to the royal rights over customs, mines, and the big Danubian fisheries, the right to impose tithes and corvée labour on all the villages.

There is no trace of the existence of state 'domains',[2] or of ones belonging to monasteries or boyars. There is no trace of the existence of feudal 'immunities' competing with the centralized monarchy. In the first centuries after the founding of the autochthonous Wallachian state, there is social chaos, the whole country struggling to control its lands, with the boyars only slowly succeeding in reducing the villages to serfdom, and taking on the character of feudal masters by gradually taking over the state's fiscal rights. It is likely that the chief of the state wanted to become a single, absolute ruler of the country, as opposed to the members of his class, who themselves had to struggle to obtain the maximum profit from the fiscal exploitation of the country. As for the peasants, they could hardly be pleased that the nomads, whom they had succeeded in throwing out of the country by force, were replaced by the class of autochthonous boyars. To master the peasants, the boyars had to uphold the centralized state. Separately, they could not have forced the armed villages to acquiesce in their own serfdom, but when they were grouped around a warrior centralized state the chances were more favourable.

Moreover, a centralized state was necessary for other reasons. The movement of goods across the country was the principal source of revenue for the state and could not be exploited except by organizing a local police along the trade routes and by placing a customs point at either end of the routes. This called for an accounting system that could establish which merchandise crossed the country and which was bought or sold within the country. In addition, the towns and their hinterlands (*ocoale*) could belong only to the state. This was also true of the mines and the big fisheries on the Danube.

But what is most interesting is that state's right to exploit the villages. Whereas a few favoured members of the boyar class could share in the profits from customs and the mines, the great majority of boyars were in competition with the state over the exploitation of the peasants. In order to understand the social life of the period, it is therefore crucial to establish what were the fiscal rights of the state and what were those of the boyar masters of the serf villages.

The internal documents appear very late (from 1369 in Wallachia and from 1384 in Moldavia) and their number is minimal. In addition,

2. Ioan Donat, 'Le domaine princier rural en Valachie (XIVe–XVIe siècles)', *Revue Roumaine d'Histoire*, volume VI, no. 2, Bucharest, 1967.

these records are only official documents, issued by the state chancellery for the benefit of the boyar class. They are also very laconic, poorly written, not in Romanian but in old Slavo-Bulgarian, that being the diplomatic language of the time, just as Latin was in Western Europe. There are, however, two categories of documents which tell us about the fiscal power of the state, and thus indirectly about the village economy. These are the documents in which the state bestows on certain monasteries goods in kind and cash, even giving them royal fiscal rights. There are also the documents of fiscal exemption given to certain favoured members of the noble class. Without going into more details, the result of these acts was that the state managed a fiscal apparatus which brought it a whole series of taxes from the peasants in all villages, both free and serf.

First, there were the *rights to collect a share of produce*, the description of which alone gives us an idea of what the peasant economy was like at the time. From them we have proof that the villages practised animal raising and agriculture, as the state had the right to take in kind agricultural produce (cereals – generally wheat and barley – wine, vegetables, and fruit) and especially livestock (pigs, sheep, cows, oxen). Beehive products (hives, honey, wax) were also of primary importance, as were timber products (wood for heating, planks, beams, etc.), fish, and hay.

The villages also had the obligation to perform a series of *public duties*. The peasants had to fight to defend the country. They were thus permanently armed. This simple fact constitutes the proof that the exploitation of the villages could not go beyond a tolerable limit. The villages were also obliged to supply a local police force. They also had to contribute, through corvées, to the needs of the army and to the construction and maintenance of fortifications, roads and bridges. They had to furnish the means of transport and the food and drink for state agents on tour through their territory.

The *corvées*, properly speaking, which had to be performed for the court of the voivode, had a more clearly feudal nature. There was also mention of the obligations of an economic nature: the maintenance of the mills and ponds of the voivode, the obligation to grow hay, to graze sheep, cows, horses, to cut wood, to hunt and fish for the court's needs. There were even cases in which certain villages, situated near salt mines, were obliged to take part in salt mining. The state also had the right to administer justice and collect fines. At a later date, the state collected taxes in cash from the villages and obliged them to make loans to the state.

The fiscal apparatus of the state

Like the nomads, the autochthonous states organized the fiscal exploitation in such a way that the villages were collectively responsible for dues (*cislă*). A total evaluation of the economic capacity of each village was made; if the village had a local lord, he was responsible for collecting the taxes. There was no separate administrative organ. The voivodes worked through delegations sent out on fiscal missions. These were composed of the boyars whom they trusted. These were called 'those sent out for the duties and services of his lordship', that is, to collect what continued for a long time to be called 'alms' (*milostenii*). This was a semantic survival from the time when it really was a case of benevolent aid, due from the villages to the warriors of the tribal aristocracy.

For every kind of tithe and corvée, a delegate of the voivode could be sent out. The list was thus very full: there were special agents for the tithe of wheat, of barley, of wax and beehives, of sheep and pigs, of fish and even of fowl, recorded in a terminology whose incoherence is itself a proof of the non-hierarchic character of the fiscal apparatus of the state. The immediate and varied needs of the voivodal court determined the demands. There were no limits but those of the 'needs of his lordship', fulfilled more or less rigidly 'according to the possibilities' of the local conditions.

The boyars forming the direct clientele of the voivode, those going out on fiscal and judicial missions, were paid a share of the revenues, or rather they directly exploited certain taxes and customs, thus having a means to increase their revenues and their social power well beyond the rest of the boyars who were not favoured in the same way.

The founding of ecclesiastical seigniories

The study of ecclesiastical seigniories provides a topic of particular interest, for, through them, we can improve our understanding of events. The churches and monasteries did not have a feudal character in the beginning and it was only by deliberate action on the part of the state that they acquired it. Their example is therefore more significant than that of the boyars. There was a time when the little wooden churches of the villages had only priests as their spiritual leaders. These were under modest monastery abbots, the 'pseudo-bishops of Greek rite', Wallachians about whom Pope Gregory IX, in his missive of 1234 addressed to the Hungarian King Bela, complained bitterly because they were insubordinate to the 'bishop of the Cumans' installed by the Hungarian royalty in Wallachia in one of its abortive attempts to conquer the route to the mouths of the Danube. But very soon after the founding of the authochthonous states a layer of feudal ecclesiastics was formed, a powerful means of spiritual domination on the part of the feudal class over the villages. The voivodes and then the great families of boyars founded monasteries and a whole episcopal hierarchy was thus organized, with the Metropolitan at its head.

These monasteries were granted patrimonies with rights to the feudal exploitation of a certain number of villages, sometimes numbering several dozen. The principal monasteries thus held vast 'domains', villages and fisheries scattered here and there over the whole country. The way in which these monasteries exploited their villages was quite curious, not in the least resembling the means habitually associated with feudal landowners. Far from being able to support themselves by the exploitation of these domains, the monasteries could only take small amounts from the villages they 'controlled'. The principal monasteries thus had to be helped by the state which periodically gave them varying amounts of goods both in kind and cash (which was called in Romanian *mertic* or *obroc*). This occurred in several ways.

The four successive types of royal donations

First, the monasteries were accorded the right to send their delegates to the voivodal court in order to receive a fixed, pre-established quantity of foodstuffs, clothing and small sums of money, taken directly from the depots or the treasury of the prince. For example, in 1374, the monastery of Vodiţa was to collect '1000 gold coins from my lordship, 300 of which must be distributed to the poor; and twelve cheeses and twelve other cheeses [i.e. two different kinds], and a measure of wax and twelve blankets. We grant this, each year, from our princely household.' The gift thus had to be called for in person, with the delegate of the monastery having to appear at the court with his own means of transport, provided, undoubtedly, by peasant corvées.

This first type of donation was followed by a second one, also of fixed quantities, this time having to be furnished directly by the fiscal agents of the state operating in the area. Thus, in 1385, 'the monastery of Tismana will receive from the county of Jaleş 400 bushels of wheat each year. And he who collects them should no longer ask our lordship's permission, but send them directly to the monastery.'

A third type, representing an even more advanced stage, consisted of giving the monasteries a share of the taxes collected by the state. The delegate of the monastery had, from this time on, an interest in accompanying the state agent to supervise the manner in which the taxes were determined and collected: 'may they receive a third of the tithes from the county of Ilfov, each year, as long as the monastery exists; and may this suffice for the wax and lighting of the holy church'.

The state could go even further, by granting certain taxes in their entirety, as, for example, in 1347: 'in the county of Brăila, they will receive the bushels of wheat destined for the state, the princely taxes, as well as the tithe on the beehives and the cash sums, in the whole county of Brăila'. Through these donations of the fourth type, the monasteries thus took over the royal rights of the state. When this transfer of rights took place in villages which were part of the monastery's 'domain', a gradual metamorphosis of public fiscal rights into private patrimonial rights could take place. The act of donation then took on an altogether different character: that of a tax exemption. The state, by renouncing its fiscal rights in favour of a monastery, created a situation clearly resembling that of a classical feudal immunity.

Stages in the formation of a private fiscal apparatus

The development of a feudal patrimony by the substitution for royal rights was slow, for the monasteries did not at first have an administration capable of handling the collection of the taxes which had been granted them. Thus the state continued to lend them its own fiscal apparatus, putting its agents at the service of the monasteries, provided they were paid for. For example, in 1482, a document tells us that the voivode had 'granted eight villages to the holy monastery of the county of Ilfov each year, in order to transport there eight bushels of wheat and eight of barley from the villages controlled by it', and likewise 'the taxes of the peasants belonging to the monastery are to be collected' by the agents delegated by the state. These agents had to be paid for by the monastery. In other cases, if the state could not render this service to the monasteries, it was specified that the monks themselves were to safeguard their rights: 'the monks are themselves to collect the bushels of wheat, and the collectors of the bushels of wheat are not to be delegated by the voivode, the monks alone having to collect them as best they can'.

The fact that from the sixteenth century, the first, second, and third types of donations were replaced by the fourth type, outright tax exemptions, shows us that the monasteries had finally succeeded in securing their subsistence by the direct exploitation of the villages serving them. Thus a feudal ownership had been born for their benefit. The exploitation of such villages continued, nevertheless, to be merely a parasitical fiscal exploitation since it had to do with tax collection and not with work directed by the monasteries. The villages went about things in their own way, according to the rules of communal villages. The monasteries only had the right to collect tithes on the produce of the village, without becoming involved in administering local economic life.

This does not mean that the monasteries did not have, from the beginning, their own areas of exploitation, worked by peasant corvée labour and gypsy slaves. But it was only a very small exploitation, barely sufficient for the upkeep of the monks and their buildings. The proof is that no mention is made of the peasants' obligation to perform a certain amount of work, measured in days or in other ways. On the contrary, the documents specify that the monasteries have a right only to 'aid', which must not exceed their immediate needs. Thus, even in the sixteenth century, in 1545, the monks of the monastery of Bistritza, holding twenty villages, were authorized to take from these villages 'only that which they need. They shall collect according to the law and nothing more and they shall not call upon the villages for anything else.' These villages were thus not liable to large tithes and corvées.

At this stage in the seizure of the villages, the documents which specify the rights of the monasteries (and it is also true for the boyars) only speak of 'villages' as entities without mentioning their inhabitants, who are neither numbered nor named. Occasionally, they address themselves directly to the peasants, the 'neighbours' (in Romanian *vecini*, a term derived from *vecinătate*, *vecinitas*), referring to them as: 'You, the neighbours of the village, you must obey and work under the direction of the abbot of the monastery.' Not until much later did this 'obedience' take the form of serfdom, properly speaking, with the village lords having the right to beat any infractors severely as though they were serfs. This took place when the village lords began to administer their own lands in order to produce saleable goods.

The first economic bases of the boyar class

As far as the Wallachian boyars were concerned, there is no case in which they needed the state's support by means of 'donations' of the first, second, and third type, as was the case for the monasteries. This proves that the boyar class had a sufficiently large patrimonial base from the beginning. In the first place, they engaged in an exploitation, by fiscal means, of the villages of the country. If not the whole boyar class, at least a part of it acted as tax collectors, judges, and tax-farmers, with full powers in the exploitation of the country, especially of the free villages which were more heavily taxed than those they owned outright and of which they were the 'chiefs'. In addition, they traded in livestock and cereals, honey, wax, salted fish and furs, either on their own account or as intermediaries in the international trade crossing the country.

These revenues were substantial enough for the boyars, led by the voivode, to lead the life of grand feudal lords, the equal of their brothers in Hungary and Poland. One has only to look at their buildings, such as the church of Curtea de Argeş, dating from the sixteenth century, or their manner of dressing, of which there is evidence in the archaeological findings, to be convinced. Even the sums of money they held are proof enough. Wanting to put an end to their struggles with the Hungarian kings, the Wallachians were willing in 1330 to pay war reparations amounting to the enormous sum of 7,000 marks (1,447.80 kg of silver). As the country had no silver mines, this had to come from trade, which must have been of very great importance. In 1445, Jean de Wavrin,[3] the Picard chronicler who took part in the crusades on the Danube, gives us additional evidence by noting the fact that the son of the Wallachian voivode told him that his father had built the castle of Giurgiu from the proceeds of the salt trade: 'il n'y avoit pierre au dit chastel qui n'eust cousté...une pierre de sel, qui se prent en roches au pays de Vallaquie.'

But the direct exploitation of taxes and commerce could not constitute a source of wealth for the whole boyar class. Those without public duties had to subsist from the tithes of the villages where they were lords, as well as by plunder. These revenues must have been quite modest, for the feudal lords of that time did not have the full powers that go along with true feudal 'landownership'. As they had barely risen, by slow evolution, from the ranks of village chiefs, the gradual transformation

3. Jean de Wavrin, *La campagne des croisés sur le Danube (1445)*. *Extrait des Anciennes Chroniques d'Angleterre*, new edition edited by N. Iorga, Paris, 1927.

of their tithes and corvées into 'feudal dues', properly speaking, had to be very slow.

We take the liberty of once again calling upon a more contemporary event. It is again with reference to the Vrancea, which seems very significant insofar as the taking over of the villages by a boyar is concerned.[4] In 1801, the voivode of Moldavia, profiting from the fact that the group of fourteen villages of the Vrancea could not produce any proof of donation made in its favour by any voivode, decided that it should be considered as belonging to the state, as it was only by chance that it had not yet been claimed by a boyar. The decision was thus taken to have the villages given to a certain important figure of the period, the boyar Iordache Roset Roznovanu. A long trial followed; the communal confederation of the Vrancea, struggling literally and judicially, succeeded in winning its claim according to which, since time immemorial long before the birth of the Moldavian state, it had already formed a small free republic to which the state had only a purely fiscal claim. The Vrancea won its case and, in 1817, chased out the conquering boyar. The region remained free. But for a short period of ten years, the boyar had taken possession of these fourteen villages.

How? Did he succeed in organizing, or at least did he attempt to organize, a direct agricultural or pastoral exploitation? Did he become, or at least did he pretent to be, the absolute landowner? Not in the least. At the most, he succeeded in collecting tithes and in instituting a monopoly over the sale of wine. He never dealt personally with these villages. He only sent agents under his orders, chosen, for the most part, from village traitors. His attempts to arrest the chiefs of the peasant revolt failed and his hostels were burned. The *purely fiscal* character of his seizure of the communal villages constitutes direct proof, supported by strong documentary evidence, that such an exploitation was possible and that a boyar could subject a village to tithes without beings its landowner and without managing his own land in the form of a personal demesne.

If an immensely rich boyar with all the powers of a modern state at his disposal could not succeed in the nineteenth century in winning anything more than a purely fiscal means of exploitation, it is unthinkable that the boyars of the fourteenth and fifteenth centuries could have done more. When the state conceded to the boyars, in the fourteenth and fifteenth centuries, the right to 'take in hand' a village,

---

4. C. D. Constantinescu and Henri H. Stahl, *Documente vrîncene* (Documents of the Vrancea), volume I, with a preface by N. Iorga, Bucharest, 1929.

the boyars could only receive the powers that the voivode himself had over these villages, that is, simple fiscal rights. In such a case, whether endowed or not with fiscal 'immunity' (of the fourth type – full immunities), these boyars entered the evolutionary schema which we have already discussed in relation to the monasteries. This is what we must look at a little more closely.

The boyar property's lack of initial security

The contents of a Wallachian document of 1407 can serve as a starting point. The voivode is addressing the villages belonging to the monastery of Tismana:

Io Mircea, voivode and autocratic lord of all Hungaro-Wallachia. I, your lord, address you, all the villages which are under the domination of the monastery of Tismana, large and small. I order you and inform you that you should belong to no *knez* or boyar of my kingdom, so that, from one day to the next, I can place you under the domination of someone else. For I have placed you, for the repose of my soul and of those of my ancestors, under the domination of the monastery, to which you will be obedient in services and tithes. . .and if another lies to you, do not believe him. . .If anyone should dare claim you, though he be one of my boyars, to take something from you or force you to work, whoever he be, beat him.

Thus the voivode expressed his power to change a village's lord 'from one day to the next'; or to control boyars who wrongly attempted to lay their hands on villages claimed by others. The peasants were authorized, in such cases, to react forcefully, 'hitting over the heads' those boyars trying to put them under their domination. How could one conceive of such a document in an actual feudal regime, with serfs bound to the soil, economic exploitation by and under the direction of the boyars, possessing their houses, livestock, tools, etc., on a *terra indominicata*? Besides, even when it was authorized by the state, taking possession of the villages had a most uncertain character. A 'landowner' always risked permanent dispossession by state order or simply by being replaced by a stronger, more fortunate competitor.

The documents in which the Wallachian voivodes grant villages to the boyars are direct proof of the above. The donation is valid 'as long as my reign lasts', or at most 'during my lifetime and that of my son'. If he wanted to consolidate these rights of domination over a village, the voivode in the beginning had no means other than the making of oaths and curses, of a religious or profane nature: 'May he who dare to take over the village be cursed by the Holy Mother of God and the 320 bishops of Nicaea.' Or the voivode curses his successors who will not respect his donation, blessing those who abide by it. Sometimes, the voivode expresses greater strength, attempting to frighten the infractors, specifying that 'he who does not respect my donation will be the object of my anger', 'he will pay with his head', 'may he not be surprised by what may befall him', formulas which, by themselves, prove the absence of a legal order. Incidentally, the cases in which boyars wrongly took over the villages of others by force were abundant.

The conclusion that can be drawn from these early documents of 'ownership' is that, in this period of social uncertainty, force and arbitrary rule dominated, with boyars competing against each other, though struggling in common against the peasant villages which they subjected, little by little, to serfdom.

Support given by the state to the boyars in the form of 'fiscal exemptions'

The feudal take-over of the villages was strongly upheld by the state, by the grant of important fiscal exemptions. Of course, this was not a general rule, for only certain privileged people, members of the personal clique of the voivode, were able to profit from such favours. This is, moreover, understandable; the principal source of taxes came mostly from the free villages which owed taxes only to the state treasury, whereas the serf villages could only be liable to minor amounts as they also were subject to the rights of the local boyars over them. To give too many free villages to the boyars as well as fiscal exemptions to the whole boyar class would have been like financial suicide for the state. The study of the fiscal exemptions is, however, interesting from several points of view, as we shall soon see.

The oldest documents granted certain feudal lords fiscal exemptions in general terms: thus, in 1374, a village was declared 'free from all labour, taxes and revenues connected with my lordship', which was merely a repetition of the Hungarian formula of the diploma of 1247 which gave the Teutonic knights the *reditum, utilitatem et servitiorum*, in the fashion of the Hungarian chancellery. Next, these documents of fiscal exemptions became more explicit, enumerating a series of rights that the state renounced, and the fiscal agents of the state were prohibited from interfering. 'These villages are henceforth exempt from the tithe of pigs, sheep, hives, wine, from fines, transport duties, etc., and not one of our boyars, large or small [there follows a listing of the state agents] must even dare show his face in these villages.' But, looking

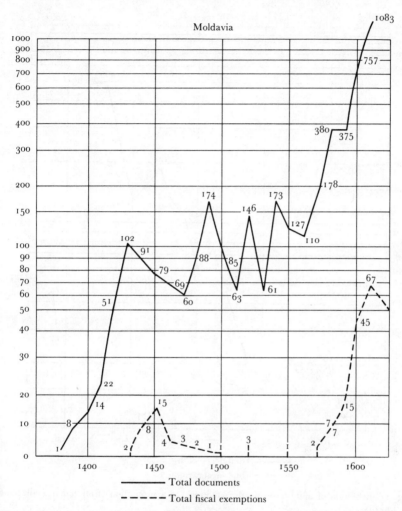

Fig. 16. Evolution of numbers of fiscal exemptions, as a proportion of all extant Moldavian documents.

at the statistics of these sorts of documents, one can see that they were rare. This is evident from calculating the percentage of such exemptions among the total number of state documents which remain extant (see fig. 16).

Towards the first half of the sixteenth century, these fiscal exemptions were no longer exercised, a sign that the boyars no longer needed them, having succeeded in the meantime in establishing their feudal 'landownership' by completely taking over the village communities (see

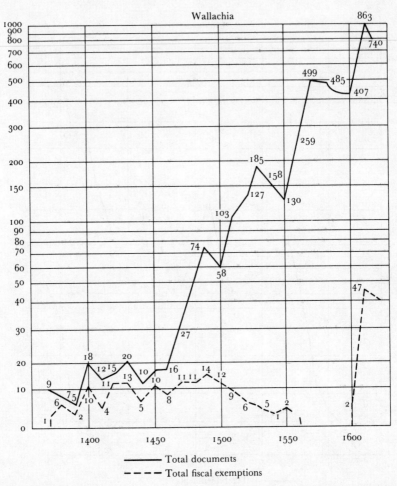

Fig. 17. Evolution of numbers of fiscal exemptions, as a proportion of all extant Wallachian documents.

fig. 17). The boyars seized the common lands of the communities with a private economic exploitation in mind; their aim was increasingly to produce saleable goods, livestock and cereals. By thus establishing an economic base independent of the state, they went after the public powers, allying themselves with the Turks against the voivode, not hesitating to betray their country if necessary. They sought to institute a new form of state by the transformation of the ancient *Domnie* into an 'aristocratic oligarchic state', in which the voivode became no more than a *primus inter pares*, holding his power on condition that he served

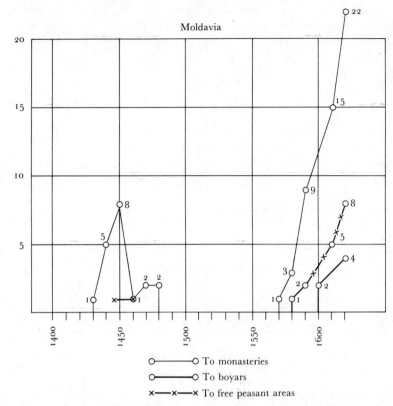

Fig. 18. Analysis of fiscal exemptions in Moldavia.

the interests of the boyars and also that he submit to the terrorist injunctions of the Turks. The Turks, in fact, began to institute a new form of fiscal exploitation of the country in a way similar to that used by the ancient 'predator states' of the nomads.

One can see, from these documents, that the fiscal exemptions, after a short period of interruption, began again. But this time, they had a quite different social significance: they were no longer meant to help the boyars set up a 'feudal property' made up of villages, but, on the contrary, to 'save the peasants' as the country had become depopulated by serfdom. There was an attempt to repopulate it by giving the peasants a softened feudal regime, as we shall see.

Let us mention, too, the chronological discrepancy existing between Moldavia and Wallachia. In Moldavia, the period when fiscal exemptions ceased began sooner and lasted longer: from 1480 to 1570, thus

Wallachia

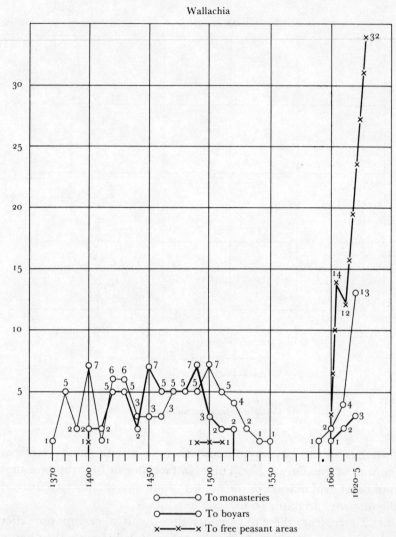

Fig. 19. Analysis of fiscal exemption in Wallachia.

ninety years. The same phenomenon began in Wallachia three-quarters of a century later and lasted only forty-two years: from 1554 to 1596. This confirms the fact that the class of Moldavian boyars, which originated on the other side of the Carpathians and conquered the country, did not need fiscal exemptions to secure its possessions, as was the case for the Wallachian boyars, who were authochthonous, coming from the local tribal aristocracy. We will have additional proof of this fact from a detailed statistical analysis in which the fiscal exemptions are classified by beneficiaries: boyars, monasteries and 'peasant communities'.

Dividing the fiscal exemptions given to the monasteries and those given to the boyars, one notices another basic difference between Wallachia and Moldavia: the fiscal exemptions were given in Moldavia mainly to the monasteries and not to the boyars, unlike what took place in Wallachia. This constitutes a new proof that the Moldavian boyars did not need the gradual aid of the state to help them become 'masters' of their villages. Having come from beyond the Carpathians and conquered the country, they had, from the beginning, a much stronger right of ownership than the Wallachian boyars, who came only from the ranks of the local 'chiefs'.

However, the new phase of transition to a liberalization of feudal conditions towards the end of the great crisis of serfdom, following a population loss, occurred at the same time in both countries, which, were, moreover, temporarily united under Michael the Brave. We have other means at our disposal for identifying this real historical turning point, the period of a total feudal take-over of the serf villages. At least, as far as Wallachia is concerned, one can study the gradual rise of the boyar class towards an economic, juridical, and political independence which came as a result of the reduction of the villages to serfdom, permitting the boyars to take over the full administration of the state.

The state's renunciation of its rights of confiscation in case of intestate succession

The old Wallachian documents contain the clause, in Romanian, *prădalica să nu fie*, which might be translated as 'may the *prădalica* not be applied'. Historians, after much hesitation and controversy, have finally agreed that the clause concerned the state's renunciation of its right to take over belongings left without heirs in the framework of agnatic inheritance rights. Thus: 'As far as they are concerned may the *prădalica* cease to exist and may everything go to the survivors' (1511); 'and if there is no son – which is not pleasing to God – may the *prădalica* cease to be, and may everything pass to the daughters' (1543); 'and after his death, may his belongings not be *prădalica* but pass to his daughters' (1576).

Let us note that there can be no question of 'disinheritance' in the free villages, as these were the collective property of a group of families constituting the local population, where the belongings of families which had disappeared entered in fact and law into the communal mass. A collective territory could only become vacant through social catastrophes, wars and epidemics, bringing death to the whole population, or by the flight of the inhabitants to other regions in the hope of escaping famine or fiscal burdens. This was not true for the boyars. The boyars thus struggled to gain the right to commercialize their villages, to handle them as they wished. For this, they had to overcome the risks of intestacy and get the state to renounce its right of possession.

Several method were used. The *pia fraus* was used to grant daughters the same rights as sons, thus transforming the agnatic family into a cognatic family. As with the peasants, whom we have studied on the basis of contemporary information, it was declared that a certain daughter was, for the purpose of the law, a son. Or they used the method of 'fraternization', an ancient custom which transformed two strangers into 'blood brothers'. Thus daughters were fraternized with their brothers, with their counsins, sometimes even with their parents. Or, to enlarge the circle of eventual successors, there were fraternizations with people who already had their private patrimonies, thus increasing the amount to be inherited. Tontine contracts were made in which two 'brothers' agreed that belongings held in common would go to the survivor.

To give these measures full effect, the state had to agree with the interests of the boyars. A struggle could break out between the state, which coveted the belongings fallen into intestacy and wished to continue exercising its right of possession, and the boyar class, which wanted to impose on the state the new rules of commercial life, the legal recognition of succession *ab intestat* and the right to will belongings to others. This whole struggle was, in fact, the consequence of an economic evolution resulting from the profound transformation of the country's social conditions, in which the boyars gradually began to exploit the communal terrains directly in order to produce goods for sale. In these circumstances, the economic and juridical character of the boyars' property changed, affected more and more by the rules of trade. Selling, buying, renting, leasing, giving, and receiving by donation of will tended to become the rule for all patrimonies at this stage of economic and social maturity.

By open struggle, by purchase of rights, by favours, the boyars forced or persuaded the voivode to renounce outright his right of possession by *prădalica* and thus to submit, willingly or unwillingly, to the new laws

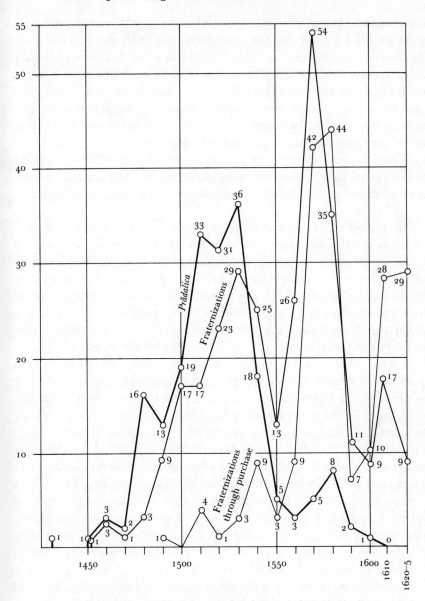

Fig. 20. Chronology of the acts of *prădalica* and 'fraternization'.

of the market. It was thus quite natural that at the time when the right of the *prădalica* was strong, the formula we are analysing was not used. On the contrary, as soon as the period of transition began in which the boyar class and the state became opposed to each other, and as the boyars became more and more successful, due to the power they held after having taken over the villages, this formula appeared more and more frequently. Furthermore, it is logical that after the boyars' victory, when their patrimonies had become merchandise, the necessity of obtaining a formal declaration of renunciation of the *prădalica* from the state was no longer useful and disappeared, replaced by statements such as 'Any man has the right to share his property with whomsoever he wishes' (1627).

The period in which this formula appeared corresponds to that of the fiscal exemptions. Thus, these formulas of 'fraternization' and of the *prădalica* began to appear, in Wallachia, towards the middle of the fifteenth century, the *prădalica* disappearing towards the middle of the sixteenth. We thus have a situation which is the reverse of that of the fiscal exemptions; these ceased at the beginning of the period in which the boyars succeeded in transforming their possessions into property not liable to the right of possession by the state.

As far as Moldavia was concerned, the documents do not provide us at all with the same rich harvest of information. The right to confiscate property which had fallen into intestacy was, however, part of the law of the state. A few rare cases may be cited. Thus, in 1528, the voivode declared that, having given to one of his boyars some property fallen into intestacy, 'We have given him, in our country of Moldavia, a village site... which reverted to our kingdom, for after his death, there was no one of his family on this patrimony.' Similarly, in 1566: 'There were no children or parents on this patrimony, which was thus retained by my kingdom. I have sold it and had masses said in his name.' Moreover, in 1631, the voivode Leon Tomşa was forced by the boyars to subscribe to an act by which he formally renounced the right of confiscation in case of intestacy.

This phase foreshadowing the great social crisis of serfdom, a period in which the boyars succeeded in becoming 'landowners' of their villages in opposition to the rights of the state as well as those of the villages themselves, is confirmed by other signs which corroborate those we have already discussed. We are referring to the right of the voivode to acquire a 'horse' when he transmitted a patrimony.

Renunciation of the gift of 'the horse granted by law to the voivode'

Certain documents show that in Wallachia the voivode received a horse whenever a change occurred in the patrimonies. Numerous controversies have arisen over the possible meaning of such a law. Most historians adopted the opinion formulated in 1904 by Ioan Bogdan stating that it was a question of a *signum domini* according to the tradition of western feudal hommage, a recognition of the state's eminent property right over all the patrimonies of the boyars, considered thus as the equivalent of feudal 'dues'. But it is hardly necessary to refer to western feudal law, for whose existence in Romania there is no proof, either direct or indirect, even from simple logic. The transfers and confirmations of property were handled by authentic documents issued by the voivode's chancellery. The favour of the voivode, supreme master of the country, did not come free: it had to be paid for. Why with a horse? A very large number of documents show that a horse was considered as cash. It was obligatory payment in the case of fiscal or penal fines. Even the word for fine, *gloabă*, means 'horse'. Horses were used in sales between individuals, boyars and monasteries. The state collected this sales tax even when gypsy slaves, mills, vineyards and other goods were sold. This kind of tax was not part of the 'dues' of western feudalism.

The villages themselves, as well as individual peasants, paid the voivode in horses for recognition of their rights. But, similarly, the villages could not be considered as 'vassals' rendering homage to their sovereign. Nor was it an 'authentification tax', as others have claimed, for the voivode was paid, not as chief of his chancellery, but as voivode, chief of the state, able to dispose of the fiscal rights of the boyar class in the precarious circumstances of early feudal 'ownership'. The boyars were subjected to the arbitrary will of the autocrat; during the first centuries the voivode was hardly in need of the sophisticated theory of *dominium eminens* and *dominium utile* in order to act as he wished.

In any case, during this same period which preceded that of the great crisis of the taking over of public power by the boyar oligarchy and the introduction of serfdom, the voivode's right to be paid before he would acknowledge the validity of a change in patrimonial ownership between boyars or between non-boyars had to undergo the same changes as the fiscal exemptions, the *prădalica* and the 'fraternizations' and thus, like them, had to disappear. The following statistics are conclusive in this regard: between 1370 and 1579, the number of

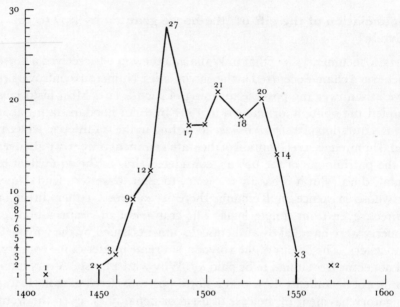

Fig. 21. Gifts of 'horses' due to the voivode of Wallachia.

documents of property confirmation rose to a total of 1,662, of which 1,058 concerned the boyars and 604 concerned the monasteries; whereas the number of horses mentioned in these documents was only 167, of which only three had to do with the patrimonies of the monasteries. In addition, in forty-one cases, the voivode renounced payment of a horse. If the donation of a horse had been a simple *signum domini*, the monasteries would not have been exempted, and the renunciation on the part of the voivode would be inexplicable. As it was not a feudal homage but rather an actual payment, it is natural that the monasteries were exempt from it and that the voivode could favour certain boyars by not subjecting them to it. Or he could, and often did, take other forms of payment. Furthermore, a document of 1639, mentioning an even older document, states that 'they gave a horse to the deceased voivode Basarab the Elder, as authentification of the charter and ownership, as was the custom in the old days'. Generally, however, after 1550 such cases vanished as transfer of patrimonial lordly rights no longer required payment to the voivode.

Again, in Moldavia, the situation was different. There is no indication as to the voivode's right to a horse. When the voivode took over Moldavia he inherited from the Tartars a whole series of towns, each having a hinterland of serf villages, the *ocoale*. Slowly, the state dissolved these domains to the profit of the boyars and the monasteries, selling the villages to them one after another. When this happened, the voivode sometimes collected not only cash but also horses. Here, however, it was not a question of one 'horse' as in Wallachia, but rather of 'horses'. Furthermore, this social phenomenon of the *ocoale* of the state, which disintegrated, was specifically Moldavian. Let us note in passing the importance of this fact. From the chronicles it appears to have been a voivode by the name of Juga who created these serf domains around the towns. But this story is contradicted by the documents which prove, on the contrary, that these *ocoale* underwent a process of accelerated disintegration and not of formation by princely edict. Thus, we have been able to count 150 cases of villages which came from the state's domain, of which seventy-four become part of the property of monasteries and seventy-six of boyars. These sales to individuals of villages belonging to the state's domain began during the last decade of the fifteenth century and become frequent in the second half of the sixteenth century, a period during which the Moldavian state took on, as in Wallachia, an oligarchic-boyar character.

Returning to the problem of horses, we can see that in Moldavia it only came up when the voivode sold those villages in the state's domain. It was never a matter of 'one horse', but of 'horses', amounting to as many as twelve. They were sold, moreover, with their 'sled', their 'carriage'; these are 'excellent horses', 'very good', 'trained', 'well fed', often quite costly. Thus in Moldavia, it was not a question of a 'symbolic sign', of 'feudal hommage', or of 'fiscal taxes'; they were actual payments, obtained by the voivode for the sale of villages belonging to him, sales which he justified by asserting that he had no other means to acquire the sums with which to pay the Turks. On the other hand, the number of villages that the voivode sold for cash was much greater than the number he sold for horses. Thus, 150 villages of the towns' hinterlands were sold, but only twenty-two of them were paid for in horses.

This is another proof that the character of Moldavian social life was very different from that of Wallachia. This merits a much deeper study than we can afford here, but does not, however, concern the village communities.

Survey of the period of transition leading to serfdom

The signs we have analysed, indicating a new social period which marked the complete victory of the boyar class over the voivode, the formation of a state dominated by the boyar class, and the institution of serfdom, were accompanied by two other signs, which we will mention only briefly here, as we shall deal with the subject later on. We are referring, first, to 'fraternizations' of a new kind which, from the fifteenth century, ceased to be a means of escaping from the voivode's right to possession and became a way of taking over free villages. In fact, the fraternization could serve, too, as we have already shown by analysing the peasant fraternizations, to admit someone by fraud into a village family line and thus to secure for him a right of citizenship, protecting him from the rights of pre-emption of property by other villagers. There was, secondly, the even clearer sign of the first cases where free village communities sold themselves, accepting serfdom in return for money.

Looking at all of these symptoms, premonitions of the great social crisis of serfdom which marked the reign of Michael the Brave (1593–1601), it seems evident to us that there were three successive phases of the social history of serfdom in Wallachia, similar, at least in their general outline, to those of Moldavia: a first period of a rather hesitant take-over of the villages (1350–1450) a second period, of a century and a half, during which the boyars succeeded in strengthening their economic base by making it independent of the state and by reducing the villages to serfdom (1450–1600) and finally a third period that can be set approximately around the year 1600, when serfdom became general but, paradoxically, also began to weaken.

10 ❧ The conquest of the village communities by the boyar class

The dual character of the feudal lords

Whether the boyar came from an old village 'chieftanship' or whether he had received a village as a donation from the voivode, his status was simultaneously that of a member of the village community and lord of the village. As 'lord', master of the village, he had the right to collect a tithe on all the villagers' products and to exact also a certain amount of corvée labour. As 'member of the community', he had access to those rights due any other member: the right to clear land, to cultivate, to plant, to graze his animals, etc., according to the same rules of joint ownership, communally valid for everyone, which were the necessary adjunct of a certain stage of development in pastoral and agricultural technology. Each lord thus had two problems to solve: organizing the collection of tithes and managing his own household, with corvée labour.

Two steps in the history of the growth of serfdom in the village communities can be distinguished. In the first period, the basis of which was a subsistence economy, the tithes were most important; in the second stage, when the boyars began to organize an agricultural exploitation for profit, with the production of market goods, the corvée became more important. The slow transition from one economic system to another was marked by a worsening of the condition of the peasants, who were reduced to serfdom. The boyars were increasingly inclined to consider themselves above the collectivity as feudal lords who were landowners.

The lineages and patrimonial communities of the boyars

We would be much more ignorant of the details of the rights of ownership the boyars exercised as village 'lords' if the villages had had as masters only the grand boyars who held latifundia. But for a long time the general rule was that the peasant agricultural collectivities were held by collectivities of boyars grouped into large family lines. The result was that at times of taking ownership, of sales, exchanges or divisions, numerous Moldavian documents were produced specifying the way in which the joint boyar owners managed their rights to the tithe. These documents have even more meaning when they are supplemented with data obtained from direct field work in our contemporary villages.

The phenomenon of the social collectivities which exploit other social collectivities is not unknown in world history, as it is found often enough at the beginning of civilizations, and even later, in the middle ages when one notes the existence not only of subject peasant communities whose remnants are found in modern times but also of 'family lines' characteristic of the families of feudal lords. In all these caes, it is a question not only of organization by family, thought to derive from ancient 'peoples' or 'clans', but also of patrimonial groups. Even given that their origin was initially from a clan, it is the common patrimony which explains their survival until so late. Every 'family' has as its base a biological phenomenon: the reproduction and raising of children. But just as essential, at least for understanding the history of family organization, is the fact that the family has a household, thus a certain economic basis. It is the evolution of this basis which explains the evolution of family forms. The non-historical biological factors are less important.

The formation of a 'family line', an 'enlarged' family, is not a biological fact but a patrimonial one. We have already seen, for example, what the particularly patrimonial social conditions were which caused the peasants from free village communities to form 'family lines' and end by setting up 'genealogical villages'. As far as the boyar 'family lines' are concerned, with the boyar patrimonies organized 'genealogically' in a way quite similar to that of the peasants, we should recall the law formulated by Marx in the following manner: every mode of exploitation of the means of production must adapt itself to the goods being exploited. The boyars exploited communal villages by tithes and corvées, thus obliging the forms of social organization of their system of exploitation to take into account the specific characteristics of the village communities being exploited.

The details of the adaptation of the boyars' family life to the necessities imposed by the existence of the village communities, as goods to be exploited, are the following. The Romanian villages had an economic value limited to the amount which the tithes could produce, which was a tenth of the produce in livestock and grain. The corvées could be demanded only within the narrow margins of a subsistence economy. We do not have direct statistical information concerning village populations in the first centuries of Romanian history. But we know that, until recent times, the villages were populated only by several dozen families at the most. And we know that the old Moldavian documents which authorized the boyars to repopulate deserted villages usually said there were ten to twenty houses per village and at the most sixty.

The life of a boyar family on such a modest base could not have been extremely prosperous, despite the fact that raising livestock did not call for much manpower. A boyar family not far removed from the early phase of clan organizations, thus still keeping alive the tradition of primitive organizations resembling those of 'gens', had a tendency to form family lines and to adopt the form of enlarged families. But the capacity of these large families to survive was limited by the productive capacity of the peasants. Increasing the amount of revenues would only have been possible in two ways. One of them was by possessing a whole collection of villages and thus forming a larger domain. But this was only possible for a minimal group of favoured boyars. Every large domain was formed at the expense of members of the same class and often at the expense of members of the same family line. It was also possible to raise the traditional tithe so as to obtain more livestock and grain. This was possible only with difficulty, and only by the strongest boyars.

The boyar families could thus form family lines only up to a certain limit. Once the saturation point was reached, the growth of boyar family lines stopped. It was possible to exploit by common ownership a limited number of villages, even if the family lines were relatively numerous. It was no longer possible once there were large domains, difficult to administer, the revenues of which had to be divided among a whole group of relatives. Similarly, a large group of joint boyar owners could not survive if it had only one village, as this lowered the level of the poor boyars to that of the free peasants.

This social process is very interesting to follow especially in Moldavia; for, in contrast to the situation in Wallachia, where large family groups were in evidence in the first documents closest to the period of the founding of the Wallachian state, the Moldavian boyars, arriving as the liberating conquerors from the Transylvanian land of Maramuresh,

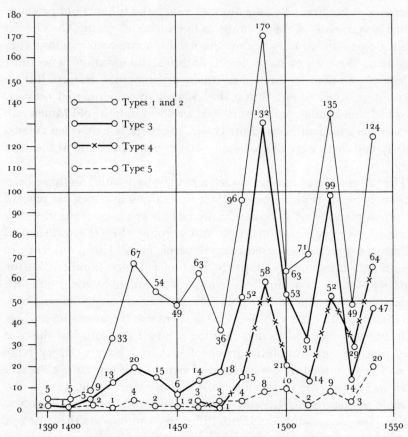

Fig. 22. Chronology of family types. Mention of families of Types I and II, III, IV and V in the documents.

settled in the existing village cells, many of which were 'deserted' following the wars against the Tartars. These villages had to be repopulated. The voivode of the country thus gave to his boyars deserted
'villages' which they had to colonize on the basis of written documents.

These Moldavian documents, which have no Wallachian equivalent,
sometimes bear but one name as the beneficiary, a name, however,
which implies a whole family. But the later documents concerning these
patrimonies are the proof that the families grew, since the documents
bore more and more names of large groups of brothers and cousins as
co-owners. Thus the simple family led to an enlarged family, but this
was a social phenomenon which lasted only a certain amount of time,
for the large families thus formed ended by splitting up, giving way to
restricted families involving only direct descendants. From a statistical

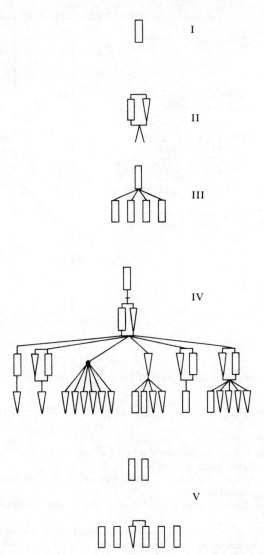

Fig. 23. Typology of family forms among nobles in the fifteenth and sixteenth centuries.

table based on the available Moldavian documents of the fifteenth century, one obtains the result shown in fig. 22. The number of joint patrimonial boyar families follows a curve, at first upward and then downward, whereas the families made up only of direct descendants experience a final ascendancy, becoming dominant in the course of the second half of the sixteenth century.

Carrying the analysis further, we have established the following types

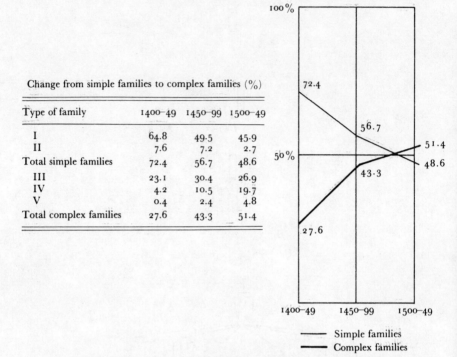

Change from simple families to complex families (%)			
Type of family	1400–49	1450–99	1500–49
I	64.8	49.5	45.9
II	7.6	7.2	2.7
Total simple families	72.4	56.7	48.6
III	23.1	30.4	26.9
IV	4.2	10.5	19.7
V	0.4	2.4	4.8
Total complex families	27.6	43.3	51.4

——— Simple families
——— Complex families

Fig. 24. Growth of complex families (Types III, IV and V) and decline of simple families (Types I and II).

of families, cited in the documents as groups of feudal lords, owning villages jointly.

Type 1: a single holder, undoubtedly head of at least a 'nuclear' family.
Type 2: other diverse forms of small families.
Type 3: diverse forms of enlarged families, containing married brothers and sisters with their own restricted families.
Type 4: diverse forms of *complex families*, containing also cousins with wives and children.
Type 5: patrimonial groups made up of family heads whose common lineage is not indicated (possibly not even existing, the group being but a collection, properly speaking, of complex family forms).

Types 1 and 2 can be considered as forming a single type, that of *simple families*.

It would be useless to reproduce in detail the statistical tables bearing on this aspect of the problem. Their final interpretation is presented in percentages in fig. 24.

One notices that the 'enlarged' and 'complex' families little by little came to dominate this first period. But this calculation only involves

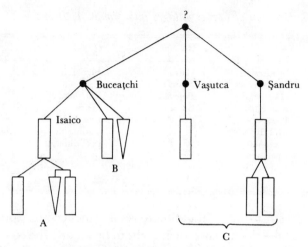

Fig. 25. Genealogy of the boyar Buceaţchi.

family forms and not the size of their patrimonies; the small number of large latifundia holders with very small families possessed a strong economic, social and thus also political base denied to large joint groups.

But from the sixteenth century on, a ceiling seems to have been reached for large patrimonial groups with joint holdings. An inverse movement toward the disintegration of family patrimonies then began. For example in 1520 there came before the voivode

our servant Christea and his sister Nastea, wife of the boyar Stîrcea, *son of Isaico*; and their uncle Stephen and his sister Madeleine, children of Buceaţchi; and likewise, their uncle, our devoted boyar Grincovici, burgermeister of the castle of Hotin, son of Vaşutca and his nephews by his brother John and his brother Iuire, son of Şandru, the Turk, all nephews of Cozma Sandrovici and of Iancou the Treasurer who wanted to divide up their twenty villages.

Associated with each 'name', there was undoubtedly a family, but we do not have the information. Their genealogy, where only the head of the chiefs' family is mentioned, is shown in fig. 25. Table 6 shows how the villages can be divided into three large groups, A, B and C.

If these feudal lineages did not possess a sufficient number of villages, or if they were reduced to a single one, it is evident that the division had to be handled in shares. Thus, for example, in 1573, a lineage made up of seventy-seven people, divided into fifteen sub-groups, all 'grand-nephews of Balog, the chamberlain', divided their village Holoboreni into eight shares. Such divisions did not occur without squabbles. For example, in 1576, a group of sixty-one people, grand-nephews of Oance

TABLE 6. *Division of twenty villages into groups A, B and C*

A	B	C
Sendreşeşti	Chiva	Iugani
Stanislăveşti	Nesvoia	Temeşani
Hălăuceşti	Deşevcani	Răchiţeni
Rurceşti	Corbeşti	Faurii
Pogăneşti	½ of Mlinăuţi	Ivancouţi
Midcău		Voropceni
Sceacăul		½ of Mlinăuţi
Ceabărcău		
Lemeşani		
9	4½	6½

Averescul, went through litigation to resolve ownership. Some claimed that, due to false documents, their right to be among the co-owners was contested, 'by not making them part of the genealogy'. The verdict proclaimed them all part of the same family line and the three villages they held were divided equally. Other documents show that this was general. After 1550 joint ownership of villages by boyar families was gradually replaced by single limited family ownership.

The 'genealogical' patrimonial form of the small boyars

We are especially interested in the small boyars, for, as we have said, it is due to them that we have information about how the collection of tithes was administered. The large holders of latifundia had no need to put in writing the way in which they managed the tithes and corvées. Masters of their domains, they were accountable to no one; whereas the small boyars, joint holders, had a mass of conflicting interests which they had to resolve by judicial decisions or by written private contracts.

We know that every communal village, given the rather primitive state of pastoral and agricultural technology, had to remain in common ownership on a territory set out in large communal economic zones: forest, pasture, ploughland, enclosure areas. The result was that the boyars could not divide the village into as many plots as there were people with a right to them, for this would have meant economic destruction. The boyars thus had to handle their rights to the tithe without touching the economic mechanism of the village. They managed this by living in the community themselves, at least as long as the boyar collectivity did not extend beyond a certain number of member families and as long as this group was still homogeneous. But as soon as the family

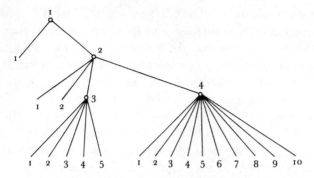

Fig. 26. Genealogical division into shares.

line went beyond a certain limit and as soon as this line fell apart, as a result of the social rise of a few families, the initial absolute joint ownership became impracticable. To put an end to it, the boyars had to apply the inheritance rules used by the free villages: division by 'ancestors'. But as it was not land but revenues in tithes that were to be divided, this form of 'division by ancestors' used by the boyars was from the beginning a division of the fourth type, bearing on both the whole territory and the revenues.

This leads us to confusion, for, at first glance, it is difficult not to confuse the genealogical division of the boyars with that of the peasants, the two juridical forms being identical although having absolutely different social functions. The peasants adopted this form to defend their rights to shares against outside trespassers on a terrain they worked themselves; whereas the boyars used it to regulate their rights to exploit the villages. But just like the free peasant's 'share', the boyar's 'share' bears on the whole village territory. It is not a land plot but a right to share in the total patrimony, thus on the entire mass of the village's corvée labour and its tithes. This right gave way to formulas which seem contradictory. For example, in 1564, a document specified the right of a boyar thus: 'May he hold the village of Runcou, that is to say half.' Or, in 1500: 'of the whole territory, the tenth part, of the field, of the forest, of the water, of everywhere, from one end to the other', etc. Or, in 1553, in the village of Glodeni, 'of half, the fourth part of the village, a fifth part' was sold for 600 zlotzi, and similarly 'of one half, the fourth part of the village, the tenth part' for 500 zlotzi. In other words, shares of $\frac{1}{40}$ and of $\frac{1}{80}$ were sold. However, the document does not tell us directly, in mathematical terms, the share that was sold, but rather reproduces in genealogical manner the subdivisions according to which the shares were calculated. The village was first divided into two halves; one of these halves was divided into four; and of these quarters, one was subdivided into five and the other into ten. The schema of these subdivisions forming the genealogical tree is shown in fig. 26.

The village thus 'walked' on two 'old men', as it was divided into two halves, as if it had been inherited by two brothers. The terms 'ancestors' and 'old men' were used by the boyars as well as by the peasants. Thus, in 1602, a boyar held 'in the "old man" of Litceşti, by heredity, part of the field, the forest, the water, everywhere, as far as one can determine, as his share in the joint ownership'.

As in the peasant genealogies, sales were disguised as fraternizations. Even without that procedure, buyers were brought into the genealogy by putting their names in the documents and in the family trees. Such genealogies thus became substitute land surveys.

Division of the tithes and corvées

But this division by 'ancestors', using the genealogy as a means of calculating shares, offered the boyars only an abstract juridical base. In fact, economic problems still had to be resolved. How did they manage? There were several means. In certain cases, two or more family groups could agree to share the village by years, each family in turn having the right to collect the tithes. The mills could likewise be divided by days. But the simplest and easiest method was to divide up the peasants. Each peasant household could thus continue to use the whole village territory in the old way, agreeing to pay the tithe to the boyar to whom it was attributed.

To distribute the peasants, the Moldavian boyars sometimes ended joint ownership in the village centre, which was divided into lots, enclosed, and organized according to the formula of possession 'by sum of lengths', each boyar having a right to the peasants inhabiting the lots allocated to him. This allotment was not, in fact, a means of dividing the land but rather the 'houses', thus the families which lived there. 'The "neighbours" [serfs] who live on his lot will obey him in all things he tells them...and he will take the neighbours who flee to the lot of another boyar and bring them back to his own lot' (document of 1755). The division by 'houses of serfs' clearly shows what was happening. It was a division of the rights of exploitation by tithes obtained by a division of men, the division of men obtained by dividing up the village centre (but only the centre as other village lands remained jointly owned).

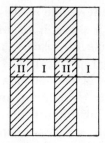

Fig. 27. Ways of dividing a village between two groups of boyars.

As the boyars also had a right to corvées, a much more difficult problem arose. If one of the boyars wanted to use his corvée rights to develop larger and larger areas of land, he could come into conflict with the rights of his co-holders. To avoid conflict, they had now to divide the land itself as well as the men, so that each boyar had to confine his labour to his own zone. Thus, in a Moldavian example dating from 1546, one can easily note that the two groups of boyars divided their territory to equalize their shares in a rather subtle manner. At the same time the village territory continued to make up a single economic unit (see fig. 27). Having thus divided the village into large zones, each boyar then had the obligation to make his serfs work only that land, both tithe and corvée, situated within his zones. This hindered the effective use of the old pastoral and agricultural technology and incited peasant protest. Furthermore, this social formula did not have very far-reaching effects, as villages with a single master became the rule and jointly owned villages ultimately vanished.

The splitting of the village community into autonomous peasant households

Grouping the peasants by 'houses' in an enclosed village centre (surrounded by a general enclosure) laid out in 'sums of lengths' was relatively easy to manage in a Moldavian type of village, repopulated by the colonizing effort of the feudal lord. But this was not possible in all the traditional communal villages characteristic of Wallachia, where the inhabitants were organized by large family lines, each one holding a 'share', a 'belt', a 'strip', giving them the right to local citizenship. But in both countries, the boyars did not directly exploit the land, but rather the peasants, by tithes and corvées, and it followed that each peasant household came to be considered as an autonomous unit of exploitation, counting as such in the boyar's patrimony.

This process was especially visible in Wallachia. In an early period when the seizure of a village was still incomplete, the group of boyars was declared to hold a 'village', taken as a whole, or else a share of the village, without any other specification. Thus in 1385, the monastery of Tismana held the 'village of Vadul Cumanilor [Cumans' Ford], half of Toporna... the villages of Hrisomuinţi and Tismana' without there being any mention of their inhabitants. There was then a second phase when the parts composing the village were specified, but the population was still only considered as a unit; thus 'half the village of Piteşti, half the serfs, half the plough fields and half the mills' (document of 1528). But soon an indication of the number of peasant families appeared, and, even more significantly, a division of the serfs and freemen of the villages. At the time of the division of the patrimony of a large boyar family, in which the voivode of the country himself was involved (1568–77), the domain was divided into two equal parts. The document tells us: 'This being the case, my kingdom has not divided the villages by villages but rather by serfs, according to the registers of my kingdom.' The voivode took for his share 578 serfs in the large villages of Greaca, Craiova and Prundul and gave his co-sharer 448 serfs and twenty-one and a half villages. As compensation for the difference between the unequal number of serfs, 578 in one share and 448 in the other, the voivode granted nine other of his own villages, containing a number of serfs equal to the balance. The peasant household was now considered as an individualized economic unit, counted as such in the state's fiscal registers. The process of individualization of peasant households went on at an accelerated pace.

Seigniorial rights measured in terms of the patrimonial rights of their serfs

To determine the value of his rights, the Wallachian boyar specified what the patrimonial rights of his serfs were. For example, in 1571, a boyar granted 'my part of the village of Vrăneşti, four serfs, namely Dragomir and Radomir and Cîrstea and Voico, among the vineyards planted on the hills, in the plough fields and everywhere else where these four serfs have a right'. Or, in 1621, there was a sale of 'a serf from the village of Izvorani, named Ivan Lupea, son of Gagor with his hereditary "strip" in the fields, in the forest and waterways, the vineyards and cleared lands, and his gardens and all his fruit trees, all his share, as well as it can be determined over the whole territory'. Or, in 1614, a boyar held a village of serfs, 'that is, Oană's whole part, Stan's whole part, Radu and Bocancea's whole parts, in the forest and waterways, in the village centre and the fields and the vineyards and mill ponds, everywhere as well as can be determined, over the whole territory, from one end to the other'; 'and they are to be serfs with their sons and their whole patrimony', for 'these are hereditary serfs, acquired by our ancestors'. The boyar thus measured his own patrimonial rights by units of serf households. A new, direct relationship 'boyar–serf' thus replaced the old relationship 'boyar–village'. Instead of a collectivity identified by a single toponym, there was now a nominal list of peasants with a description of their economic value.

Selling a serf thus meant selling the seigniorial rights of feudal exploitation of the patrimony held by the serf. Now merchandise, the patrimonial rights of the boyars, were calculated in 'serfs'. A whole series of commercial documents appeared, in which 'serfs' and their 'shares' were sold, bought, leased, willed, exchanged, etc., according to the general rules of commerce. The serfs themselves were able to participate in these commercial transactions, their contracts bearing only on their rights of use, burdened as they were with tithe and corvée obligations.

There was an important detail: in commercial relations with their own boyars, their liberty itself was actually if not legally at stake, for in buying the boyar's right to the tithe and corvées, or in repurchasing the lease of which they were the object, they freed themselves of any obligation to tithes and corvées, a problem we will return to. They even had the right of *protimisis* (right to withdraw) in case their village was sold or leased.

As proof that the transactions between boyars concerning a 'serf' did not yet legally involve his personal liberty, we have a certain number of documents concerning not serfs but 'serf' women. On the other hand, it is certain, that women were never subjected to corvées nor bound to the soil. Each time a woman appeared in a contract as 'serf', it concerned her patrimony and not her physical person. These cases existed when the woman was a widow, when she had the role of head of the family, or when she herself held a hereditary lot, giving her the right to 'everywhere' on the village territory.

Abolition of the citizenship right of serfs

When a boyar wanted to sell his patrimony, he had the possibility not only of selling a village in its totality or simply a share of the village, but also of selling a single serf, or rather the right of exploitation he held in this serf. Thus one could sell a peasant household as a member of the collectivity. The economic unit of the peasant household thus became merchandise that could be bought, leased, inherited or willed, on the condition that the serf was specified 'with his strip', that is, his patrimony, his share of the village community. The point of enslavement still had not been reached. Properly speaking, a right over the physical person of the peasant, who had not yet become 'merchandise' himself, did not exist.

The first formula spoke of 'a serf and his strip', thus his patrimony. But the inverse formula was not long in coming: 'the strip with its serf'. In 1583, there were sold 'one hundred lengths, insofar as they can be separated from the common ownership, from over the whole territory, in the fields, waterways and in the hills', with the concise affirmation, 'and these lengths are four serfs'. Under this form, the serf's person was still not at issue. It was still his patrimony, symbolized by his name. In 1578, for example, 'two and a half serfs' and 'a half a serf, called Stan', could be sold, clearly indicating that it was a question of patrimonies and not of the physical person of the peasants.

Measurement of the patrimonial rights of a lord by the extent of the common patrimonial rights of his serfs constitutes the proof that in Wallachia these serfs continued to be members of a village collectivity, able to own their own goods, a right deriving from the possession of a strip. Thus can be seen, at this period, the existence of rules of the type of social organization we have been able to observe directly in the twentieth century, according to which a peasant's rights derived from the fact that he was a member of the collectivity. His citizenship with full rights was proved by his holding a 'share', a 'strip', a 'belt', an enclosed field, divided by 'sum of lengths'. This possession of a 'strip' granted the right to use the common goods. Each year newly cleared land could be ploughed, vineyards and fruit trees planted where one wanted, clearings made in the forest, beehives set up, mills built, fish ponds made, etc. Even a serf, as a peasant holding a 'strip' within a communal village, had a right to all these benefits. This explains the fact that any serf's name entering the patrimony of a boyar had to be accompanied by the specification that he owned a 'strip', thus that he had a right to the whole territory. Without this specification, an inventory had to be drawn up of all the 'holdings' that the serf, through his labour, had secured.

The direct proof that the peasant serf was really master of his patrimony is supplied by the documents by which the boyar purchased certain patrimonial rights belonging to his own serfs. Thus, in 1579 a boyar donated to a monastery 'two mills with their fields and the enclosed terrain on all sides...which he bought himself at the price of 2000 silver aspers from his serfs of the village of Clăteşti: Sarul and Voico and Vladul and others of their joint group'.

The direct relationship established between a feudal lord and the patrimony of a serf was not legally defined. But, in fact, the manner in which things happened is known. In the beginning, if a peasant fled from a village, or if his whole family disappeared, his goods reverted to the community, which had to pay the taxes of the defaulting peasant. But the boyar, substituting himself for the community, succeeded in holding on to these patrimonies without serfs. In 1607, 'When Badiul died, he left no one after him. And as Badiul was the hereditary serf of the *vornic* Staicu, his patrimony remained in the hands of Staicu.' In fact, this involved 'Badiul's part of the fields, of the forests, of the waterways and the mountain, as well as it can be separated from the common ownership, over the whole territory'.

It was the same for the 'shares' left by the serfs who fled. The sixteenth as well as the seventeenth centuries experienced an excessive worsening of the conditions of rural social life which grew more difficult every day. Continual wars followed by terrible famines, plague epidemics, and unbearable fiscal exploitation to satisfy the demands of the Turks caused the villages to lose population. Inhabitants fled and those that remained were decimated by epidemis and famine. As a result, from the time of the sixteenth century, there is a bizarre state of affairs in the documents concerning sales: the existence of numerous patrimonies without peasants. There were cases where in a certain village there was only one serf and there were even villages that were completely 'deserted'. From then on any document of sale had to specify the state of the local population. For example, in 1615, it was noted that of the sixteen 'strips' which had belonged in 1592 to serfs, there were only seven 'living', whose names were given. 'Living serfs' became an expression to designate the serf patrimony of an existing serf, as opposed to the 'dry', 'sterile' strip designating patrimonies without a peasant holder.

Once the distinction was made between serfs and patrimony, the exchange between boyars of 'domains for domains' and 'serfs for serfs' became possible. In 1614, the village of Tataru was sold with six serfs, but as the seller was only able to provide five serfs, he was obliged to find another – 'serf for serf'. Alternatively, land was exchanged for land and serfs were sold for money.

The boyar had finally found the means to improve his juridical and social foundations. Now a landowner, at least of the 'sterile' patrimonies, he had the chance to break the tie which held the 'living' serfs to their 'strips', thus to their right of citizenship, by changing the unusual rule of sterile patrimonies into the normal rule for all village patrimonies, even those not deserted. The patrimonies of 'living' serfs ended by falling into the private patrimony of the boyar. The sale of villages 'without serfs', in spite of the fact that the village was inhabited, became frequent, though for a time it was deemed abnormal and contrary to ancient custom. In 1619, for example, the voivode of Wallachia, having to judge such a sale, asked the question: 'How is it possible for a boyar to purchase a village without serfs?' To study the case, he named, according to the old custom, a commission of arbiters made up of twelve boyars, who confirmed that actually 'the village has been sold without serfs, the seller wishing to transport his serfs to another one of his villages and have thus both the money and the serfs'. Thus any tie between the population of the village and the land was definitely broken. Land began to be sold for money, in Moldavia in 1439 and in Wallachia in 1451.

Ostensibly, the boyar possessing patrimonies without peasants was stripped of revenues, but in fact he acquired a right he never had before, that of landowner. In a deserted village, the boyar no longer had to undergo the competition of a village community or to respect the traditional customs. He had undoubtedly to procure new peasants as quickly as possible in order to work his property. 'There was no village on this land; but Radu the *clucer* [a petty noble title] bought neighbours and built the village calle Urîţii', a document of 1572 tells us. These peasants were newcomers and no longer had a right to their ancient legal status. Like those of Moldavia, they were no longer holders of 'strips', no longer members of a traditional community. Once they had reached this point, serfs were considered as merchandise and they began to be sold without land. 'Micou bought Oancea, a serf from the village of Boteni, for 400 aspers', reads a document of 1570.

There was now another danger to ward off: as long as the peasant held his own patrimony in his native village, he tried to remain there, at all costs. Once he no longer had this, nothing held him to the soil and as soon as life got too hard, he tried to escape. There was only one way to hold him back: to bind him to the soil. This development was not long in coming.

11 ❧ The great social crisis of serfdom

General characteristics of the period of serfdom

The series of transformations affecting the relations which bound the peasant class to the boyar class, increasingly clear from the second half of the sixteenth century, was the sign of a deeper upheaval, touching the whole social life of the period, bringing successive surprises and contradictions. On the one hand, a large number of villages fell into serfdom; serfdom itself was transformed from being patriarchal to become a binding to the soil. On the other hand, another group of serf villages succeeded in repurchasing their liberty by paying large sums of money. Increasingly, the peasant class fell into various categories. There were peasants belonging to free village communities, free peasants without land, serf peasants, some bound to the soil but others not, free peasants with serfs, peasants with serfs who sold themselves into serfdom with their serfs, and even serf villages with lordship over another serf village.

Similarly, within the boyar class, at least as important a cleavage was taking place. A small number of large seigniorial families became, by purchase or force, masters of gigantic serf domains, at the expense not only of free villages but also of other noble families, which dwindled, some even falling into the class of free peasants.

Before attempting an analysis to help us determine the importance of each of these dissimilar social processes in the whole intense mix-up of the social life of the times, we have to ask a preliminary question: where could the large sums of money come from which the large owners of latifundia and the peasant serfs needed, the former to acquire their domains, the latter to buy back their freedom? There is only one possible answer: trade. Let us recall the general features of the commercial history in the region. For a long time historians have studied the great trade routes which crossed Romania, binding Western

Europe with the Near East and Asia.[1] Already in the thirteenth century, Genoese and then Venetians had their ports all around the Black Sea, from the mouths of the Danube, Maurocastron (Ancient Tyras, Cetatea Albă or Ackerman), Lycostomo (Chilia) and Vicina, to far away Kaffa and Trebizond. The commercial registers of the period prove that at the mouths of the Danube fish, salt, grains, and, of course, slaves were purchased. The Danubian ports were united, across Moldavia, to the routes coming from the Baltic and Central Europe, passing through the Polish cities of Lvov and Cracow.

On the other hand, western trade sent its products toward the Orient by way of Bohemia, Austria and Transylvania, where powerful towns located at the entrance to passes crossing the Carpathians were great commercial centres. The most important was Braşov, opening the way toward the Danubian port, Brăila, as well as Bistriţa, which, along the Moldavian Seret, led towards the Danubian ports and towards the great 'Tartar route' heading in the direction of Russia and Asia. Another Transylvanian town, Sibiu, also a link with western trade and also located at the entrance of a Carpathian pass, led towards the Balkan fords of the Danube and from there either to Constantinople or to the Adriatic, where Ragusa played a most important role.

This network of routes, the object of constant struggles between diverse competitors (Tartars, Hungarians, Poles), was certainly not the only cause of the creation of the autochthonous states of Moldavia and Wallachia, as some have maintained. But its presence explains the prosperity of those countries from the time of their foundation in the fourteenth century. In fact, Transylvania, Wallachia and Moldavia formed an economic unit, a locus of trade, enabling Europe to handle a large part of its trade with the Orient. Undoubtedly this trade was not one of simple transit; Moldavia and Wallachia must both have participated with their local goods: salt, fish, sheep, horses, cattle, honey, wax and grain. The tartar domination of these regions does not seem to have upset this traffic between west and east. The Tartars had established themselves as masters over a network of routes and customs points in order to exploit a commerce in which they were parasites but also guardians.

Everything changed once the Turks occupied the Byzantine Empire and conquered the whole Balkan peninsula, Wallachia, Moldavia, Transylvania and a sizeable part of Hungary. After they had inflicted defeat upon the Serbian kingdom in 1389, crushed a European army

1. Chiefly N. Iorga in his excellent studies of commercial routes and customs in our country.

at Nicopolis in 1396, taken Constantinople in 1453, subjected Hungary at the Battle of Mohács in 1526, they did not stop until 1529 at the gates of Vienna. Thus they cut Europe off from the route to the Black Sea and the Danube, seizing Trebizond in 1461, Kaffa in 1475, Chilia in 1463, Ackerman in 1484, Brăila in 1540, Giurgiu in 1417, Belgrade in 1521 and Pest in 1530.

However, though the sea routes towards the mouths of the Danube were cut, one must not neglect the fact that as the Turkish Empire reached the summit of its power towards the middle of the sixteenth century, it held under its direct influence not only Wallachia and Moldavia but also Transylvania. The economic unity of these three countries was achieved, thereby permitting trade to continue, at least by land if not by water, towards Central and Western Europe.

It is true that the Turkish administration imposed a heavy tribute on these countries, as well as a monopoly on the purchase of certain foodstuffs at arbitrarily fixed prices. But Turkish trade maintained, in a way, local bank operations, or at least loans with interest. The cosmopolitan group of businessmen from Constantinople – Greeks, Jews, Armenians, Turks – was aware enough to be interested in renewing the ties, momentarily broken, with Central Europe. There is proof that a land trade existed with the west up to the time when the decay of Turkish power enabled the Black Sea and Danube routes to reopen in the eighteenth and nineteenth centuries.

In addition, one should not forget that, towards the middle of the sixteenth century at the dawn of the new capitalist and colonial system, the nature of the European economy was changing with serious consequences for the system of prices and currencies as well as for the export of food products from Eastern Europe to the manufacturing cities of the west. Of course, the Romanian countries did not feel the effects as deeply as did the Baltic countries. However, if the Romanian countries did not export cereals in large quantities, it was because the overland transport of cereals was extremely difficult, due to the almost total absence of good roads. On the other hand, livestock exports continued at an increasing rate.[2] The export of grain could not begin until the Turkish monopoly over the sea routes leading to the mouths of the Danube was broken. From the sixteenth to the nineteenth centuries, the export of pigs (which the Turks did not buy), cattle and

2. Someone who knew the country well, the Italian Graziani, expressed the importance of this trade as follows: 'Animals are incredibly numerous...It is from Moldavia that they export this multitude of cattle whose meat feeds not only the people of Hungary and Russia but also those of Poland, Germany, and even Italy, especially Venice.'

horses, as well as eastern goods in transit, was of the greatest importance. Romanian merchants travelled to sell these goods at the great European fairs and returned with products manufactured in Flanders, England, France and Germany. This international trade carried with it, in its transit between the Levant and the west, Wallachian, Moldavian and Transylvanian goods, and it was thus, through local commerce unifying these three countries, that large amounts of capital could be accumulated in Romania.

Cash is not, in itself, the sign of the penetration of capitalist trade, for this 'universal commodity' is to be found even in prehistoric times. But when money comes to dominate the market, it can be considered a sign of the transition to a cash economy. This does not mean that the fundamental structure of a country is uprooted. A country can pass from the phase the Germans call *Naturalwirtschaftliche Feudalismus* to that called *Geldwirtschaftliche Feudalismus*. This seems to have been the characteristic phenomenon as of the sixteenth century in the Romanian countries.

We have only to look at the sums the Romanians had to pay the Turks as annual tribute, without counting the equally large sums due as *bakshish* (an eastern custom), to be aware of this phenomenon. In 1456 Moldavia paid in tribute the sum of 2,000 gold coins, 4,000 in 1501, 8,000 in 1514, 12,000 in 1541, 17,000 in 1551, 30,000 in 1553, and 65,000 in 1593. Wallachia paid 10,000 in 1415, 12,000 in 1505, 16,000 in 1538, 24,000 in 1542, 50,000 in 1588, 60,000 in 1577, and 140,000 in 1582.[3] Things worsened in the following centuries. The exact amount of these tributes is undoubtedly subject to controversy. But it is certain that the Turks got from the Romanian countries an ever higher sum in tribute and that Romania was able to pay. These sums could only have come from trade which, in all likelihood, could not have been only that carried on with the Turks. Such sums could not have come exclusively from customs taxes. They must also have been furnished by direct taxes. Boyars and villages must themselves have had the means to procure the necessary sums.

Furthermore, in the sixteenth century, the boyars began to accumulate large domains. There was, for example, the great Buzeşti family, owning more than 300 villages in Wallachia, and the Costin family in Moldavia with 250. A study of the domain of the voivode Michael the

3. M. Berza, 'Haraciul Moldovei şi Ţării Româneşti în sec. XV–XIX' (The tribute paid by Wallachia and Moldavia from the fifteenth to the nineteenth centuries), in *Studii şi materiale*, volume II, Bucharest, 1957.

TABLE 7. *The domain of Michael the Brave*

	Villages	Sums paid in aspers*
Domain acquired coming to the throne	44	1,515,700
Domain acquired as voivode of the country	149	1,023,330
Total	193	2,539,030

* In 1590, 100 aspers = one gold coin; in 1600, 170 aspers = one gold coin.

Brave affords us some very interesting details on the manner in which these domains were born.[4] In the days when he was just a simple boyar, Michael the Brave had at his disposal sums large enough to establish his domain, by purchasing villages, a domain which he subsequently enlarged beyond all measure once he occupied the throne (1593–1601).

In brief outline, the history of this domain is shown in table 7. Undoubtedly, force was used to acquire these villages, as was made evident by the lower price he paid as absolute master of the country for a much larger number of villages. But still he had to have the money. Where did he get it? Undoubtedly, he had creditors in Constantinople. But such credits were only given with the assurance that they would be repaid. Buying domains had thus become a serious commercial affair. For a large boyar it was not a question of having villages to provide for the livelihood of his household, even if it was a princely one, but rather of going beyond the subsistence economy towards an exchange economy. The feudal domain, in the course of the sixteenth century, had really become the means of securing quantities of merchandise to export to Transylvania for the transit trade towards the west.

Michael the Brave was not, furthermore, the only voivode engaging in commerce. In Wallachia, they even gave the nickname 'Shepherd' to the voivode Mircea Ciobanul (1553–4 and 1558–9), because of his large trade in sheep. Peter Rareş (1527–38 and 1541–6), before becoming voivode of Moldavia, engaged in the fish trade and Alexander Lăpuşneanu (1552–68) was one of the largest Moldavian merchants of his time dealing in pigs.

The first glimmers of commercial capitalism thus began to appear in the sixteenth century, giving way in the Romanian countries to a

4. Ioan Donat, 'Satele lui Mihai Viteazul' (The villages of Michael the Brave), in *Studii şi materiale*, volume IV, Bucharest, 1960.

period of primitive capital accumulation, about which we will later give some details as it concerns the seizure of communal villages transformed into villages of serfs bound to the soil. A first significant fact is that the taxes owed by villages, instead of being collected exclusively in produce, began to be collected in cash.[5]

In the beginning, when the state claimed its right to bushels of wheat, to cows, pigs, honey, wax, etc. it was a question of goods in kind, even specified by the name of the tax to be 'paid'. Soon, taxes became evaluated not by quantity but by cash value. Even when money was only used as a legal standard, it was nonetheless a symptom of the fact that the produce in question already had assumed a commercial value and thus had begun to appear on the market. Eventually, the state requested of its tax payers sums payable in cash, the name of the taxes clearly indicating what was involved. The relatively large number of villages which repurchased their freedom by paying large sums of money provides direct proof of the fact that many peasants, even serfs, held capital.

Towards the middle of the sixteenth century, the villages, as well as the individual serf patrimonies, has taken on the clear character of 'merchandise', with a market price varying according to whether they were poor or rich villages. To buy itself back, every village or serf had to pay this market price, a price, furthermore, which rose over the course of the succeeding centuries. The sums paid for this often represented very large amounts, paid in silver 'aspers' or in gold, the 'galben' being valued at 140 aspers. There were villages paying 18,000, 26,000, 30,000, 80,000 and even 130,000 aspers. Sometimes the serfs of a village were even richer than their boyar, as in the case in 1599 when a boyar received from his serfs a loan of 1,500 aspers, enabling them to lease their own village, that is to say, their liberty, until the time when he could acquit his debt. This constitutes proof that even peasant serfs participated in local commerce, for it was only possible to accumulate this money through commerce.

Of course, only a limited category of peasants and boyars had such sums of money. But the fact that such privileged categories existed, struggling commercially to lay their hands on the village lands, is irrefutable proof of a commerce which had caused the old structure of social classes to break up, rich and poor entering thenceforth into commercial conflict, though still within the surviving feudal relations.

5. D. Mioc, H. Chircă, S. Ştefănescu,, 'L'évolution de la rente féodale en Valachie et en Moldavie, du XIVe au XVIIe siècles', *Nouvelles études d'histoire*, volume II, Bucharest, 1960.

The conquest of the free villages of Wallachia

The simple fact that the Wallachian boyars first had to break the ties existing between the peasants and their land plots, the 'strips' which gave them a right to use the whole village territory, in order to reduce them to serfdom proves that these serf villages had a 'communal' character. This system of common ownership in the serf villages was identical with the one we were able to observe directly in the contemporary free villages. Thus the boyars struggled to bring about disintegration of the communities.

The existence of peasant communities as the normal form of social organization at the time is again made clear by the fact that in the second half of the sixteenth century the boyars began to buy free villages, and the documents concerning these purchases give us all the details necessary to show that these free villages were organized in communities, some in the 'archaic' form, others in the 'evolved' form, according to the same models that we found surviving between the two world wars.

These purchases of free villages were carried out in several ways, following each other in steps. The first was that of fraudulent fraternizations.

Purchases disguised as 'fraternizations'

These purchases exactly resemble those we analysed by direct field work in the contemporary free villages, the only difference being that the buyer in the sixteenth and seventeenth centuries was a boyar and not an individual; also, at that time, in buying the land, one purchased *ipso facto* the freedom of the seller.

The big problem in penetrating a free village was first to become accepted as a member with citizenship rights, for this status alone gave firm rights to use and ownership. To accomplish this, the boyars fraudulently employed the formula of fraternization, with the donation ritually accompanying fraternization becoming the selling price. The boyar thus purchased a peasant's land by engaging in 'brotherhood'. As 'brother' of one of the villagers, he became 'brother' of all the other villagers, his future serfs. From that time on, he no longer needed to 'fraternize' with anyone else, for his status as brother, once acquired with one of the members, gave him the same position towards the whole collectivity, thus enabling him to purchase, lot by lot, the entire village.

Purchases of villages 'lot by lot'

Documents of the second half of the sixteenth century prove that the purchase of free villages, following a preliminary fraternization, had become a social phenomenon as new as it was significant. These boyars were buying up free village communities and not autonomous landed properties. Let us cite several cases which can better help us understand both the internal social mechanism of the bought villages as well as the purchase technique. A document of 1610 describes the manner in which a great boyar took over the village of Pîrcicoveni. He had first fraternized with a peasant. The princely document ratifying these purchases confirms

that my honorable dignitary, the *joupan* [title of nobility] Stanciul, grand chamberlain, holds at Pîrcicoveni half of Nicola's part, through inheritance as well as taxes, over the whole territory, for Nicola came before his lordship in person in order to fraternize with my honorable dignitary and donate his entire part, both inherited and bought, so that they might be two brothers indissolubly linked. And thus, my above named boyar for this fraternization made him many gifts and treated him with great honour and clothed him and never did he have to pay taxes his whole life, for my dignitary as named above exempted him totally. And Nicola, seeing so much esteem, care and gifts from my above named dignitary, closed the agreement with a curse so that no man after his death, whether he be of his lineage or blood, could touch the agreement. And may any man of his blood who tries to annul the agreement be three times accursed by the 318 saints of Nicaea.

Thus, a grand chamberlain, at the top of the court nobility, was 'brother'with a poor fellow, who must be clothed, given gifts and exempted from taxes. It was certainly not a brotherly gesture but rather a precise commercial calculation: the boyar, once fraternized, began to buy all he could, succeeding in monopolizing half the village. He bought

the part of Stoichiță and of his brothers, namely Luca and Radu and Stoia and Necoară and Vasile and the priest Luca with all their parts, as well as they can be determined, in the fields, in the woods, the waterways, the mill ponds and in the village centre over the whole territory; for these above named men were all free; but subsequently, they themselves, of their own free will and without force, sold all their share of inheritance to become his serfs for the sum of 17,600 aspers.

Among those selling, Stoia also had a lot which he had bought which was sold separately for the sum of 1,400 aspers. The document then enumerates other groups of sellers: nine (so-called) brothers, among whom there were two women, who sell themselves into serfdom for 20,300 aspers; four brothers and two sons who sell themselves for 4,000 aspers; two brothers who sell themselves for 4,000 aspers, another for 500 and still another for 2,000 aspers.

The high degree of disintegration of this communal village is apparent not only from the multiple and unequal purchases but also from the fact that the sellers were sometimes individuals, sometimes a joint group. There were among them even some who had succeeded in having their own serfs and who sold themselves into serfdom with their own serfs. Thus the boyar purchased

the share of the wife of Datco, daughter of Badea of Vilsăneşti and the first cousins of his wife, Vlădaia, the whole share of the field, of the forests and waterways, of the village centre and of the whole territory, the serfs included, that is to say, all that belongs to them through inheritance and purchase, all that was bought from Radul, son of Gogu, the share of Necşuleşti, for 2,300 aspers and also the share of Necoară, his share in the Necşuleşti plot, for 2,200 aspers, and also Cazan's part, in whole, for 2,000 aspers, as well as the serfs named Cazan and Badea and other serfs which can be identified; for the honorable dignitary of my kingdom bought this patrimony from the wife of Datco and from her first cousins for the sum of 6,010 aspers, in cash.

By another means of purchase, the boyar 'fraternizes and buys' all the villagers, as a unit, in the case of a community that was closer to the egalitarian archaic type. Thus, in 1573, 'the honorable grand boyar and first in my lordship's council, the *joupan* Dragomir *vornic* [title of nobility], fraternizes and buys' the following family lines:

1. Puiu of Ruşi, who sells 750 lengths at 5,763 aspers;
2. Fratea and his brother Nan, 250 lengths at 3,600 aspers;
3. Ignar and his brother Cazan, 250 lengths at 3,560 aspers;
4. Drăghia, 250 lengths at 3,342 aspers;
5. Puiul and his brother Tadul, 167 lengths at 2,841 aspers.

The price was paid in kind, consisting of clothing, horses, boots, etc., evaluated at a total of 5,736 aspers. In addition, the boyar 'gave to all the above-named brothers thirty cows, that the brothers divided among themselves, each according to his share...Thus bringing the total to 22,120 aspers, for they gave, established and fraternized.'

Loss of the initial meaning of the term 'brother'

Little by little the term 'brother' lost its real meaning of blood relationship and even its acquired meaning of relationship by 'fraternization' to become synonymous with 'co-owner. This semantic evolution was significant for the social system of communities organized along large family lines in the process of being transformed into simple local communities. The term 'brother' continued to be used, though no longer signifying anything but joint ownership. 'Blood brothers' became 'patrimony brothers', 'plot brothers', with anyone able to become a brother by simple purchase, without having to perform the ritual of fraternization. There were thus cases of fraternization between two villages as, for example, in 1570, when two villages involved in a lawsuit with each other were awarded in common the patrimony in question, 'by fraternization between these two above-mentioned villages, they will hold the patrimony in common. . . half and half'. Or, in 1575, a boyar alone held half a village, the other half being owned by a monastery. Their litigation was treated thus: 'my lordship fraternized them so that they might possess the village together'.

The same loss of the original meaning of the term 'brother' was noticeable in the cases involving possession obtained by force. Thus, in 1570, a monastery received a notice giving it the right to defend its fish ponds, 'so that none dares to fraternize. . . And any one daring to fraternize wrongly will be beaten and punished by the abbot of the monastery.' The term 'brother' had thus come to mean all those who, in one way or another, possessed in common and who according to the old rule would actually have had to be 'brothers' or at least have had to 'fraternize'.

To possess goods 'as brothers', whether it was a village, land, mill or a certain number of serfs, no longer had any meaning other than that, thenceforth, the parties would share equally as though they were brothers. The expression is, moreover, common in modern Romanian.

Direct sales and their social consequences

These sales disguised as fraternization only began to appear in the middle of the sixteenth century and they rapidly became unnecessary as soon as serfdom was accepted as the normal situation of all non-free peasants. Thereafter purchases were no longer camouflaged as fraternization but declared outright. The fraudulent character of these sales by fraternization between lords and peasants is evident in a large number of documents. In 1620, it was noted that a peasant, Stan, had fraternized with the boyar Barbul, at the time of Michael the Brave. 'But Stan, having seen that he could not continue living next to Barbul, tore down his house and moved to another piece of land he held, at the other end of the vineyards.' He, then his sons, lived in peace. But the descendants of the boyar brought the descendants of the peasant to justice, claiming that under the form of 'fraternization' it was his actual freedom that Stan had sold, meaning that all his descendants were considered to be serfs. The voivode judged the case, concluding that only the land had been sold and not Stan's liberty, as Stan had taken the precaution of not selling all his land but had reserved a piece for himself. Selling one's land thus came to mean that one had also sold one's liberty. From a legal presumption, the sale of land rapidly became proof of accepted serfdom. To escape from this, peasants had to specify, at every sale, in clear terms, that they 'have sold only the land and they still have a piece for themselves so that they might be free' (1609).

If a serf village rebought its freedom, granting the boyar a share of the territory, it was specified that 'we, the village of Cartojani, who have written above, have negotiated with Para, the *postelnic*, and have given him, in the lower share, the fourth part, domain without serfs' (1617).

The term 'dry land' was given to a piece of land sold by a free peasant, taking the precaution to mention that he was giving 'dry' land without 'his head', thus his personal liberty. For example, in 1598 it was recorded: 'they did not sell themselves as serfs but only dry land'. Here is one of the formulas: 'We have not sold our heads into serfdom; we have only sold all our land, from one end to the other, dry land, with no man' (1641). The boyar himself, at the time of purchase, attested to the truth of these clauses. Thus, not having land of one's own came, in law and in fact, to mean one was the serf of he whose land one worked, unless it could be demonstrated in writing that one belonged to the new social category of peasants without land but still 'free' – free to die of hunger elsewhere or to accept new work conditions if one was able to arrange something with another boyar.

Why did the free peasants sell their land? The boyars had several means of 'convincing' them to accept such sales 'willingly' (as the documents read): usurious loans, taxes too heavy for the free peasants, three times heavier than for the serfs, use of voivodal power to grant tax exemptions, the unfortunate cases in which a peasant fell under the penal code, either because of his own offences or as a consequence of the collective penal responsibility which considered all members of a social group together in case of the misdemeanor of one, or when there were crimes, committed by strangers on their territory, and even by forcing old people with no inheritors to sign themselves into serfdom. The frequent great famines of the period in fact helped such 'fraternal' buyers.

Let us cite, as convincing evidence, the cynical sentence of a document of 1573: 'All these men have sold and subjected their land of their own free will, some during a bad famine, others when they sold their sons to the Turks, and others while dying of hunger along the roadside, at the time of the voivode Radul.' A whole region could fall into serfdom. Such was the case in 1587 when, at the time a new voivode had come to power, a boyar wished to flee to Transylvania. But as he was crossing the Carpathians, twenty-three villages at the north of the counties of Gorj and Vîlcea in Oltenia caught him and stole all his belongings. The boyar gave up all thought of flight, returned to the new voivode, who pardoned him and ordered the twenty-three villages to repay damages. Not able to comply, these villages agreed 'willingly' to become his serfs.

Large-scale purchase of whole villages or of strips of free villages

At this point, there appeared a new way of taking over villages: the purchasing of villages, as a whole or by plots. A free village could sell itself for a sum of money and accept serfdom. Even as late as the 1864 reform, at the time the Rural Law was promulgated abolishing corvée labour, there were still situations before the courts involving free peasants who had sold or leased out their liberty for a certain period of time.

By analysing the diverse means of payment when villages were purchased as a whole, one can again see that in the second half of the sixteenth century there existed a whole gamut of diverse forms and steps in the procedure which paralleled the social development of the village communities. Thus, if the village was still at the archaic phase of absolute joint ownership, the buyer only had to pay one lump sum. For example, in 1596, the voivode Michael the Brave confirmed the purchase of the village Lupşani by one of his boyars, specifying that 'in this village they were all free. But then all the villagers came before me, submitted and sold their whole share in the inheritance to my honourable dignitary, the *joupan* Udrea, for 26,000 aspers paid in cash, so that they would become his serfs forever, willingly, in the sight and knowledge of all their neighbours, and in my presence.' This sort of formula, however, was not always proof of the archaic organization of a sold village, as it was likely and sometimes certain that it was only the writer of the document who, in order to simplify his task, used this formula, omitting the details of a sale which easily may have been made by multiple purchases.

A variant of this formula was that in which there was the payment of a total sum for the whole village but with a list of the sellers' names. In 1596, the 'whole' village of Moşăştii was bought from Pistrui. It was formerly a free village which the peasants had to sell 'due to their great poverty and to their excessively heavy taxes'. The village was sold by ten people, whose names are given, for the total sum of 12,000 aspers.

According to a second formula, the village was divided into several large family lines with equal rights. Thus, in 1598, the two hamlets of the village of Găvănești were bought 'from top to bottom, all together', the sellers being 'Dragotă, his brothers and their joint group; and Prodan, his brothers and their joint group', for the total price of 58,000 aspers.

A third formula corresponded to a more advanced stage of disintegration in the village community, each family line selling its patrimony separately, the prices for all family lines being, however, equal. Thus, in 1604, the village of Vladești was sold for the total sum of 36,000 aspers, paid in eight parts of 4,500 each, given to eight family lines, each holding an equal number of three 'strips'.

A fourth formula denoted an even greater degree of disintegration in the village community, the shares being unequal but still based on an initially egalitarian calculation. Thus in 1605, the village of Nucșoara sold its forty-one 'strips' for the total sum of 41,000 aspers. The sellers held unequal shares. The calculation was as follows: four family lines receiving in payment 1,000 aspers; eighteen family lines receiving 2,000 aspers; and two family lines receiving 500 aspers, each 'strip' being valued at 1,000 aspers. It turned out that the village was initially divided into forty-one equal parts. But at the time of the sale, four family lines owned only one 'strip', eighteen family lines owned two, and two had no more than one half each. The village continued, however, to live as a community, for the boyar paid the sale price giving the village collectivity 6,000 aspers in cash, five horses at 2,500 each, six oxen at 2,000, six cows at 1,750, a total of 35,000 aspers' worth of livestock. The manner in which these villages managed to divided up the cash and animals is, however, not described.

A final formula involved a series of sales made within the same village but by households holding unequal shares no longer traceable to an initial division into equal 'strips'. It was the same case we have already analysed, without any preliminary fraternization being necessary: one after another, all the villagers were bought up, with the mention that all were paid for 'and none may say he was not paid...and there was no longer a free man in the village'. In 1592, the peasants from the village of Rabega 'forced by their great poverty and want, due to taxes', sold their liberty. The village was divided into 'lengths' which were

TABLE 8. *Payment for the village of Rabega, 1592*

First section	Second section
3,000 aspers to 4 men	3,600 aspers to 1 man
2,500 aspers to 1 man	2,400 aspers to 1 man
2,000 aspers to 2 men	2,140 aspers to 1 man
1,500 aspers to 5 men	2,100 aspers to 2 men
1,000 aspers to 1 man	1,600 aspers to 2 men
750 aspers to 2 men	1,200 aspers to 1 man
	1,070 aspers to 1 man
	900 aspers to 1 man
	800 aspers to 2 men
	740 aspers to 1 man
	600 aspers to 2 men
	400 aspers to 2 men
	300 aspers to 1 man
	200 aspers to 1 man
28,500 aspers to 15 men	28,500 aspers to 19 men

purchased in two slices. The payment received by the men in each section is shown in table 8. The first slice was acquired at the cost of twenty-five aspers per 'length', the second at a lower price of twenty aspers per 'length'.

Numbers of sales into serfdom

The documents do not provide us with exact statistics on these kinds of self-sales, either by individuals or by whole units. Their terseness and formalistic clauses, often deliberately misleading, raise controversies and make them difficult to interpret. It is especially difficult to determine their chronology, as many purchases were only confirmed by later documents which related simply that a certain village sold itself 'at the time of the ancient voivodes', or 'a long time ago'. Even when the name of the voivode was given, it does not help much, for during the period from 1521 to 1627, there were twenty-four voivodes, but forty-three changes in the throne, the voivodes struggling among themselves by intrigue and revolt to oust each other. Thus there were reigns lasting only a few months, others lasting several years, and voivodes who succeeded in coming back to power three or four times.

As a result we must order the sales documents by voivode and not chronologically (see table 9). However, a general trend can be discerned, marking *grosso modo* an ascending line of purchases. There were four distinct periods: two when the purchases began; another, under the

TABLE 9. *Trends in purchases according to sales documents, in order of voivode*

		Self-sales		Repurchases		Lawsuits			
						Villages		Individuals	
		Villages	Individuals	Villages	Individuals	Won	Lost	Won	Lost
Neagoe	1512–21	—	1	—	1	—	—	—	—
Vlad Vintilă	1532–5	—	—	—	1	—	—	—	1
Radu the Monk	1535–45	1	—	7	1	—	—	—	2
Mircea the Shepherd	1545–59	—	—	—	1	—	1	1	—
Pătrașcu the Good	1554–7	—	—	1	1	—	—	—	—
Radu Ilie	1552–3	1	—	—	—	1	—	—	—
I Total		2	1	8	5	1	1	1	3
Peter the Young	1559–68	23	5	3	2	—	2	1	3
Alexander II	1568–77	1	—	7	5	—	4	1	—
Mihnea Turcitul	1577–91	4	—	5	1	—	34	—	—
Peter Cercel	1583–5	—	—	1	1	—	4	—	—
II Total		28	5	16	9	—	44	2	3
Ștefan Surdu	1591–2	2	1	2	—	—	—	—	—
Alexander the Bad	1592–3	8	4	—	—	—	2	—	—
Michael the Brave	1593–1601	185	14	—	1	6	9	1	—
Nicolae	1601	1	—	—	1	—	—	—	1
III Total		196	19	2	2	6	11	1	1
Simion Movilă	1601	8	7	4	—	1	6	—	—
Radu Mihnea	1601–23	6	6	33	20	13	16	10	19
Radu Șerban	1602–20	41	12	10	1	1	14	8	1
Gavril Movilă	1616–20	1	1	21	6	2	3	4	8
Alexander Iliaș	1616–18	—	1	11	6	—	3	1	5
Alexander Cuconul	1623–7	8	9	5	17	1	8	2	9
IV Total		64	36	84	50	18	50	25	42
TOTAL		290	61	110	66	25	106	29	49

reign of the voivode Michael the Brave (1593–1601), when a maximum was swiftly reached, and finally a fourth when the sales began to dwindle. They disappeared totally only towards the beginning of the eighteenth century.

12 ✦ First signs of the failure of serfdom

The trend toward liberation of the serfs by repurchase

Paradoxically, the crisis which raged in the village communities and resulted in the purchase of free villages and the transition to serfdom was accompanied by an opposite trend that ultimately ended serfdom. At first rather timidly, then more and more strongly, these liberations of serfs grew and ended in the decrees of Constantin Mavrocordat which, in 1746 in Wallachia and in 1749 in Moldavia, abolished the boyar's property right over the peasant's physical person.

A distinction must be made, however, between peasant collectivities which repurchased their liberty and their lands and individual peasants, hereditary serfs from long ago, who freed themselves without any longer having a right to land, thus 'only with their head', or only free in their physical person.

Reconstruction of the free peasant communities, by repurchase from serfdom. The purchase in whole, or by large or small lots, of a total peasant collectivity was often followed by repurchase, the serf community again becoming a free community. What were the motives and the circumstances which prompted the boyars to accept repurchase of their serfs?

It is not possible to deny the fact that there were cases in which human charity played a part. For example, in 1622 a boyar, himself having fallen into slavery during the war, commanded his family to liberate his serfs. It was particularly liberations made in wills which had this character, though their greatest frequency in the seventeenth century was a sign that a change of opinion had already been felt. It was a sign in itself of the beginning of the decline of serfdom as a social institution. Similarly, in 1617, a princely document liberating a whole village stated that the boyars, husband and wife now old, first intended to give this village to a monastery as charity. But later they thought that this would serve no one, only increasing their sins and multiplying the curses upon them, for it was a question of Christian Wallachians and not gypsies. And thus the boyaress Baloşina and her husband Dima decided to free these serfs as an act of charity, with all their 'strips' and their cleared lands and all their buildings, so that they might feed themselves and be *cneji* [free] and perform charitable deeds so that they will no longer be serfs, ever, for anyone.

The voivode spoke thus 'to the village of Vîlsăneşti and to all the old men and inheritors of the village, so that the "strips" and territory and clearings of Vîlsăneşti be in peace and free from all serfdom, for all'. This document was certainly sincere, for the donating couple took care to leave their family line 12,000 aspers so that no one would complain.

Such liberations by testament, common in the seventeenth century, invoked charity 'for the repose of the family's souls' (1617 and 1620), and 'for the repose of my soul and that of my relatives and may this be a perpetual gift' (1627)'. The donor sometimes took care to provide 'that the village and the serfs be pardoned and from thenceforth no one be allowed to give them orders except God and the voivode of the land then in power...but [this] only after the death of my wife' (1620). This sort of liberation in testaments thus provided the condition that until one's death and that of one's family, the serfs had to continue caring for them and maintaining them: 'May they be near me as they were before they were sold [back].' 'May they obey and nourish us and work for us as much as we need, until our death.' These phrases often occurred in these documents made 'under the influence of the fear of death'.

But in most cases, the appeal to the sentiments of human pity was no more than a simple stylistic form. Giving the peasants the right to repurchase themselves constituted a source of revenue tempting to the state and the boyars once they were short of money. Thus the monastery of Cotmeana, 'losing its belongings and its livestock', agreed in 1617 to let one of its serfs repurchase himself by paying two cows with their calves and 1,000 coins in cash so that 'he might be free on his hereditary patrimony'. Or, in 1625, the voivode of the country stated that a boyar 'guilty of a deed against me, as he killed a serf from his village named Anghel', did not have the money to pay his fine. He thus freed three of his serfs for the sum of 19,900 aspers, 'so that they might be free, as they were earlier'.

This dual motive for freeing serfs, commercial and humanitarian, was perfectly expressed in a document of 1619 in which the great boyar Preda Buzescu, son-in-law of Michael the Brave, and his wife Florica, 'desire from the bottom of their heart to render charity but also to obtain money' by freeing ninety-one men from the village of Slaveni for 30,000 aspers (ten men for 500 aspers, thirteen for 1,000 and five for 2,000). Another document, concerning the same boyar, proclaimed that

it has happened that the *joupan* Preda the *postelnic* [chamberlain] and the boyaress Florica, his wife, had many financial difficulties and obligations, and not having the money necessary to pay what they owed, they went to their villages to get the money, by repurchase from serfdom. But only the village of Gostavăţul had the means to rebuy itself from serfdom.

In fact, only half this village was able to repurchase itself (1617):

Michael the Brave himself, though so rapacious a buyer of serfs, sold their liberty to numerous villages which he had just recently bought. Thus a document of 1614 tells the story of such a village, which had sold itself, against its will, because of a debt of 15,000 aspers:

Then his lordship became very worried because of insufficient funds to pay his mercenaries who were accompanying him to German lands. So the late voivode Michael had no solution but to send his boyar Panait, the ban of Hotărani, to all the inheritors of the village of Întorsura de Sus...so that they might pay money to rebuy themselves from serfdom to the state and become free.

'When Michael the voivode was master of Transylvania', states another document, 'all the villages of the country rose up to free themselves and the villagers of Loloieşti, they, too, rose up and went to Belgrade to Michael the voivode and cried at his feet saying that they had been forced to sell themselves.' Mentions of such occurrences at Belgrade (now called Alba Iulia) in Transylvania are numerous in the documents of the seventeenth century.

Even in the days of Michael, there were already protests against unfair sales, which explains why, in certain cases, Michael sensed the need to justify himself: 'And I can only swear, because the Good Lord is himself witness that these men came of their own free will, forced by no one, and sold their patrimonies, giving me also their old documents of inheritance.' But his successors were not of the same opinion, claiming that 'Michael the voivode took many villages by force which he reduced to serfdom', being 'an unfair voivode' (1619).

The great crisis of serfdom raging at the time of Michael the Brave, once passed, gave way to a whole series of law suits. All those, boyars as well as peasants, who had suffered under the hard social order of this voivode, came to protest before the voivodes who succeeded him and who, for the most part, were his bitter enemies. Simion Movilă, his Moldavian rival, who replaced him on the throne, stated that 'the deceased voivode Michael once bought this village and many others, with money from the state treasury. Then he lost all these villages, as well as his country, because of his betrayal of the honoured Emperor, and lost even his head.' As a result, Simion resorted to a radical measure, confirmed by a later document: 'After Michael the voivode, it was voivode Simion who became prince and master of Wallachia. Hence his lordship called all the villages of the country which had been bought by the deceased voivode Michael so that they might appear together before him in order to buy themselves back from serfdom.' Radu Şerban, who succeeded Simion, 'took pity and freed all the villages belonging to the state domain so that they might be free again with their patrimonies just as they once were', although they had to pay him.

For, in fact, all these repurchases had, at base, as goal, the hardly philanthropic desire to fill the state coffers. Thus, in 1615, the village of Caraula, composed of fifteen family lines, brothers and sons, as well as 'all their patrimonial brothers', reduced by Michael the Brave to serfdom due to unpaid taxes, came before the voivode Radu Şerban who freed them, arguing that: 'This being my kingdomn, seeing so many tears and sins among these men... I took pity on them and freed them, just as I did with other villages bought by Michael the voivode', which, however, did not prevent him from collecting the sum of 300 gold coins, worth at least double the original purchase price.

This was not an exceptional case. The village of Întorsura de Sus had sold itself for 15,000 aspers, and it bought itself back for 40,000. Retaken by force by another boyar, this time it paid the sum of 98,000. Thus, originally bought for 15,000, it repurchased itself for a total of 138,000. The village of Homurile sold for 7,000 aspers and bought itself back for 13,000, the document stating that 'this village gave two aspers for one so that it might be free' (1614). The village of Sulariul sold itself for 40,000 aspers and rebought itself for 80,000; that of Craioviţa gave 60,000 for 36,000 (1619), and so on.

The voivodes of the country only had a right to free the villages of the state domain or those belonging to them privately. Thus it had to be determined for each village bought by Michael the Brave whether it had been bought by him as boyar, from his own pocket, or as voivode, from the state treasury. A 'register of the villages of the voivode Michael' was used, which, unfortunately, has not come down to us. This register could not have been very precise, however, as there were controversies. In 1623, the villagers of Grozăveşti, claiming they had sold themselves as state serfs, demanded to rebuy themselves. When Michael's register was consulted and the village was not found listed in it, the request was rejected. In 1619, the village of Crăişani made the same request and the voivode declared himself willing to grant it liberty. But the boyar Preda proved that this village had been bought by Michael when he was a simple boyar, obliging the voivode not to grant repurchase, the decision depending on the evidence in Michael the Brave's register.

Sometimes the voivode went beyond this rule, despite the grievance he caused another boyar, who undoubtedly was not one of his friends. The village of Glubavi, composed of fourteen 'names', had sold its freedom to Michael the Brave. 'But at the time of the voivode Şerban, all the villages belonging to the state domain bought by Michael the deceased voivode' could be repurchased. However, in the meantime, the village of Glubavi had been given to a boyar. In the reign of Alexander this village offered the sum of 330 gold coins to regain its freedom. The boyar refused. 'But Alexander, seeing that the boyar did not want to accept the money, took the money from the villagers and gave them their liberty.' Under Gabriel Movilă, the boyar reclaimed the village which was restored to him. The village offered at this time forty *ughi*. The boyar took the money but refused to recind the original sales documents. The villagers fled to the other side of the Danube, to the Turks, 'destroying the village and the taxes completely because of serfdom'. The voivode recalled them. They returned. But they again protested that the boyar 'once again oppresses them to reduce them to serfdom'. The law suit was judged, and, when the village paid an additional sixty *ughi*, it was freed.

There were cases where the perseverence of the peasants in pursuing their freedom was quite dramatic. Let us cite the twin villages of Pleniţa and Păstăi. The 'large and small' villagers came before the voivode Peter Cercel (1583–5) to retake their freedom. They invoked old documents emanating from Mircea (1545–59) and from his son, Peter (1559–68). The boyars on their side invoked documents emanating from Vlad the Monk (1521–2), Radu (1523–4) and Vlad (1530–3), documents which have not come down to us. The boyars won their case. The peasants had already protested twice in vain, in the reigns of Pătraşcu (1554–7) and Mihnea (1577–83). Then, they returned a fourth time under Michael (1593–1601), again under Radu Şerban (1602–20) and during the course of the two reigns of Radu Mihnea (1601–2 and 1611–13). But as their adversaries were the powerful boyars of the

Buzeşti family, they did not succeed in safeguarding their liberty. In the same way a serf bought his freedom by paying to the woman who held him three oxen, and 400 silver aspers, then to her sons two oxen and a horse, and again to their inheritors 2,100 aspers (1617).

If a boyar was not short of money, he categorically opposed any attempt on the part of his serfs to buy their freedom. The most numerous cases were those in which a boyar sold freedom to his serfs, immediately following which another boyar, with a right to pre-emption or with other rights, proclaimed his right, 'throwing the money' to the serfs and forcing them to belong to him. An early document of this kind was the one of 1533 in which the voivode stated that the buyers of 'parts' of a village, the priest Stanciul and another, named Nagîlea, were serfs and consequently gave the right to a boyaress to 'throw money at these serfs' and to take over their rights. The trial was said to have been judged 'according to the ancient law of the Good Lord'. The same procedure was to be applied more and more frequently, from century to century until the Law of 1864.

Let us cite a few other cases. In 1571, the sons of the boyaress Calea sold to their serfs the tenth share of the village of Cepturile, for 2,000 silver aspers, 'of the field, the forest, the hill, of vineyards as well as eight acres of vineyards'. But their mother Calea knew nothing of this sale. Profiting from this fact, another boyar, declaring himself 'patrimonial brother' with Calea, restored the 2,000 aspers to the serfs who, from then on, had to belong to him. In 1614, the boyar Buzescu protested because, when he had donated a share of one of his villages to a monastery, the monastery sold this share to the serfs. The boyar did not agree, saying, 'he does not want to accept being brothers with these serfs, in his village'. He thus returned the sum of 20,000 aspers paid by the serfs.

In 1624, Staicu, the cup bearer, freed his serfs 'due to his needs and granted them the possibility of freeing themselves from him'. They reached agreement amicably and the village of Frăţeşti gave 205 *ughi*. 'But the *joupan* Trufanda, grand *postelnic*, having learned that these serfs had rebought themselves and were free in the same village as himself, did not want to accept it and subjected them, according to law, before the Divan, and returned the paid sum 'for the honoured dignitary of my lordship held in the above-named patrimony of Frăţeşti, as well as a number of serfs, a third part, much more than other boyars; and it was a question of hereditary serfs who had never been free' (1624). This was a most important detail as it was the only one enabling us to assume the existence of two kinds of repurchase, that of formerly free serfs and that of hereditary serfs.

The law suits between boyars and serfs judged by the voivode concerning liberty, were concluded for the most part in the boyar's favour. In all, we have been able to number 209 litigations, only fifty-four of which were concluded in the peasants' favour (see table 9 above). Once they lost, the peasants saw themselves destined not only to remain serfs but also to undergo rather serious arbitrary punishment. Thus, for example, they were 'placed outside the Divan to their great humiliation' (1620). 'Having betrayed us like a thief, a peasant's documents were destroyed and we sent him away from the Divan of my kingdom, mistreated' (1620). 'I shaved the head of a serf from the village, as well as his beard, and sent him to work in the salt mines, for he lied to gain his liberty' (1615). 'Having used a false and a dishonest document, they were sent away from the Divan in great humiliation, imprisoned, and fined' (1624). 'I beat him, my lordship, very hard' (1623). 'I sent them away from the Divan of my lordship, humiliating them and having them soundly beaten before me, in the middle of the courtyard, for having lied, as they had cheated before all the voivodes to escape from serfdom' (1622).

The appearance of free peasants without land

Binding the peasants to the soil was a way of securing sufficient manpower when it began to run short, but paradoxically, the wish to bind the peasants to the soil was accompanied by the wish to empty a village of peasants once they became undesirable. A peasant could be undesirable for two reasons: first, if he was indigenous with a hereditary patrimony in a traditional village community, the boyar would prefer to throw him out and replace him with a newcomer with no ties to the land, having only personal relations with the boyar. The boyar would grant the newcomer the right to use the land according to conditions agreed upon more or less amicably. Secondly, peasants were undesirable if their number exceeded that needed by the boyar to cultivate his lands.

At the same time that the peasants were being bound to the soil, boyars began forcing 'liberations' of a new kind, making the peasants leave the village in order to free their patrimonies for the boyars. Thus the boyars obtained manpower by breaking the ties which bound the serfs to their 'strips', transforming them into serfs *adscripti glebae* and, on the other hand, they got rid of the undesirable peasants by 'freeing' them, 'their head only', that is, while keeping their land and making them leave the village. In 1623, the serf Bolovan paid his boyar the sum of 17,000 aspers and four horses to be freed from serfdom, 'but only him and all the sons God grants him, not his brothers or his nephews or his hereditary lands'.

There were disputes. In 1610, some boyars claimed that certain peasants were their serfs; the serfs maintained they were not and that their houses had been burned and that they had been chased from the village. Liberations by testament were also made in the same way: 'the servants he had in the village of Balomireşti, if they want to remain in the village and work for the holy monastery that will be good. But if they do not wish to, they are free to go where they wish and no one will bother them' (1609). A document of 1622 categorically stated: 'he may go where he wishes; but he takes with him his tax load'.

The formula 'they may go where they wish' became common, even during the high point of serfdom. The point was clear, freeing a peasant was very often a way of getting rid of him. In 1621 a boyar who sold his village mentioned clearly that he sold territory, not an inhabited village, for 'the inhabitants have bought their liberty, they became free peasants and were chased out of the village'. Let us note clearly: not 'left willingly', but 'chased out'. Sending them away from the village 'so that they might go where they wished, in the country of my lordship' thus became the new formula, indicating a new set of social conditions different from the old ones.

Demography and social forms

All serfdom is related to a demographic problem. As long as a boyar's village is sufficiently populated, there is no need to tie the peasants to the soil. It is only lack of manpower that makes serfdom necessary. But underpopulation can be absolute or relative. It is *absolute* when there is a loss of population due to the death of inhabitants following wars, epidemics, or famines. It is *relative* when it is caused by social conditions forcing the peasants to desert their village.

This is a most complex problem, subject to an internal dialectic, in the course of which absolute and relative population loss form a single system, involving vast geographic areas in which there is a double disequilibrium, both demographic and social. In the whole area of south-eastern Europe the continual wars between Turks, Russians,

Romanians, Hungarians and Austrians successively devastated one region after another. Wishing to escape the brutality of war, not only the massacres but also enslavement and deportation, the inhabitants fled in masses, hiding in the mountains, in the forests or in other sheltered areas. Once the crisis had passed, the country slowly became repopulated. It would have been normal for each to return to his homeland. But the runaways preferred to seek new areas rather than to return to those where they had lived before.

This was crucial. The boyars of depopulated areas wanted to repopulate them at all costs. When they were not able to do it by force, *manu militari*, they at least tempted the runaways by offering them, on the basis of 'contracts' agreed to amicably, better living conditions than those of their native villages.

On the other hand, the boyars owning well-populated villages wished to prevent their villagers from fleeing toward the areas where better 'contracts' could be made and where peasants could be freer. Thus they tried to impose their right to bring the peasants back by force, that is, to bind them to the soil. So, in the course of this bitter competition raging within the boyar class, two social orders were born and conflicted: that of serfdom and that of 'corvée' villages where peasants were not legally bound to the soil. The peasant masses had a choice between these two orders, but only by running away and at their risk and peril. Those from the devastated regions whose origins had been lost moved easily. The Romanian peasants did not hesitate, if need be, even to cross the boundaries heading either towards the Ukrainian steppes or towards the Balkans, crossing the Danube in winter when the river was frozen. It was even more usual for them to travel to another one of the three Romanian countries, Wallachia, Moldavia or Transylvania. On the other hand, other peasants crossing the same boundaries in the other direction arrived in masses. A demographic mix-up developed during the seventeenth and eighteenth centuries, with a double movement of emigrations and immigrations, irregularly depopulating and repopulating vast areas. Social currents followed the emptying and filling of areas and the new forms of social life were consolidated, indicating two distinct levels of social evolution.

The free peasant areas

Let us first look at the state's fiscal interests. Taxes were not the least of the ills the peasants had to suffer. Not only war, epidemics and famine but also taxes forced the peasants to flee. When a peasant could no longer bear his poverty, burdened with debts beyond his means, he no longer had any choice but to flee. 'To pay one's taxes with flight' has remained until today a common expression meaning any desertion. To prevent these fiscal evasions, the state, while forbidding the running away of peasant debtors, softened the taxes, at least near the border areas of the country, even forbidding collection during the winter when the Danube was frozen. 'To make someone cross the Danube' is, incidentally, another Romanian expression, still common, meaning to make life hard for someone.

But the Turks judged harshly those countries that became depopulated, making the Wallachian and Moldavian voivodes responsible for their poor administration. The latter thus did their best to bring back the runaways as well as encouraging the immigration of foreign peasants. Through its messengers, the state opened discussions with the runaways, inquiring about the reasons for their refusal to return, tempting them with promises.

For example, in 1756, the voivode Constantine Racoviţă of Moldavia claimed that in his country there were too many places with a dearth of people, the villages having been abandoned long ago. Some of them had been abandoned for no one knew how long nor did anyone know who owned them. The times were very difficult and taxes excessive. But in the border countries there were many inhabitants and runaway Moldavian peasants. The voivode therefore sent emissaries to discuss the problem with the delegates of the runaways who were two or three priests and four or five peasants. The voivode's emissaries tried to convince them to come back. Even 'the serfs will have nothing to fear from their masters, as no one will take them from the homes they have chosen' (1742). 'Try', the voivode advised his emissary, 'to encourage as many people as possible to recross the border; and to get them to settle in the country' (1742).

To get them to return, the state offered them the conditions of a new type of life in the form of peasant 'freedoms' (*slobozii*). It offered them real advantages, most interesting to us as they tell us directly what the free peasant communities at the time must have been like: there was a striking similarity to what we already know of this type of village from direct field research in contemporary communities. In 1602, the voivode Simion Movilă decided that the system offered to 'certain Albanians of Cerveni Voda who came from Turkey to the land of my lordship, to the village of Călineşti in the county of Prahova [in Wallachia]', would be the following:

May they be in peace concerning the payment of oxen, bushels [of grain], hay, the tithe of bees and the tax on sheep and pigs and all the taxes going to the state, for the tithe on home products and their belongings; and they will not have to give horses for the *olac* nor the wine tax. And may the 'bans' of the county not apply in this village, and likewise may they not be judged by the servants of my lordship or those of the boyars.

They were thus given a total fiscal exemption. Even the payment of the *bir*, the cash tax, was eliminated for a period of ten years. The state then proposed, once this period had elapsed, a system of 'subscription'.

May they pay only the *haraci* [tribute owed to the Turks] owed to the honoured Emperor of the Orient, 15,000 aspers per year; and may they pay these aspers, half on the day of St George and half on the day of St Dimitrius. And may the tax collectors not enter their village but may they send this sum directly to the treasury of my lordship.

As for the internal system of the village, the greatest liberties were granted:

Any man who is guilty will be judged by the holders of the village elected by the peasants themselves. And he who incurs the death penalty will be bound by the elders and brought to my court to be judged and hanged...And likewise, any man who comes to settle, be he Bulgarian, Greek, Albanian or Hungarian, if he is a righteous man and if the village and village elders accept him, may live in peace and quiet. But he who causes trouble, upsetting the village or he whom the village and the elders will not accept, will be chased out and have to return to where he came from.

Thus a free village was instituted, without a local boyar, according to the model of the free villages.

In 1615, the village of Popşa was transformed into a privileged village:

And not only the serfs there but also any other wishing to settle in this village in the country of my lordship, any man without a master, whether from the villages of my lordship or from the villages of the boyars or the monasteries, only free without owing any back taxes or tithes, if they wish to obey and work for the holy monastery, are free to take up residence here.

In 1614, a boyar received a village belonging to the voivode, depopulated for more than twenty years. A total fiscal exemption was granted for three years to any man 'who would like to come settle in this village, whether he be Serbian, Hungarian, Moldavian, Greek, or of our country; but he must be free from any back taxes or tithes'. At the end of these three years 'my lordship decided amicably with them that they were to give me sixty Hungarian gold ducats in two payments each year, bringing them themselves to the state treasury'.

These oases of relative liberty among the mass of serf villages thus had the quality of encouraging not only the return of the runaways but also the territorial displacement of 'free peasants without land'. Even the serfs bound to the soil as well as the insolvent debtors were tempted to leave their villages by fraud to go to the privileged villages. Moreover, a good number of boyars, wishing to repopulate their villages, received from the state, if not the concession of a complete system of peasant 'freedoms' (which would not have pleased them), at least fiscal exemptions rendering the life of the peasants lighter and thus increasing their chances of paying the tithes they owed. The state also had its own interest in offering the villages a fiscal system completely different from that of the old tithe in kind, that of fiscal 'subscription', paid in cash, at already fixed rates and terms.

The villages with voluntary contracts

Even without the support of the state, an increasing number of boyars offered newcomers much better work conditions than those of serfs. It was no longer a question of binding them to the soil nor of taking possession of their physical person, but rather of considering them simply as free workers, agreeing by contract to live in the village, perform the necessary work, as much to support their families as to work the lands that the boyars themselves wished to exploit. In the eighteenth century these villages with voluntary contracts began to increase in number and ended by being in the majority.

In 1700, the peasants from the village of Jiblea had fled, unable to pay the interest on a loan. After having wandered around the country, they returned to the village and drew up the following contract with their master: they accepted working three days in the spring and two days in the autumn. They also worked with shovel and axe, when this was demanded. If they refused, they would be driven out and would have to go earn their bread elsewhere.

In 1702, some peasants agreed to a contract obliging them to provide 'two days of ploughing and two others for any other work. And when the time comes to plough and the abbot tells them to provide the corvée, we must be ready to do it in the same day working in common agreement, all on the same day, but only those who are married with their own households.'

The clauses of these contracts varied greatly depending on the local circumstances, the poverty of the men, and the power of the boyar. The small boyars offered better conditions than the large boyars did, with the documents of the period testifying even to flights between contract villages towards the villages of the small boyars.

Rivalry within the boyar class

This new state of affairs, the growth of free areas and contract villages, could hardly appeal to the boyars from areas that were not depopulated, who saw their peasants fleeing one after another, tempted by the better life offered elsewhere. In 1626, a first alarm was given, appearing in a document coming from the synod presided over by Cyrille, patriarch 'of the new Rome and the whole world', archbishop of Constantinople. There it was written

that those who live in 'freedoms' were exempted from all legal duties, taxes and tithes, whereas the others were burdened with taxes; there was the risk that soon no one would do the work necessary to pay the tithes and taxes due to the Emperor and that all would flee to the free areas or that the country would get barer and barer, that it would be completely depopulated with the peasants who were not living in the 'freedoms' emigrating across the border as soon as they had the chance. In the impossibility of remedying these misfortunes, having judged the situation many times and from all angles, and bearing in mind the public interest and justice, it became evident that all the free areas of the boyars, the monasteries and the foreigners had to be annulled, as bringing prejudice against their masters and leading to the destruction of the other Christians and co-workers. Thus, may all pay alike the taxes of the empire as inhabitants of the same ancestral country and undergoing the same duty.

The Metropolitan thus annulled the oaths and curses which formerly bound the contracts of the 'freedoms', 'so that there might not be any more such areas'. However, this did not prevent an exception being granted in favour of the free areas belonging to the Holy See of Alexandria and a few villages of a certain boyar, six villages in all. But this attempt to slow down a social process that the new conditions of the country imposed was in vain. The 'freedoms' and, even more, the contract villages continued to grow in number and to become, little by little, the general rule of the country. There was a clear economic reason for this shift. The work of the serf peasants and those bound to the soil could not equal that of the peasants who were free, though liable to corvée. Moreover, towards the beginning of the eighteenth century, the boyars' domains which were worked by peasant corvée labour could furnish a larger amount of livestock and grain, enough to enter the cycle of international and internal commerce. This was not possible for the villages of quasi-slave peasants.

The boyars' increasing interest in corvées was noticeable at this period. The tithe was set, once and for all, at a rate of 10% which could not be exceeded. But the corvées, of secondary importance in the time of a subsistence economy, were becoming the principal source of profits. They were not fixed at a traditional rate, so they could be reworked for one's benefit. The struggle between these two social systems thus seemed not only inevitable but also necessary to ensure the failure of the quasi-feudal system of exploitation of the village communities by tithes and corvées in favour of the rise of a system of boyar domains worked entirely by corvée labour. This did not prevent the boyars loyal to the old order from seeking a means of defence by reinstituting serfdom, which was thus a belated serfdom that appeared only at this turning point in history, like the last gasp of a world in the process of disappearing, just at the beginning of a new movement towards the capitalist development of the country.

The end of serfdom

But the agony of this second serfdom was very slow. Desperate efforts were made to oppose the flight of serfs bound to the soil, forcing them to return to their village. Documents justifying the boyars in 'laying their hands' on the runaways 'to take them by the neck', numerous in the seventeenth and at the beginning of the eighteenth century, were proof of an excessive severity. The boyars struggled against the competition of the 'freedoms' not by lightening the feudal duties but by aggressive, exaggerated claims of their property right over the serf's physical person.

In 1701 the voivode proclaimed, concerning the serfs who had fled, 'that they are to be seized wherever they are found, in the villages of the state, of the boyars or of the monasteries or in the"freedoms" or among the artisans. They are to be taken with all their belongings and forced to live in their native village(s).' Or 'One has the right to take them with all their property and establish them where one wants', 'they are to be taken by the neck, brought with their wives and their children', 'and they are to be bound and taken by the neck and forced to stay in the village'. A manhunt was organized to please the boyars whose villages had been depopulated, the inhabitants having fled to the contract villages. These boyars had formerly made all efforts to break the traditional ties established between villagers and their patrimonies. They had reached their goal, transforming the 'natives' into 'inhabitants'. But at the same time, they had given them the possibility of leaving, as they were no longer held to the land by anything but force.

It became more and more difficult to bring back the runaways. The rights of the boyars with serfs conflicted not only with the rights of the boyars who had given asylum to the runaways, but also with those of the state. Moreover, once they had settled in another village, the runaways were entered in the fiscal registers. To change the accounts in these registers was not possible. There are even some documents telling the runaways to return home, taking their fiscal debts with them. But the means of controlling these payments could not have been very easy. Thus one sees an increase in the documents in which the state decided that the runaway will have the right to settle where the fiscal census registered him, having to repay the boyar to whom he belonged the amount of six small coins. 'As concerns the serfs registered for taxes, they are to stay where they are registered, paying for their corvées with six coins, called *ort*' (1734). 'They are to pay two *lei* per year, just like the other serfs belonging to other monasteries, who are scattered about' (1745).

Liberation of the peasants by the laws of Constantine Mavrocordat

This social struggle between the peasant class and the feudal class, as well as the struggle within the feudal class between boyars owning serfs bound to the soil and boyars who had made voluntary contracts with their peasants, could not last forever. The system of contract villages had such obvious advantages, not only of decisive economic benefit but also of being able to end the rural revolts and the demographic mix-up caused by the flow of inhabitants from the villages bound to the soil to the contract villages, that finally it had to be admitted that serfdom had become uneconomical, and its psychological and moral anachronism was acknowledged.

On the other hand, the Sultan himself ordered the voivode Constantine Mavrocordat, in 1744: 'You will try, in this period, to raise up and repopulate the country, using softer means, proving your good will; and reestablishing public order, you will bring back all the inhabitants, subjects or non-subjects of the Sultan, serfs or poor, scattered all over because of abuses.' Mavrocordat,[1] imbued with the new political literature of the French Encylcopaedists, and especially desirous of introducing a modern state administration benefiting the country's development, proclaimed a generalization of the system of contract villages. He began by proclaiming in 1746 that all the emigrants who had returned to the country would not have to pay any taxes for six months and would have the right to settle where they wished, with only

1. D. C. Sturdza, *L'Europe orientale et le rôle historique des Mavrocordato*, Paris, 1913.

the obligation of providing six corvée days and the tithe of their produce. The former serfs were freed and given the right to appear before the council of the voivode to obtain passes guaranteeing their new status as peasants, not serfs.

Another step was taken the same year, this time to the benefit of all serf inhabitants, by a document recognizing that the country had 'some old laws which not only were of no usefulness but also were damaging to Christian souls, as, for example, the old and bad custom of serfdom'. Thus it was decided that

any boyar family or monastery with villages of serfs bound to the soil would continue to hold the land, which would belong to them as in the past, but as for the heads of serfs without land, those boyars who wished, of their own free will, to liberate them, from charity, would be looked on with favour; but if they do not wish to do this, to save their souls, the serfs must get along as best they are able and get money to buy their liberty, paying for each soul the sum of ten thalers, either amicably, if their master agrees, or lacking agreement if their master will not take the money, by coming to make a petition at the princely council.

The same voivode, having gone from Wallachia to Moldavia, proclaimed the same rules there in 1749. The assembly of boyars stated that people considered serfdom synonymous with slavery, as many boyars had taken to the habit of selling their serfs like slaves, dividing them up as though they were gypsies, listing them in their dowry papers, separating the children from their parents, taking them as servants in their houses, and making them move from one place to another. It was solemnly declared that serfs were not slaves, but rather peasants without land who did not have the right to leave.

Worsening of the corvées and the trend toward the system of 'urbariums'

In the new type of village born in the period of the Mavrocordat reforms, every local lord considered himself absolute master of his 'domains'. The peasants, in his eyes, were now merely workers of the land, permitted to inhabit his village providing they furnish not only the tithe but also the corvées necessary to work the lands he held. However, this did not mean that the ancient social forms of the village communities disappeared. As we have already seen, it was not only an old tradition, strongly anchored in the customs of the time, that assured the survival of the village communities, but also – and especially – the primitive state of the technology of cultivation and animal raising. Whether one wanted it or not the peasants, even those of the peasant 'freedoms' and even more those settled by voluntary contracts, re-organized their life according to the ancient model of the peasant communities, thus claiming a *right* to cut firewood, to use the land, with free access for their herds, and to make clearings. We have seen, furthermore, that these rights of the peasants remained unchanged even at a later date, the period of the 'corvée' villages of the eighteenth century and until 1864.

It was from another point of view that the village created by the reforms of Mavrocordat was different from the one where serfs were bound to the soil. Apart from the disappearance of the right over the peasant's physical person, there was another fact to consider: the assiduous effort of the boyar class to increase its corvée rights. This was a clear sign of a new economic era being born at this period, that of a seigniorial economy by direct exploitation which increased in importance until it became the major base of the life of the country. One can judge the importance of these increasing seigniorial exploitations by the increasing number of corvée days.

Formerly, the tithes formed the base of the subsistence economy of the boyars. But at this time, they had fallen, in the corvée villages, to second place among the boyars' interests. It was no longer a question of supporting the lord's family and court alone, but rather of producing the maximum amount of wheat merchandise. The corvées and not the tithes thus became first in importance. In addition, the tithes had been traditionally fixed at a tenth of the harvest and could not be raised arbitrarily, whereas the corvées had never followed a fixed rule. We have seen that there was a time when the boyars were forbidden to demand more corvée labour than was necessary to maintain their household. But this 'necessary' amount continued to grow and, when peasants became simple serfs bound to the soil, the boyar was able to impose a system of corvées at will. But at the time of the Mavrocordcat reforms, the serfs bound to the soil disappeared, melting into the mass of so-called 'free' peasants, whose treatment, however, continued to vary from one area to another. To avoid chaos and especially to leagalize the boyar's right to a greater number of corvée days, a series of 'urbarial' rules and administrative decisions appeared, proving that a substantial change had occurred in the relations between boyars and peasants. Aside from the 'establishments' and 'voluntary contracts' between boyars and peasants, the legal and actual situations became equalized in the course of the century, after the Mavrocordat reforms.

Several years earlier, a decision had been reached which called for every man living in the monastery villages to provide six free days of work a year. The peasants do not seem to have been pleased. In the same year, in a letter addressed to a village, Mavrocordat wrote:

Since you were living on the monastery's domain, you were formerly rendering to the monastery as many corvées and other services as the monastery ordered; and in spite of that you were content. But now, my highness, to better your lot, has removed all that and taken the decision, in the document I gave to your abbot, that you only have to work six days a year at any task assigned you and no more, which is a real alleviation, and in spite of that you do not wish to work.

Consequently, the voivode threatened to hang them or send them to forced labour in the salt mines. In 1742, the same voivode, at the request of the monasteries, decided that all those who, while not serfs, lived on church domains, must provide twelve work days. By the proclamation of the abolition of serfdom, Mavrocordat decided in 1749 that all peasants on any domain, whether ecclesiastic or belonging to boyars, would have do to twenty-four days of corvée. The figure then wavered between twenty-four and twelve days, sometimes more, sometimes less.

In 1755, the boyars affirmed in a collective document addressed to the voivode that 'formerly the serfs worked like the gypsy slaves. But liberated by Mavrocordat, they were set at twenty-four corvée days; nonetheless, they continue to work according to custom', thus without a fixed rule. Due to the resultant chaos, the boyars demanded that, as with the tithe, the corvée days be established at a tenth, thus at thirty-six days. This was refused them, but two years layer, they were given two more days. In 1783, the figure came back to twelve days; then, in 1805, it was decided to fix the days at forty. The Organic Regulations again reduced them to twelve.

However, there was an important consideration: no longer able to raise the number of days, the boyars found another means to reach their goal, by giving another definition to 'corvée days' which became calculated not in hours but in quantity of work. Thus it was established what a corvée labourer ought to do in a day, clearing land, working already cleared land, how many hay stacks he ought to make, etc. This system of calculation, in the form eventually given to it by the Organic Regulations, formed the object of a very significant study that Marx wrote in one of the chapters of *Das Kapital*, which ought to be reread for a correct understanding of the problem.

Let us only note that from the time of these 'urbarial' laws the corvée village was officially constituted. As we have already seen, this type of village continued to be 'communal', though in the process of disintegration. The social struggle which followed concerned the boyar's right to more and more corvée days, as well as his right to have more and more of the land worked, and the opposite, conflicting right of the peasants to use all the land sufficient for their needs, and to furnish as little corvée labour as they could get away with. In fact, it was two forms of life, two social conceptions which conflicted: the ancient communal serf village and the new latifundia, of mixed style, larger domains of capitalist production worked by corvée peasants.

We have thus come to modern times. We have tied together the two ends of our study, the one going from the present back into the past and the other, beginning with ancient times, meeting the contemporary period. It only remains to give a general outline of the theoretical conclusions we can draw from our study, while attempting also a chronological reconstruction of the different steps we have described in related sections.

Conclusions
Some theoretical considerations

The communal village: the underlying fabric of Romanian social history

We hope that the reader has been convinced of the special importance of the existence of the peasant communities as a mass phenomenon for Romanian social history. That some of these communities survived into the first decades of the twentieth century underlined this fact. To our knowledge, nowhere in Europe except Romania did such peasant communities remain alive so long and take such a wide variety of forms that, by studying them directly, a social theory could be established.

The result was a deep understanding of the laws by which such communities are born, exist, change form, and eventually dissolve. In the years 1928–46, when our research was carried out, most of them still had a visibly archaic character, so we were obliged to consider them as vestigial remnants of a very distant past. This prompted us to take them as the starting point in an inverse study of social history, which returned, step by step, to ancient times, when the Romanian countries, after they had been abandoned by the Roman administration and had lived for a thousand years under the domination of a whole series of nomadic peoples from the Asiatic steppes, succeeded in the thirteenth century in setting up their own states through 'reconquest'.

The problem of 'feudalism'

The first document confirming the existence of state-like forms set up by Romanians dates from 1247.[1] It says that there was already a dominating aristocracy (the *maiores terrae*) with a warrior force (an *apparatus bellicus*), able to collect tithes on agricultural products from the

---

1. Câmpina, in his 'Le problème de l'apparition des Etats féodaux roumains', tries to put the date back to the tenth century.

villages as well as to demand certain corvée labour (*utilitatum et redditum ac servitiorum*). It is even more likely that in the following centuries, when these many forms were united into a single state, and when the voivode declared himself autonomous and absolute master of his territory, this aristocracy emerged clearly as a distinct 'social class', so to speak, ruling over a peasant class.

What was the nature of such a social form? Was it a feudal system, as others believed? We first have to define 'feudal system'. Some consider it a structure belonging to a ruling class. Thus 'without vassals, without fiefs, without a social and political organization based on the private ties of a particular nature, there can be no feudal system'. But others conceive of the feudal system as the particular social structure of a whole society, according to which a landowning class imposes on the class which actually works the land the obligation of providing tithes and corvées, 'serfdom' and not the 'fief' being the distinctive sign of this system. We are rather inclined to accept the second definition of 'feudalism', for if in the Romanian countries serfdom existed, the fief system did not.

Nevertheless, a good many historians believe otherwise. According to them, the first Romanian state forms can be seen as an exact replica of western feudalism, characterized by the existence of a class with landed property *ab initio*, able, as landowners, to impose on the peasants the harsh system of the *adscripti glebae*, with heavy tithes and corvée labour. The nobles are also seen as having been bound by vassal oaths to a sovereign, the voivode of the country. However, this explanation of a social state by the invocation of a few legal principles, such as that of 'property' and of the supreme right of the monarch, is not acceptable. Property and monarchical rights cannot explain a social problem since they, too, must be explained.

It is better never to consider a human society as the result of legal principles but rather as a link in a long historical chain of events that are forever unfolding. Thus, one can only understand western feudal society by refusing to explain it entirely by the rules of feudal law. Instead it is necessary to study the social conditions which made feudalism possible and which, according to the scholars specializing in this topic, fell generally into the following pattern: in the old Roman provinces, the society of the early middle ages was built on the ruins of slave-based and colonial latifundia, following the conquest by barbarian warriors who took over by force the pre-existing social forms, thus replacing the old landowners and inheriting their slaves or colonized peoples. In quasi-autonomous groups, their armies then took over an already formed society which they divided into a hierarchical order of many levels along a descending ladder with sovereigns, vassals and subvassals. They had many immunities, making up numerous small states within one large state, more nominal than real.

Could such a social system have been born in areas which, not having been part of a Roman province, did not have any slave-based or colonial latifundia and where the conquerors were not like the confederated Germanic armies which settled on the land of the conquered country? It must be remembered that in 1247 the lands inhabited by the Romanians had not been part of the Roman Empire for almost a thousand years. There is no question here of large slave or colonial domains or of a class of large local landowners. Even at the time of the Roman conquest, we have absolutely no proof of the existence of such domains; and furthermore, after the Romans left Dacia, the Romanian countries experienced only the rural life of the village communities: The barbarian conquerors of Dacia did not settle permanently on Romanian soil, with the single exception of the Hungarians, who conquered only one of the three Romanian countries, Transylvania.

The social premises of western feudalism were lacking completely in the Romanian countries. We must thus refer to a different theoretical schema from that of western feudal law in order to understand the social character of the first Romanian states. Let us not get involved in the theory of feudalism, whatever it may mean. Rather, let us analyse the facts themselves. The theoretical framework to be adopted must take into account the following:

(a) The existence of village communities, at the dawn of Romanian history, organized by large tribal confederations under the leadership of a tribal aristocracy of *knez* and voivodes that had emerged from ancient local 'chieftainships'.

(b) The existence of a nomad conquest, exploiting this mass of village communities through a purely fiscal system, like that used by the nomads over all their huge empires. In the absence of any written information concerning the Romanian countries, we must make use of what we know about this system of fiscal exploitation as it was used in Russia under the Tartars and in Asia under the Mongols.

(c) Knowing the social laws of the village communities and the system of fiscal exploitation of the nomads, we must be aware of what the relations between the village communities and the conquering nomads must have been in order to understand the social formation which the first autochthonous Romanian states inherited.

The problem of the 'predatory states'

The nomads set up in each of their conquered countries 'predatory states'. The horsemen of the steppe did not take possession of the land. They were content with subjecting the local population, which was allowed to live according to its own customs. There was a purely fiscal exploitation bearing on all aspects of economic life; customs duty on all transit commerce, international and local, customs duty on all large-scale river fishing, customs duty on the salt mines, duty in the 'towns' on all manufactured products, duty on agricultural production in cereals and livestock, and, in addition, the imposition of non-economic corvées – the construction and maintenance of the *olac* roads, the construction and maintenance of fortifications, the improvement of the road network, and the imposition of corvée labour to transport men and goods along the same roads.

With the rhythm of successive waves of nomadic peoples, these 'predatory states', in turn, all took on the character of 'substitution states', the new arrivals inheriting the system set up by their predecessors and simply adding a new ruling layer. In such circumstances, an assimilation of the indigenous population with the nomads could not take place. At most a kind of symbiosis between the nomad aristocracy and the local aristocracy was possible, that is, between nomad chiefs and village chiefs charged with the task of collecting the tithes for the nomads (but also for their own profit) and simultaneously responsible for collecting the tribute. This layer of local aristocracy was thus able to become a social class of its own, bearing the Turanian name of 'boyars'.

From the time that the great Turanian migrations of peoples ended, as the Petchenegs, Cumans, and Tartars finally withdrew, this new class of local boyars was able to 'reconquer' the land at the expense of its former masters and, in its turn, take its place in the state system created by the nomads. It continued to collect tribute, no longer as agents of the nomads, but for itself.

What could the character of the Romanian state formations have been? At any rate, not that of feudalism. The class of Romanian boyars was never a hierarchic class, with a sovereign at the top of a descending ladder of vassals and subvassals. We have no record of the existence of real immunities granted by the state, at least at first. The laws of the Tartar *Tarcan* in the form of fiscal exemptions, which were used in the Romanian countries, have nothing in common with feudal immunities.

Nothing of classic feudal law is to be found aside from a few stylistic clauses in the format of the documents; this was only an imitation of the diplomatic norms of foreign chancelleries.

The Romanian countries had a completely different state social formation, called *Domnie*, which was just a central organ of the boyar class, meant to administer the country insofar as was necessary to bring in the taxes, police the roads, organize a customs network, and oblige the villages to pay the tithes. Hence it was still a matter of fiscal exploitation, by 'tribute', not based on landownership but rather on the titular power of the state chief, that is, the chief of the warrior class (*voivode* meaning 'warrior chief'), who, though master of the country, did not also own it. The economic base of this class of boyars, who did not yet possess large holdings or fiscal immunities, was weak, and they were in competition with the central royal power. Their only recourse was to become parasitic exploiters of the communal villages. In the beginning the boyars were only 'masters' of a few villages, as chiefs of the local population and at the most as 'nominal' owners of the village lands. They had the right to certain tithes and corvées, inheriting the fiscal law that had been established by the nomads. They were able to extend their rights only very slowly by gradual modifications in the village popular assemblies as well as in the fiscal laws of the state, which favoured them, moreover, with *fiscal* exemptions.

To understand the social status of this class of boyars at the next stage when they took full control over their villages (except for the free villages which continued over the centuries to be attached only fiscally to the central organs of the state), it is necessary to know first how these village communities administered themselves, that is, what were the rights and duties of the village assemblies. The status of the 'feudal landowners' (if one is willing to use the term) was an exact copy of the status of the assemblies, as the village chief had succeeded in conquering his former co-villagers by a gradual take-over of the rights of the assemblies. By making a parallel between the status of the assemblies and the status of the boyars, the mechanism of the feudal conquest of the villages can be convincingly explained.

The problem of 'Asiatic despotism'

These state formations were not 'feudal' (and even less 'slave states'). It is possible, however, to consider them as belonging to the category of 'Asiatic despotism'? Let us put aside the negative connotation of the words 'Asiatic' and 'despotism' and look at the question purely factually. An 'Asiatic despotism'[2] is a system of social life characterized in the following way:

> existence of an absolute state power, responsible for an administration with an economic goal, which in most cases is the construction and maintenance of a network of irrigation canals;
> thus, it is mostly a 'hydraulic' society, at least in the countries where this kind of social life was born, before spreading to the 'marginal zones';
> existence of an administrative class, of a 'bureaucracy';
> existence of an economic base made up of village communities;
> from this comes the 'stagnant' character of this kind of social life, which could not evolve except through the introduction of outside forces.

Except for the existence, as an economic base, of village communities, none of these characteristics can be found in Romanian history. The voivode was not an absolute despot; he had no economic responsibility to fulfil concerning hydraulic works; he did not have access to a bureaucratic social class; and we maintain that, far from being stagnant and isolated, the Romanian countries evolved rapidly, from one social type to a completely different one in several centuries, within a continental complex comprising both west and east.

But does this mean then that we are dealing with a social formation that does not fit any of the types established by classical theory as it was once formulated by the Marxist school (slave, feudal, capitalist, socialist), with the type 'Asiatic despotism' only a lateral link in this unilineal typology? In our opinion, this type of social formation, the Romanian *Domnie*, is *sui generis*. We are dealing with a 'tributary regime'. It is also called a 'predatory state' (*stat de pradă* in Romanian) a term established long ago by the great Romanian historian Nicolae Iorga, if not in the larger sense we give it, at least to describe the nomad states and even the Ottoman state.

It is undoubtedly a state founded on conquest. To understand the role that conquest can play in the formation of a state, we should refer to one of Marx's texts authorizing even the most dogmatic of his interpreters to reexamine this problem. In a letter Marx wrote to Engels, after having read Mieroslawski's book on the social history of Poland, there is the following passage:

In Mieroslawski you will notice yourself... that the fate of the 'democratic' Polish *gmina* was inevitable. The dominium proper is usurped by the crown, the aristocracy, etc.;

2. Karl A. Wittfogel in his *Le despotisme oriental: étude comparative du pouvoir total*, Paris, 1964, says that 'For practical purposes all historically important agro-despotic systems which perform no hydraulic function seem to have originated from pre-existing hydraulic societies.' This general law of Wittfogel seems to me to be incorrect insofar as Romania is concerned.

the patriarchal relations between the dominium and the peasant communities bring about serfdom; optional parcellation gives rise to a sort of *peasant middle class*, the *Equestrian Order*, to which the peasant can rise only so long as war of conquest and colonization continue, both of which, however, are also conditions which accelerate his downfall. As soon as the limit has been reached this Equestrian Order, incapable of playing the role of a real middle class, is transformed into the lumenproletariat of the aristocracy. A simiar fate is in store for the dominium and the peasant among the Latin population of Moldavia, Wallachia, etc. This kind of development is interesting because here serfdom can be shown to have arisen in a purely economic way, without the intermediate link of conquest and racial dualism.[3]

Marx was right to note the importance of 'the conquest' and, in the case of Moldavia and Wallachia, it is particularly important to stress that it is not a question of conquest of one people by another, of a 'racial dualism', for actually the boyar class was itself Romanian, as were the peasants. However, there was a 'conquest', or rather a 'reconquest', carried out at the expense of the nomads and by a replacement of the rights and powers of a conquest state. In Transylvania, there was actually a 'conquest' made by the Hungarians against the indigenous Romanian peasants, with several elements of 'substitution' in the ranks of nobles created by the former Romanian voivode and *knez* formations.

The problem of the 'second serfdom'

Towards the end of the fifteenth century the fiscal exemptions given to the boyars were used only rarely and eventually they disappeared altogether. This was a sign that the boyars no longer needed them, having succeeded in the meantime in claiming their feudal 'property' by a complete take-over of the village communities. They had already seized the communal lands of the communities, to exploit them directly, increasingly with the aim of producing livestock and grain for market. They had thus succeeded in creating an economic base independent of the state. In attempting to take over the public power, they allied themselves with the Turks to combat their voivode, not hesitating when necessary to betray their country in order to institute a new form of state by transforming the former *Domnie* into an 'aristocratic oligarchic state'. The voivode became no more than a *primus inter pares*, with no power unless he served the interests of the boyars, while at the same time submitting to the terrorist injunctions of the Turks, who instituted a new kind of fiscal exploitation of the country which was itself a kind of renewal of the nomad 'predatory state'.

3. Letter of October 30, 1856, in *Karl Marx and Frederich Engels: Selected Correspondence*, Moscow/London 1956, pp. 114–15.

Thus, only towards the end of the fifteenth century could the boyars, finally masters of the state, start to use corvée labour for their purpose. Only then could they reduce the peasants to bound serfdom. In the sixteenth century the village communities disintegrated and lost their rights; the peasants, as semi-slaves, could now be sold and bought as their masters wished. Large feudal domains were formed and there was a primitive accumulation of capital. To understand this process one must keep in mind the social mechanism enabling the whole social base of the boyars to be transformed, from 'tribute' to actual 'feudal dues', established on the basis of a regime of feudal landed property. We are dealing with a struggle that the boyar class led against the village communities and which consisted in reducing the free villages to serfdom and aggravating the servitude of the villages they already controlled until they were able to reduce the peasants to total serfdom. This struggle ended in the slow disintegration of the social system of the village communities, through infiltration into the communities due to a reversal of the laws of communal life in such a way that they became dead letters.

The principal lever consisted in cutting the ties that formerly bound every peasant member of the community to his hereditary patrimony, the 'strip', giving a right to a total use of the common territory. It is thus through a knowledge of the social laws of the village communities that we gain the clue to the understanding of the forms taken by the class struggles of Romanian social history. A peasant community could be reduced to serfdom only in a completely different way from that of the serfdom of the ancient slave and colonial latifundia. Instead of a movement from slavery to an increasingly relaxed serfdom, we have an opposite process, in which a mass of free or quasi-free autonomous peasant formations became progressively bound to the land.

War and famines and the fiscal administrative domination of the Turks characterized the eighteenth century. There was a strong demographic shift due to the fleeing of peasants who left their villages to avoid being bound to the soil, or to escape famine and fiscal terror. To hold them back and repopulate the villages, there was again recourse to fiscal exemptions, this time to encourage the runaways to return home, with the promise of agreeable working conditions. The feudal lord, now uncontested landowner of the terrain, offered peasants who were no longer part of a traditional peasant community and who had no claim to land rights a contract with reciprocal duties and obligations. This last form of exploitation of the villages (feudal domains worked by corvée labour), more economic than serfdom, spread until finally Mavrocordat legally abolished serfdom and issued a set of decrees regulating the conditions which had to be offered to the peasants as obligatory rules for all villagers ('urbarial' regime).

In these circumstances, in what sense and at what period can one speak of a 'second serfdom'? Let us recall that this 'second' serfdom is nothing but a 'belated' serfdom, 'second' in the European chronological order, not necessarily re-appearing a second time in places where it had temporarily disappeared. Some areas had a 'second' serfdom without having a 'first'. Nevertheless, the problem raises many controversies. Did the reform of Mavrocordat not 'free' the peasants, by abolishing all serfdom? And it cannot be denied that the corvée labourers who then came into existence faced an even worse fate, as they had not only lost their former rights to use the land but were also bound to ever harsher corvées which in the end were so excessive that they resembled the worst forms of serfdom.

One must not take the 'liberation' of the peasants proclaimed by Mavrocordat literally. Let us recall that liberation from serfdom could be accomplieshed in two ways: the 'magnanimity' of the boyars could be called upon to urge them to free their serfs of their own accord; or, on the other hand, the peasants had the right to repurchase their freedom with cash, just as in 1864, when they also had to pay to buy back their corvée obligations.

In quest of money, most boyars agreed to repurchase by the peasants. But there were peasants who did not have the necessary capital and boyars who did not want to free them gratuitously. After the laws of Mavrocordat, serfdom did not disappear overnight, nor was its disappearance a direct result of those laws. The disappearance of the property right over the peasant's person was a much more complex historical process, going far beyond the will of a legislator. Mavrocordat only transformed the possibility of repurchase into *right to repurchase*. He accelerated and gave a legal base to a development which had begun before these reforms. They in no way constituted a break in the historical chain of events, interrupting serfdom, annulling it temporarily to have it return a second time. The social process which took place in the Romanian countries in the second half of the sixteenth century was that of a serfdom which progresssed without interruption, worsening, step by step, experiencing nevertheless a period of exacerbated social crisis at the time of legal 'serfdom' when the boyar actually had a right over the serf's person. It was only this right that disappeared as a result of the laws of Mavrocordat, without interfering with the fundamental process which had begun before Mavrocordat and continued precisely because of these reforms. That is to say that the movement from the patriarchal feudalism of a subsistence economy to a monetary feudalism that ended as the belated feudalism of the capitalist period, serving a capitalist commerce, forms a continuous line. This is what constitutes the 'second serfdom', in the real sense of the term, and across which history stretches for several centuries without a break. In other words, Romania's serfdom was a 'second' serfdom that was never preceded by as classical western 'first' serfdom.

Specific forms of the 'primitive accumulation of capital'

Even in the eighteenth century, the villages continued to maintain or to reinstitute the modes of agricultural and pastoral exploitation of the land, according to the communal rules, imposed objectively by the necessities of a primitive agricultural technology. But this time they were in sharp rivalry with their boyars who were increasingly enlarging their 'demesnes' (corvée lands) at the expense of lands left to the peasants (tithe lands). To settle this conflict, the division into thirds was made to regulate which shares were to go to the boyars and which to the peasant community (Organic Regulations of 1832). Finally the corvées were ended (Rural Law of 1864), causing the almost total disappearance of the former way of life of the rural communities in favour of a capitalist system.

The factor which unleashed the social transformations of this whole period and determined the outcome of the struggle which the boyars led against the peasants was undoubtedly of an economic nature. The laws of the capitalist order penetrated into the country through commerce and succeeded in casting their influence over the production of cereals in the Moldavian and Wallachian principalities. This process, moreover, was felt over a much vaster geographic area, extending over the Romanian Banat which, under Austrian administration, was develped and colonized by Joseph II, a process which brought about its participation in the international wheat trade. The Ukraine also felt the effects of a spreading capitalism, and at the same time that Romania was building a series of Danubian ports the great port of Odessa was created.

This economic evolution was everywhere accompanied by a parallel demographic evolution, for in all of these regions a population explosion took place and in some districts the population quintupled in half a century. The radical social transformations that occurred at this period are particularly interesting and cannot be better described than by Marx's own, 'primitive accumulation of capital'. 'The so-called primitive accumulation is but the historical process separating the producer from the means of production. It seems primitive because it makes up the prehistory of capital and of the capitalist mode of production.' Marx observed primitive accumulation as it was practised by the western promoters of capitalism, expressed principally by their colonial policies. In the Romanian regions, it was obviously not a question of the same policies. The country was more than two centuries behind, like a 'feudal' social enclave in a capitalist world in the process of conquering the globe. But in the beginning of western capitalism, feudal ties had to be slowly loosened by precisely the same means used in Romania, that is, by claiming 'as private property, in the modern sense of the word, goods to which they had only feudal rights'.

This is exactly what we believe to have happened in the Romanian countries during this whole period which began with the reforms of Mavrocordat and ended with the Rural Law of 1864, when the boyars deprived the peasants of their joint rights over common land and did not hesitate to use the worst forms of violence in order to become 'landowners'. We must stress that this split between the man who worked the land directly, always the peasant, and the principal means of production of the period, the land, took place not at the dawn of the capitalist order but rather during the middle of the capitalist era, that is not in the sixteenth century but in the eighteenth and nineteenth centuries.

The factor which set off the social struggles between boyars and peasants was the persistent desire on the part of the boyars to transform the collective lands into private property, for their profit alone, in order to produce a marketable wheat crop. The boyar wanted at all costs to exploit the land directly, though of course with the use of peasant corvée labour, in order to produce as much wheat as possible. Though their relations with the westerners who came to buy their wheat were capitalist, the boyars remained fundamentally large feudal lords in their relations with the peasants. This mixture of capitalist and feudal forms was the characteristic phenomenon of this whole period during the course of which the serf village communities disintegrated and finally disappeared. Only the 'free' villages continued as testimony to ancient times, and fortunately a few survived into our century to help us understand the past.

Index

Adrianople, Treaty of (1829), 96
Adriatic Sea, 33, 176
Alexander Lăpuşneanu, voivode, 179
ancestors, 36, 44–5, 73–9, 81, 105, 168
Anderson, Perry, x
Argeş, 13, 17, 143
aristocracy, *see* modes of production, feudal; village chieftains
Armenians, 177
Asia, 29, 176, 213
Asiatic despotism, *see* modes of production, Asiatic
Attila, 29
Aurelian, P. S., 51n, 53n, 117
Austria, Austrians, 4, 7, 11, 40, 107, 176, 199, 200
Avars, 24

Bălcescu, Nicolae, 80, 129
Balkan Peninsula, 29, 33, 103, 176, 199
Baltic Sea (*see also* Ponto-Baltic), 4, 176–7
Bărăgan Steppe, 50
Barbu, Katargiu, 84n
Basarab the Elder, voivode, 156
Bauer, F. G., 103
Bauer, Otto, 7n
bees and honey, 47–8, 138–9, 143, 180
Bela, King of Hungary, 30, 139
Berni, Nicolas, 124
Berza, M., 178n
Black Sea (*see also* Ponto-Baltic), 4, 31, 33, 96, 176–7
Bloch, Marc, xi, 1, 8
bocage (absence of), 62
Boeresco, B., 84n, 100n
Bogdan, Ioan, 155
Bohemia, 176
Bond of Michel (*see also* Michael the Brave), 129–32
bourgeoisie, 3
Brăila, 13, 17
Braşov, 176

223

Bucharest, 13, 17
Bukovina, 13, 17, 25, 40
Bulgars, 24
Byzantium, 29, 176

Calimacus, voivode, 118
Câmpina, Barbu, 30n, 211n
Cantemir, voivode Dimitriu, 25–6
capital accumulation, 179–80, 218, 220–1
capitalism, *see* modes of production, capitalist
Caragea, voivode, 126
Carpathian Mountains, 13, 17, 23, 29, 176, 186
  sub-Carpathian depressions, 12, 46
Carra, Jean Louis, 50n
cash, 178, 180
cattle, 51, 176, 180
Cazacu, A., 131n
censuses (*see also* population), 10–13, 32, 108–9
cereals (*see also* wheat), 3–4, 29, 53, 92, 112, 115, 131, 138, 143, 176–7
Charlemagne, 133
chieftains, *see* village chieftains
China, 29
Chircă, H., 180n
Cîmpulung Bukovina, 13, 15, 17
Cîmpulung Wallachia, 13, 15, 17, 73, 76–8
clan, 160–1
class struggles, 65, 70–1, 79–82, 88–91, 97–100, 111–22, 208–9, 221
Claudian, Ion, 47n
clearings, 47–62, 92–3, 97
Codrescu, T, 79n
Colescu, Leonid, 10n
Colescu-Vartic, C., 50n, 80n, 100n
colonial and semi-colonial societies, x, 5, 7, 135–6, 221
commons, 52, 55–6, 58
communal village, *see* village, communal
Congress of Paris (1858), 50, 95, 100
Constantine Racoviță, voivode, 200

village(s) (*cont.*)

  chieftains, 7, 26–7, 32, 42, 134, 139, 143, 159, 215

  communal, ix–x, 7–8, 11, 15, 20–9, 33, 35–62, 96, 100, 104–5, 107–10, 123, 127–8, 132–4, 136, 159–60, 166–7, 169, 172, 181, 183, 211, 213–15, 217

  confederations, ix, 25–7, 31, 213

  conquest of, 14–15, 36, 79–81, 90, 100–2, 111–15, 132, 144–74, 181–90, 215, 217

  corvée, 95–128, 199, 206–9

  free, 7, 9–15, 17, 22, 35–82, 100, 107–10, 122, 133, 138, 146, 181–8, 191–7, 221

  law, 38–42, 54–7, 101–2, 123–6, 213

  ownership of, 135, 140, 145–6, 148–51, 162–74, 179, 180

  serf, 8–15, 22, 38–9, 66, 81, 83–93, 100–2, 122, 125–6, 128, 138, 146, 156–7, 170–4, 185, 221

  solidarity, 39–40, 109, 173

vineyards, 59, 124–5

voivodes, 24–7, 32, 46, 106, 134, 136–7, 139, 140–1, 143–6, 148–9, 152, 154–7, 159, 170, 189, 194, 200, 213, 215, 217

Vrancea, 13, 15, 17, 25, 38, 42, 47, 55, 59–60, 144

Wavrin, Jean de, 143

wheat, 4, 97–8, 139, 141, 180, 207, 220

Wittfogel, Karl A., 216n

Wojciechowski, Zygmut, 7n

World War, Second, 26, 46

Yacubovskii, A. I., 31n

Ypsilanti, Voivode, 113, 117, 126

Zakin, S. D., 4n